SERVICE QUALITY IN AIRLINES

The Significant Role of Frontline Employees in Airline Industry of India

SERVICE QUALITY IN AIRLINES

THE SIGNIFICANT ROLE OF FRONTLINE EMPLOYEES IN AIRLINE INDUSTRY OF INDIA

Dr Manmohan Chaudhary

KALPAZ

ISBN: 978-93-5128-216-7

Price: ₹ 1050

First Published, 2016

Published by

Kalpaz Publications
C-30, Satyawati Nagar,
Delhi – 110052
E-mail: kalpaz@hotmail.com
Ph.: 9212142040

Printed at: G. Print Process, Delhi

Cataloging in Publication Data—DK
Courtesy: D.K. Agencies (P) Ltd. <docinfo@dkagencies.com>

Chaudhary, Manmohan, author.
Service quality in airlines : the significant role of frontline employees in airline industry of India / Manmohan Chaudhary.
pages cm
Includes bibliographical references.
ISBN 9789351282167

1. Aircraft industry—Customer services—India—Quality control. 2. Airlines—Customer services—India—Quality control. I. Title.

HE9871.Z7S47 2016 DDC 387.730954 23

Contents

Abstract

Background. Frontline employee commitment has been a topic of interest since the researchers realised its importance especially in service organisations. However, researchers primarily focused on investigating job satisfaction and its impact on numerous work outcomes, with turnover intention the most thoroughly researched. An enrichment of this research stream was therefore the recent study on employee commitment to service quality. Due to the growing importance of this topic, it was undertaken for the research. The main objective of the study was to investigate the antecedents and consequences of Frontline employee commitment on job satisfaction and also to study whether job satisfaction serves as a mediator between different antecedents and their consequences for which hypothesized relationships were developed. This study has examined various antecedents and consequences of FLSE commitment to service quality which includes organisational support, reward, employee empowerment, training, Service technology, supportive management, servant leadership (antecedents) and frontline employee commitment to firm, frontline commitment to service quality, frontline employee commitment to service recovery performance, frontline commitment to job performance, cooperation, extra role customer service behaviour (consequences) that affects the employees commitment towards the organisation.

Method. For this Descriptive study, quantitative approach has been undertaken. Three research frameworks are developed.The data collection was done by both primary and secondary sources. For primary data, a structured questionnaire was developed and administered to a sample of 263 respondents of six domestic airlines in Delhi. The sample consisted of the members of cabin crew, CSA- ticketing, CSA-Check in and the Traffic control assistant By using the statistical method of correlation, regression and mediation analysis, the entire conceptual model was tested by using the Statistical Package for Social Sciences (SPSS, version 19) software for investigation of the antecedents and consequences of frontline employee commitment to service quality and the potential mediating role of job satisfaction.

Results. The correlation analysis was done and the results showed that the correlations among the frontline employees commitment to firm and frontline employees to service quality was the highest ($r = .782$, $p<0$). The regression results clearly indicated a significant relationship between rewards, training, service technology, servant leadership, supportive management and the mediator job satisfaction. Among the antecedents, servant leadership displayed the largest effect on FLSE's job satisfaction ($\beta = .488$ $p<.05$). The results showed the effect of Job satisfaction on fl_cf to be the highest among the consequences ($\beta = .835$ $p<.05$). The discovery that employee empowerment and organisational support has a significant negative influence on FLSE CSQ was not expected. The mediation analysis was conducted using bootstrapping method with bias correcting confidence variances. In the present study, the 95 per cent confidence interval of indirect effects was obtained by 1000 bootstrap resamples. The direct and the indirect effect in case of organisational support was found to insignificant which means job satisfaction do not mediate the relationship between organisation support (antecedent) and the consequences. Full or complete mediation was found in the case of service technology.

Conclusion. The results of the study provides a more nuanced picture of these relationships than the other studies related to the employees commitment to service quality.The conducted study has significant relevance for understanding the various antecedents and consequences of FLSE commitment to service in Indian public and private sector airlines and its implication on employees and organisational effectiveness and also the mediating role of job satisfaction. The refinements and extension of the present problems may be undertaken. Further work on the general framework is required. Specifically, it would be of value to examine further variables within the objective, event, and dispositional classes of antecedents; broaden the domain of consequences to include more objective data; to examine possible recursive effects between job satisfaction and both antecedents and consequences, and to replicate the results of this study in other settings.

Acknowledgement

Many people have contributed and helped me in completing this Research Work. Without their valuable cooperation and suggestions, this would have been a difficult task to accomplish. First of all, I wish to thank my internal advisor, Dr Bilal Mustafa Khan,for his support and assistance in the process of completing this study and making this a meaningful learning process. His help and support was invaluable when I struggled with the formulation of concepts and models for this study. His immense wealth of knowledge was an inspiration for me. I gratefully acknowledge his suggestions, advice, and encouragement at every stage of my project. He was always ready to extend his cooperation. His guidance and comments have given me a tremendous inspiration.

I would also like to thank my external guide Dr A.S. Ahluwalia, who had been continuous source of inspiration throughout the course of this research. He has taken a special interest in the project despite his busy schedule.

I am fortunate enough to have a great family and friends who supported me throughout the entire period of my study. Special thanks to my husband for motivating and encouraging me.

I also thank all the known and unknown respondents who were willing to participate in the survey. I am indebted to them for having spared their valuable time to fill up the questionnaire, which I had developed during the course of my research.

I am also thankful to the faculty members and staff of my institute for their continued support throughout the study. My special thanks to all the respective authors of various articles, textbooks and websites from where I consolidated the required data and information.

Dr Manmohan Chaudhary

Abbreviations

GDP	: Gross Domestic Product
FLSE	: Frontline Service Employee
IATA	: International Air Transportation Association
CSQ	: Commitment to Service Quality
MCSQ	: Management Commitment to Service Quality
FLSE CSQ	: Frontline Commitment to Service Quality
OCBs	: Organisational Citizenship Behaviours
CSA	: Customer Support Assistant
SPSS	: Statistical Package for Social Sciences
AIL	: Air India Limited
NACIL	: National Aviation Company of India Limited
INR	: Indian Rupee
US$	: United States Dollar
CIT	: Critical Incident Technique
SMTs	: Self-managing Teams
LISREL	: Linear Structural Relation
SEM-	: Structural Equation Modelling
IM	: Internal Marketing
PLS	: Partial Least Squares
ECSQ	: Employees' Commitment to Service Quality
FHEs	: Frontline Hospital Employees
HLM-	: Hierarchical Linear Modeling
WRC	: Willingness to Report Service Complaints
CO	: Customer Orientation

CSE	:	Core Self-evaluations
AMOS	:	Analysis of Moments Structure
BI	:	Behavioural Intentions
ROS	:	Return on Sales
ROA	:	Return on Assets
POS	:	Perceived Organisational Support
ANOVA	:	Analysis of Variance
ROE	:	Regulation of Emotion
UOE	:	Use of Emotion
SEA	:	Self-emotional Appraisal
OCB	:	Organisational Citizenship Behaviour
KMO	:	Kaiser-Meyer
PCA	:	Principal Component Analysis
OS	:	Organisational Support
RE	:	Reward
EMP	:	Empowerment
TRG	:	Training
ST	:	Service Technology
SM	:	Supportive Management
SL	:	Servant Leadership
JS	:	Job Satisfaction
FLSE_CF	:	Frontline Employee Commitment to Firm
FLSE_SQ	:	Frontline Commitment to Service Quality
FLSE_SRP	:	Frontline Employee Commitment to Service Recovery Performance
FLSE_JP	:	Frontline Commitment to Job Performance
Co_p	:	Cooperation
ER_sb	:	Extra Role Customer Service Behaviour
IV	:	Independent Variable
DV	:	Dependent Variable
UL	:	Upper Limit
LL	:	Lower Limit
CI	:	Confidence Interval

List of Tables

List of Figures

Chapter - 1

Introduction

1.1 Introduction

Service sector is the lifeline for the economic growth of a country. It is the largest and fastest growing sector globally contributing more to the global output and employing more people than any other sector. Among fast growing developing countries, India has also accepted the role of service sector in the growth of the country. Where earlier developers grew on the basis of exports of labour intensive manufactures, India has concentrated on services Eichengreen and Gupta, (2011).

The rapid growth of this sector especially in the post-reform era has played a critical role in the country's emergence as one of the fastest-growing economies in the world in recent years (Chanda and Gupta 2011). It has placed India in the top fastest growing economies of the world despite the Eurozone crisis and North American economic instabilities. It has witnessed massive and continuous growth, especially over the last 2 decades, and today stands at a monumental 64.4 per cent of the GDP of India (2011-12) (Singh 2012) .The share of services in India's GDP has increased from 33.5 per cent in 1950-51 to 55.1 per cent in 2010-11 and to 56.3 per cent in 2011-12. If construction is included, the share increased to 64.4 per cent in 2011-12. In Q1 of 2012-13, the share of services in GDP of India is 6.9 per cent. (Economic survey, 2012-13) Although there are other emerging markets where the share of services in

GDP exceeds the share of manufacturing, India stands out for the dynamism of its service sector (Eichengreen and Gupta 2011).

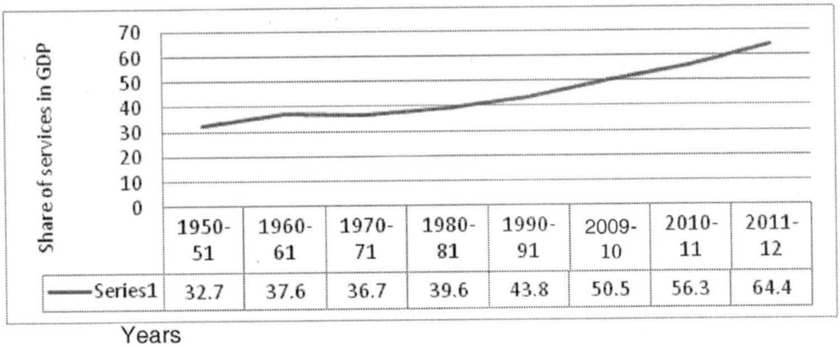

Fig. 1.1 Share of the service sector in the total GDP of India (in per cent).

Service organisations to a large extent depends upon the delivery of services and that is why the service organisations worldwide are shifting their focus to service quality as a priority in the current competitive environment (Zeithaml, Berry and Parasuraman, 1996). High service quality allows service providers to differentiate themselves from their competitors and thus gain sustainable competitive advantages in the global market place (Gounaris, Stathakopoulos and Athanassopoulos, 2003).

Table 1.1 Performance of India's Aviation Sector

Sector	***Aviation***
Indicators	Airline passengers (domestic and International)
Unit	Million
Period	
2008-09	49.5 (a)
2009-10	54.5 (a)
2010-11	64.5 (a)
2011-12	70.2(a)
2012-13	67.5(a)

Source: Directorate General of Civil Aviation.

Note: (a) calendar years, for example 2007-8 for 2007.

Airline industry too has turned to focus on airline service quality to increase service satisfaction by retaining customer patronageand with this comes the market share. In India during the five years i.e. 2008-2013, the performance of airline industry has improved as depicted in Table 1.1.

Delivering high-quality service to passengers is essential for airline survival, so airlines need to understand what passengers expect from their services. Understanding exactly what customers expect is the most crucial step in defining and delivering high-quality service. Since service quality is an important factor for airlines, several researchers have applied service quality related theories and methods in the airline industry (Alotaibi, 1992; Chang and Yeh, 2002; Chen, 1997; Kaynak, Kucukemiroglu and Kara, 1994; Ostrowski, O'Brien and Gordon, 1993; Sultan and Simpson, 2000 shows the performance of the aviation sector of India.

To gain competitive advantage airlines have resorted to various strategies such as intensive marketing, advertising and promotion as well as ticket price wars. These are not sufficient measures to remain competitive. Another important strategy is to improve service quality delivered by employees of the airlines to retain customers. A study by Ostrowski *et. al.,* (1993) shows that airlines could acquire and retain customer loyalty by continuing to provide perceived high quality services. Empirical studies of demand for airline service shows that service quality is central to the choice of airlines by passengers, both for business and leisure travel (Abrahams, 1983; Etherington and Var, 1984; Young *et. al.,*1994).Thus, providing superior service quality should be the main agenda for all airlines in order to remain competitive.

But at the same time customers try to evaluate the worthiness of the services delivered to them.The evaluation of service processes can be divided into three distinct stages: pre consumption, consumption, and post-consumption (Kasper *et. al.,* 2006). Mirroring this framework into the airline industry, the three corresponding stages are pre-flight, in-flight and post-flight activities (Leong, 2008). Among others, the pre-flight activities are check-in, security, and waiting at the gate, whereas the in-flight process covers seating and accessibility of service offerings. Finally, the post-flight activities comprise baggage claim and customs among others. Each stage respectively contains several customer-oriented activities that contribute to the total customer experience (Leong, 2008) and in each process FLSE plays a major role.

The contents of service quality may be different in different industries. According to the IATA (International Air Transportation Association), service items for airlines include seat reservation, selling ticket, airport check-in, cabin service, baggage delivery and the subsequent services after arriving at destinations, etc. In general, from a passenger's perspective, the service items of airline should include flight frequency, flight safety, cabin food and beverage, seating, flight on schedule, etc. On the other hand, from an operator's perspective, the airline industry generally pays more attention on safety, comfort, convenience, accuracy, and hospitality, etc. (Chen & Liu, 2002).

Gourdin, K. (1988) categorised airline service quality in terms of three items: safety, timeliness and price. Elliott and Roach (1993) proposed food and beverage, timely luggage transport, seat comfort, the check in process, and in-flight service dimensions. Haynes (1994) used the processing of luggage, seat cleanliness, and the check-in process, the convenience of transit, timeliness, and handling of customer complaints as the standards of service quality.

Delivering high-quality service to passengers is essential for airline survival, so airlines need to understand what passengers expect from their services. But at the same time it is equally important to know how efficient and satisfied their employees (especially the FLSE) are with the service environment of the organisation as it affects the behaviour and the attitude of FLSE towards the service. Frontline service employee's (FLSE) attitudes and behaviours significantly influence the quality of service operations, as these employees present the face and the voice of their organisations to customers (Hartline and Ferrell 1996; Schneider, Wheeler, and Cox 1992). The organisation has high stakes on how the service employee behaves in service encounters. These service employees are faced with multiple challenges on a daily basis ranging from technical faults to badly behaved customers. It is the manner in which these challenges are dealt with and the degree to which one can cope with the strain of boundary spanning roles, which distinguishes excellent service providers.

1.1.1 The Boundary Spanning Behaviour of FLSE

The frontline is the touch point of the company; therefore, the service that frontline employees provide is critical in developing customer relationships, gathering customer information, and in creating customer satisfaction, loyalty, and brand commitment (Burmann and Konig, 2011; Fang, Palmatier, and Grewal, 2011)) They are the first lines of contact in the organisation and plays a boundary spanning behaviour to create the first and long lasting impression on the organisation and project a positive image in the minds of customers..

The boundary-spanning behaviour relates to the behaviour of customer-contact employees or the FLSE's of service firms that derives from their unique position as boundary spanners of the firm (Bettencourt, Gwinner, and Meuter 2001). They have a strategic function: they are being placed between the external environment, including organisation's customers, and the internal organisation (Aldrich and Herker 1977). Operating in the so-called 'boundary-spanning' role can be fraught with stress and has led academics and practitioners alike to seek to understand how to better support such roles and also enhance the service offered to customers (as cited by Harrison 2013). Based on the services marketing and management literature, three types of boundary-spanning behaviour are identified by Bettencourt and Brown (2003). External representation behaviour represents the extent to which the frontline employee is a vocal advocate of the organisation, its image and its assets to outsiders of that organisation (Bettencourt and Brown 2003). This type of boundary-spanning behaviour can be considered partly customer-oriented and is more likely to be considered relatively more extra-role (Bettencourt, Brown, and MacKenzie 2005). The second type of boundary-spanning behaviour, internal influence behaviour, reflects the individual initiative taken to communicate to the firm and co-workers in order to improve the service delivered (Bettencourt and Brown 2003). Internal influence behaviour is clearly employee-oriented and is also more likely to be considered relatively more extra-role (Bettencourt, Brown, and MacKenzie 2005). Service delivery behaviour refers to the behaviours that directly impact customers: serving customers in a conscientious, responsive, attentive and courteous manner (Bettencourt and Brown 2003).This third type of boundary-spanning behaviour is clearly customer-oriented and is more likely to be considered relatively more in-role (Bettencourt, Brown, and MacKenzie 2005). As such, the three dimensions of boundary-spanning behaviour are each belonging to a specific category of prosocial organisational behaviour.

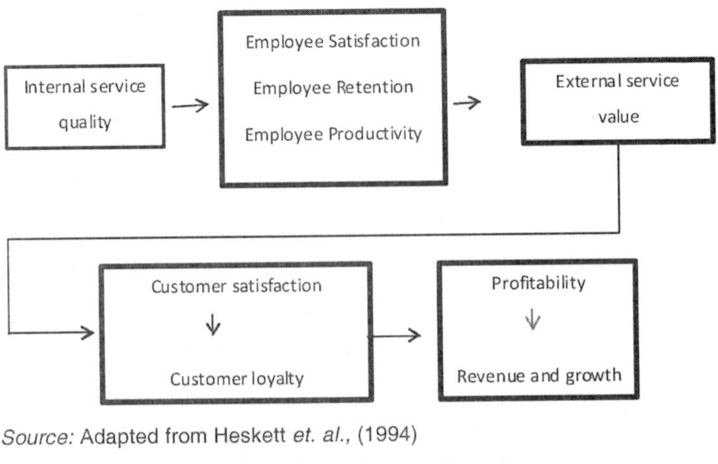

Source: Adapted from Heskett *et. al.*, (1994)

Fig. 1.2 Service profit chain.

Because they span the boundary between the firm and its customers, these employees are directly responsible for service quality, customer satisfaction, and ultimately the overall performance of the firm (Hartline and Ferrell 1996). The framework postulated by Heskett *et. al.* (1994) lists the relationship between employee satisfaction, customer satisfaction and profitability.

1.1.2 Service failure and Service recovery

According to Zeitham *et. al.* (2013), service failure can be defined as a mismatch between service performance and customer's expectation perception which lead to dissatisfaction. This concept is applicable in service as well as manufacturing sectors. Based on this concept service failure occurs when consumers are dissatisfied with service when performance/ quality of product falls below their expectations.

Since the frontline employees are the ones who interact directly with customers, they would also be the first ones to get to know about a service failure. Moreover, knowing that frontline employees act as boundary spanners for the service organisation, most complaints are put forward by customers to these employees and are known only to them. When this complaining encounter between the employee and the customer occurs, the organisation loses control and it is up to the employee to interact with the customer. The employee will from that point hold the responsibility in handling the service failure. How well the employee will serve the customer will depend on how skilful or how motivated, he or she is. With this realisation, it is therefore important to properly manage frontline employees. This is especially true for tourism and hospitality organisations like airlines and hotels that involve a big volume of service encounters in its day-to-day operations. Failures are indeed pervasive in service encounters (Maxham and Netemeyer, 2002) which forces the service organisation to engage in "dissatisfaction management" and service recovery processes to attain successful service provision (Liao, 2007).

Specifically, these circumstances often need to be initiated by frontline employees where various actions are to be taken to alleviate service failures and restore customer satisfaction.

The inability of the service organisations to deliver as per customer expectations constitutes service failure. According to Zeithaml and Bitner (2000), failure can occur if the service is unavailable when promised, is delivered late or too slowly, the outcome is not as per expectations .or the employees are indifferent and uncaring. The problem of service failure is further compounded by the fact that there is increased competition in most service industries .Thus the customer has many options to choose from.

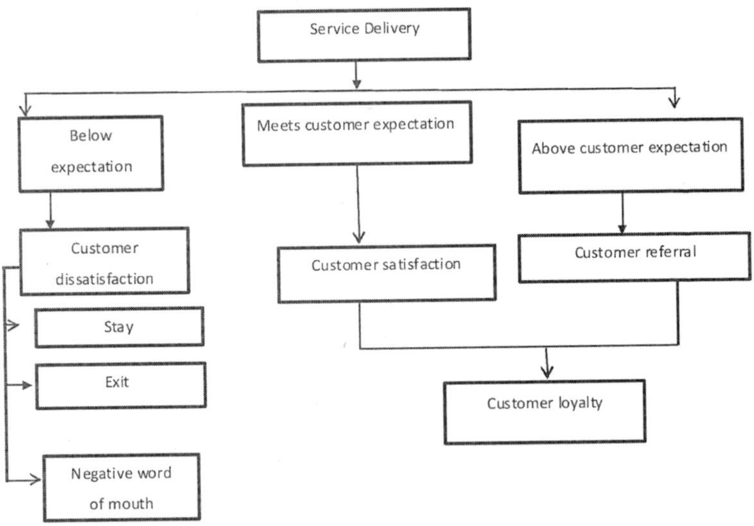

(Adapted from Zaithaml and Bitner 2000)

Fig. 1.3: Service Recovery Process.

Gronroos (1983), in his six criteria of good perceived services quality gives due importance to service recovery. The service recovery process has been shown with the help of a figure 1.3. Service recovery is possible only if an immediate action is taken to keep the situation under control and thereby finding a new, acceptable solution. Thus, service recovery involves what a service provider does in response to service failures (Weun *et. al.* 2004).

1.1.3 Commitment of FLSE to service quality

The most important basis for the assessment of quality is the individual's experience of a service that comes from the internal quality service of the internal customer (all the organisation's employees). Their commitment and willingness to serve is in the best interest of the customers, which incidentally is a prerequisite for achieving service quality (Kandampully, 2002). Clark *et. al.* (2008) defined commitment to service quality as the "dedication of employees to render service quality and the willingness to go beyond what is expected of them". Past findings have also established that employees who are committed to the organisation will remain loyal and are inversely related to turnover (Hartline *et. al.,* 2000); Clark *et. al.,* 2008; Elmadag *et. al.,* 2008). In such conditions, employees were known to spend more time and energy in assisting the organisation realize its goals and they also put their own self-interest aside (Porter *et. al.,* 1973; Tsai, 2008; Sohail and Shaikh, 2004; Yiing and Ahmad, 2008). They would subscribe to the idea of being a citizen of the organisation and be fully committed to the goals of the organisation (Rashid *et. al.,* 2003).

There are other researchers also who agree with the performance benefits accrued from increased employee commitment and have been widely demonstrated in the literature. These benefits includes, increased job satisfaction (Vandenberg and Lance 1992), increased job performance (Mathieu and Zajac, 1990, Lambert, S.D. 2002), increased total return to shareholders and sales (Barber *et. al.,* 1999), decreased employee turnover (Cohen, 1993), decreased intention to leave (Balfour and Wechsler, 1996), decreased intention to search for alternative employers (Cohen, 1993), decreased absenteeism (Cohen, 1993). Lack of commitment from employees can be harmful to an organisation, resulting in poorer performance arising from inferior service offerings and higher costs (Caruana, A., P. Calleya, 1998). Research tells us that workers that are committed (i.e. identify and involve themselves) to their organisations perform to a higher standard (Meyer *et. al.,* 1989; Mowday *et. al.,* 1979) and with higher perceived service quality (Malhotra and Mukherjee, 2004).

Many authors have described CSQ on the basis of different factors affecting their behaviour. Peccei and Rosenthal describe CSQ as "the relative propensity of a service employee to engage in continuous improvement and exert effort on the job for the benefit of customers" (1997). Recent studies have emphasised the influence of service employee CSQ on customers' perceptions of service (Hartline and Ferrell 1996; Schneider, White, and Paul 1998). Customers desire relatedness, assurance, empathy, and reliability, and often view service employees as the means by which an organisation conveys these components of service quality (Brady and Cronin 2001). According to Loveman (1998), capable employees who are committed to service quality increase customer satisfaction. However, research suggesting that firms lose customers because of poor or indifferent service (Boulding *et. al.* 1993; Liu, Sudharshan, and Hamer 2000; Zeithaml, Berry, and Parasuraman 1996) indicates that service employee CSQ is often deficient and that an immediate challenge for many service organisations is to improve it.

1.1.4 Antecedents and Consequences of Employee Commitment to Service Quality

It is very important that the service provider guarantee that whatever is delivered can delight and make the customers happy. But that would be a difficult task for every service provider. There are many hitches that may limit them from performing as required. They may not be able to perform well if the power that is given to them is restricted, or if they are not allowed to make simple decisions or if they only have restricted flexibility in their jobs. On the other hand, the levels of their service may also be affected if they are not in a positive mood to do their job. These conditions may have some impact on the value of quality that they deliver which may well have some influence on the customer's evaluation and possible dissatisfaction. In these kinds of circumstances, empowering employees could result in more employee commitment towards delivery of services.

The empowerment of employees appears to be capable of generating feelings of commitment to the service encounter (Barbee and Bott, 1991). Therefore, a range of initiatives such as autonomous workgroups, quality circles, suggestion schemes, job enrichment (Lashley, 1997), joint consultation, employee shared ownership and communications programmes (Kelly and Kelly, 1990) could be introduced and implemented for employees as a key to accomplishing organisational strategies. Empowerment is described as working arrangements which engage empowerment at an emotional level (Conger and Kanungo, 1988). Accordingly, various forms of empowerment that are introduced for employees in order to enable them to make some decisions, take control over their jobs and deliver greater enthusiasm will result in increased sense of ownership of the service encounter which leads to smooth generation of the required emotional display (Lashley, 2001b)

Elmadag *et. al.* (2008) examined the effects of alternative developmental and reward-based antecedents and affectivee and behavioural consequences of frontline service employee commitment to service quality. According to the author, MCSQ generates affective responses of frontline employees' job satisfaction (feelings towards the job) and affective organisational commitment (feelings towards the organisation), which in turn directly influence frontline employees' service recovery behaviour. A synthesis of the relevant literature suggests that training, empowerment, employee rewards, supportive management, servant leadership and investment in technology are relevant indicators of the MCSQ construct (Babakus *et. al.,* 2003; Berry *et. al.,* 1994; Pfeffer, 1994; Bowen and Lawler, 1995; Heskett *et. al.,* 1997; Lewis and Gabrielsen, 1998; Lytle *et. al.,* 1998; Schneider *et. al.,* 1998; Hartline *et. al.,* 2000; Rogg *et. al.,* 2001; Yoon *et. al.,* 2001).

According to Elmadag ( ) management commitment to service quality leads to affective outcomes (job satisfaction and organisational commitment) which in turn leads to service recovery performance. Findings of the study indicated that managerial coaching has the strongest influence on frontline service employee commitment to service quality. The effects of developmental and reward-based interventions on frontline service employees' commitment to service quality (FLSE CSQ) have also been studied by Sun *et. al.* (2012).The results revealed that formal training, coaching and rewards have positive relationships with FLSE CSQ. Moreover, FLSE CSQ was found to be positively related to job satisfaction, commitment to the organisation, job performance and organisational citizenship behaviours (OCBs).

Babin and Boles (1996) results of the study suggested that employee perceptions of co-worker involvement and supervisory support can reduce stress and increase job satisfaction. Other results indicated a positive relationship between role conflict and job performance, a positive relationship between job performance and job satisfaction, and that job performance mediates effects of role stress on satisfaction.

1.2 About the study

The present study was carried out on six domestic airlines out of which one is public sector airline and rests of the five domestic airlines are private sector airlines. The purpose was to investigate the antecedents and the consequences of the FLSE commitment in providing the services to the passengers. The other important objective was to find out the mediating role of employee job satisfaction in these airlines.

Out of the selected, the public sector domestic airline, Air India is the oldest airline of India and the other five private domestic airlines also have nationwide presence. The selected private domestic airlines have also started operating in an efficient way. The study was conducted at the Indira Gandhi international airport, New Delhi. As the study was related to the FLSE performance, samples were collected from the FLSE that included the members of cabin crew, CSA- ticketing, CSA-Check in and the Traffic control assistant. To measure their commitment towards the service quality, a standard questionnaire was used. Later the data was coded and fed into computers using SPSS 19 (Statistical Package for Social Sciences) as software for data analysis. The collected data was processed and analysed with the help of SPSS package to statistically prove different hypothesis included in the study.

1.3 Need for the study

In a world of increasingly global competition, as the organisations try to have loyal customers it is at the same time important for the organisations to have committed employees towards the delivery of superior service quality to the customers. It is important as it increases revenues, reduces costs, and enhances customer satisfaction. While dealing with the different types of customers and their complaints, these organisations faces lots of problems as the different airlines have different way of dealing with them. According to Webster(1990) the service organisations need to establish a way out for the effective implementation of the strategies needed to overcome these problems through the support of frontline employees (Harris and Ogbonna, 2000). It has also become more difficult to meet the expectations of customers due to problems resulting mainly from the intangibility, inseparability, heterogeneity, and perishability characteristics of services. In this regard FLSE plays a very important role in satisfying the customers. But at the same time their commitment towards the firm is equally important and that can be estimated only by considering the quality of services rendered by them. Frontline employees may be a useful source of knowledge (Rust, Stewart, Miller, and Pielack, 1996;), and play critical roles in service delivery and recovery (Boshoff and Allen, 2000), but their role is often not defined clearly in service organisations (Kelley, 1992). Accordingly, service organisations should consider the crucial roles of frontline employees in the effective establishment of a service organisation.

A study conducted by Lambert, S.D. (2002) concluded that employees who are more committed demonstrate higher job performance, less job displeasure, more ethical behaviour, diminished intent to leave, less stress and organisational citizenship. Furthermore they perceive the value of organisational goals and think of their goals and those of the organisations in personal terms, thereby a lot of cost efficiencies accrue from committed employees. But the commitment of FLSE towards service delivery is also affected by certain variables and these variables need to be identified in case the objective of the organisation is to increase profitability, market share and at the same time managing increasing cost. For all these reasons, this study was undertaken to ascertain the various factors affecting FLSE behaviour.

1.4 Research Questions

In order to study the effect of different variables on FLSE commitment to service quality, the following research questions require answering-

1. What are the antecedents of Job satisfaction of FLSE?
2. What are the consequences of FLSE commitment to service quality?
3. What are the effects of antecedents on job satisfaction of FLSE?
4. What are the effects of consequences on FLSE commitment to service quality?
5. What is the role played by the job satisfaction as a mediator between antecedents and consequences?

1.5 Research objectives

In order to address the research questions as outlined in preceding section, the study was designed to accomplish the different research objectives, presented as under:-

1.5.1 General objective

The general objective of this study was to analyse the effect of antecedents and the consequences on the services delivered by FLSE.

1.5.2 Specific objectives

1. To identify the antecedents of Job satisfaction of FLSE.
2. To identify the consequences of FLSE commitment to service quality.
3. To analyse the effect of antecedents on job satisfaction of FLSE.
4. To analyse the effect of consequences on FLSE commitment to service quality.
5. To study the role of job satisfaction as a mediator between antecedents and consequences.

1.6 Scope of the study

Today the Airline industry has been experiencing privatisation, increasing competition, technological innovation and customisation.This industry is different than the other service organisations because airlines present a unique work environment. The FLSE of the service organisations play a very important role as they are the key to the firm's success. The way they deliver service actually affects their as well as organisations productivity. The relationship between the delivery of service quality and employee productivity is a continuing debate in the services literature (Parasuraman, 2002; Singh, 2000). If a service is delivered in an efficient way, it will result in an increase in the satisfaction level of customers which further would results in a more loyal customers and an organisation can have loyal customers only if it has loyal employees. In the case of service organisations, Loyalty and commitment go hand in hand. Research shows that employees who are more committed demonstrate higher job performance, less job displeasure, more ethical behaviour, and diminished intent to leave, less stress and organisational citizenship .Furthermore they perceive the value of organisational goals and think of their goals and those of the organisations in personal terms, thereby a lot of cost efficiencies accrue from committed employees. This is the reason why the study has taken the perspective of the employees who deals directly with the customers.

This research focuses on the antecedents and the consequences of FLSE commitment to service quality in the airline industry of India. The research is based on Indian Public and private sector airlines only. Besides this the research also focuses on the importance of job satisfaction as a mediator. For the purpose of the research one public sector airline and five private sector Indian airlines operating in Delhi have been chosen. The study is about the role of FLSE in providing services to the passengers. As it focusses on the different factors that affect their behavior, the management of the airlines would be in a condition to solve certain problems that are related to the performance of the employees.

This study will also help Aviation industry managements to better diagnose the loops and holes in the service delivery of the employees of different airlines. It will also play a role in planning future strategies regarding better service delivery to passengers. The study also reveals the role of employees in service quality delivery and comes up with a developed theory that can be applicable to other airlines and provide the guidelines for other airlines to improve the service delivery.

The study covers the following categories of airlines-

Full Service Carriers- Public Sector which includes Air India (Domestic)

Full Service Carriers- Private Sector which includes Jet Airways and Kingfisher

Low cost Carriers-Spice jet, Indigo and Go airlines

1.7 Brief outline of the methodology

The research was carried out using a quantitative approach. Detailed literature survey and review on FLSE commitment towards service quality in airline industry was done by reviewing articles published in various journals. Based on literature review, gaps in the current research were identified and accordingly research objectives were set and hypotheses were formulated. For quantitative study, a questionnaire based approach was used. The sample was collected from both the private and public sector domestic airlines operating in Delhi. The collected data was analysed using Statistical Package for Social Science version 19 (SPSS). Regression analysis was used to test the hypotheses. The mediating effect of job satisfaction on the antecedents and the consequences was also studied.

1.8 Outline of the thesis

The outline of the thesis is presented in Fig. 1.4.

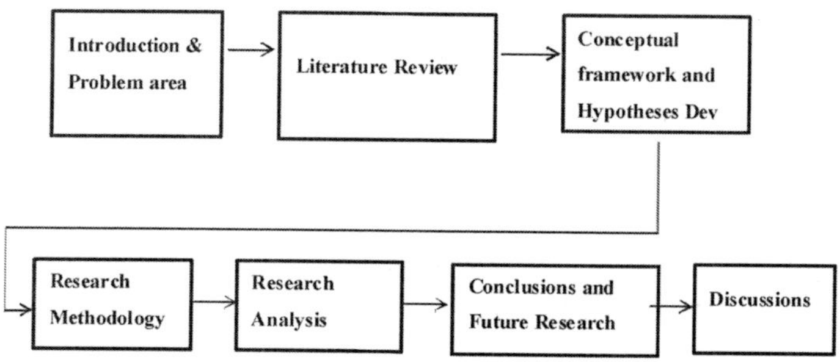

Fig. 1.4 Outline of the study.

1.9 Chapterisation of the Thesis

The total thesis is divided into seven chapters. The chapter wise plan along with the brief description is as follows:

Chapter-1 Introduction of the study: The introductory chapter describes briefly about the study, need for the study, Objectives of the study, Scope of the study, brief outline of the methodology.

Chapter-2 An overview of the airline industry: It includes the current Indian service sector scenario, History of airline industry in India and the Overview of major players in airline industry of India.

Chapter-3 Review of Literature and Earlier studies: A detailed review of literature is carried out at the various stages of the study. Various reports, journals, articles, text books had been reviewed regarding the commitment of FLSE towards service quality, Antecedents and consequences of service delivery and service quality in airline industry, and the management commitment towards service quality. It also explains the research gap based on the available literature.

Chapter-4 Conceptual framework and Development of Hypothesis: A model was conceptualised and on the basis of the model, hypotheses were drawn.

Chapter-5 Research methodology: It included research approach, research design, problem statement, research framework I, II and III, adaption of various measures, Universe of the study, Sample unit and sample frame, Measures used in the study, Outline of the study, Questionnaire development, Procedure of data collection, Primary and secondary source data, Survey duration, Data analysis and the Statistical treatment of the data.

Chapter-6 Data Analysis and Interpretations: It includes Descriptive and Inferential analysis of the collected data.

Chapter-7 Results and Discussions: This chapter elaborates the results of the study followed by discussion of the result.

Chapter-8 Summary and Suggestions: This is the final chapter which starts with the summary of the study. It also reports the major findings, implications of the findings, intervention strategies of the study. Few suggestions and limitations are included for the FLSE commitment in different domestic airlines. Finally the chapter ends with conclusions of the study and the scope for further research.

1.10 Description of terms used in the study

The description of different terms used in this study is given in the form of a table that shows the different definitions given by different authors.

Table 1.2: The terms used in the study

Terms	*Author*	*Definition*
Services	Gronroos (1990)	An activity or series of activities of more or less intangible nature that normally, but not necessarily, take place in interactions between the customer and service employees and /or physical resources or goods and/or systems of the service provider, which are provided as a solutions to customer problems
Service quality	Zeithaml and Bitner (2003)	Service quality is a focused evaluation that reflects the customer's perception of specific dimensions of service: reliability, responsiveness, assurance, Empathy, tangibles. Satisfaction, on other hand, is more inclusive: it is influenced by perceptions of service quality, product quality, and price as well as situational factors and personal factors.
Service climate	Schneider, 1998	Service climate refers to the shared perception of employees concerning the practices, procedures, and kinds of behaviour that get rewarded and supported in a particular setting.

Employee Commitment	Porter *et. al.* (1974)	It is the strength of an individual's identification with and involvement in a particular organisation.
	Allen and Meyer (1990).	The degree to which employees feel a sense of connection, obligation, and reward in working for the organisation.
Training	Landy (1985)	It is a set of planned activities on the part of an organisation to increase the job knowledge and skills or to modify the attitudes and social behaviour of its members in ways consistent with the goals of the organisation and the requirements of the job" (p. 306).
·	(Patrick, 2000)	Training is systematic development of the knowledge, skills, and expertise required by a person to effectively perform a given task or job.
Rewards	Armstrong (2006),	Total reward is a combination of financial and non-financial rewards available to employees.
	Manus and Graham (2003)	It means all types of rewards – indirect as well as direct, and intrinsic as well as extrinsic.
Organisational support	Eisenberger, Huntington, Hutchison, and Sowa, (1986) and (Scott and Bruce, 1994).	Organisational support is the extent to which employees perceive that the organisation is concerned about their well-being and encourages, respects, and recognises those who outperform.
Empowerment	Chebat and Kollias, 2000; Forrester, 2000).	Empowerment means enhancing a person's ability and motivation to develop and make the most constructive use of their talents and experience.
	Bowen and Lawer (1992)	Empowering employees means: "(1) providing them with information about the performance of the organisation, (2) rewarding them based on the organisation's performance, (3) creating a knowledge based that makes it possible for employees to understand and contribute to the performance of the organisation, and (4) giving employees

(Contd...)

		the power to make a decisions that influence organisational directions and performance. (p. 31-39)
Job satisfaction	Burke, 1989; Brown and Peterson, 1993	Job satisfaction is a product of the evaluation of the job, taking into account all aspects of the job such as pay, benefits, supervisor style, communication and discretion.
	Locke, 1976; Spector, 1997	Job satisfaction has been defined as a positive emotional state resulting from the pleasure a worker derives from the job.
Supportive management	Beck and Beck, 1986; Hartline *et. al.*, 2000.	It means management concerns and support for employee work and represents the degree to which they create a facilitative climate of support, trust and helpfulness.
MCSQ	Ahmed and Parasuraman (1994)	The conscious choice of quality initiatives as operational and strategic options for the firm and engaging in activities such as providing visible quality leadership and resources for the adoption and implementation of quality initiatives. (p. 89)
	Hartline and Ferrell (1996)	"The manager's affective desire to improve his or her unit's service quality" (p. 53).
	Babakus *et. al.* (2003)	Employees'appraisal of an organisation's commitment to nurture, develop, support, and reward its employees to achieve service excellence" (p. 275).

1.11 Summary

The present study has been undertaken to examine the impact of different variables on the employees' commitment towards the delivery of services in public and private sector airlines operating in New Delhi. This chapter presents a background of the study which includes research question, research objective, need of the study, scope, limitations, some definitions, significance, outline and cauterisation of the thesis and research methodology. Airline scenario in general and History of Airlines of India is discussed in Chapter-2.

Chapter - 2

Indian Aviation Sector Scenario

2.1 Introduction

The Indian Aviation Industry is among the world's fastest growing industries. It has undergone huge transformation following the liberalisation of the aviation industry in India. It is redefined by changing regulation policies, increased privatisation of airports and growing infrastructure developments. And the major development is the emergence of private and the low cost airline industry.This chapter deals with the present scenario of the aviation sector of India. Section 2.2 discusses about the past history of the airlines in India. Section 2.3 explains each of the domestic airlines undertaken for the study purposes. Section 2.4 summarises the chapter.

2.2 History of Airline Industry in India

In India the first airline Tata Airlines in 1932, a division of Tata Sons Ltd. (now Tata Group) started by J. R. D. Tata. On October 15, 1932 the founder, J. R. D. Tata flew a single engined De Havill and Puss Moth registered VT-and carrying air mail (postal mail of Imperial Airways) from Karachi's Drigh Road Aerodrome to Bombay's Juhu Airstrip via Ahmedabad. The aircraft continued to Madras via Bellary piloted by Royal Air Force pilot Neville Vincent. Following the end of World War II, regular commercial service was restored in India and

Tata Airlines became a public limited company on 29 July 1946 under the name Air India.

The airline was set up under Air Corporations Act, 1953 with an initial capital of Rs 32 million and started operations on 1 August 1953. It was established after legislation came into force to nationalise the entire airline industry in India. At the time of independence, the number of air transport companies, which were operating within and beyond the frontiers of the company, carrying both air cargo and passengers, was nine. It was reduced to eight, with Orient Airways shifting to Pakistan. These airlines were: Tata Airlines, Indian National Airways, Air service of India, Deccan Airways, Ambica Airways, Bharat Airways and Mistry Airways.

The Open-sky policy came in April 1990. The policy allowed air taxi- operators to operate flights from any airport, both on a charter and a non-charter basis and to decide their own flight schedules, cargo and passenger fares. The operators were, however, required to use aircraft with a minimum of 15 seats and conform to the prescribed rules. In 1990, the private air taxi-operators carried 15,000 passengers. This number increased to 4.1 lakh in 1992, 29.2 lakh in 1993, 36 lakh in 1994 and 48.9 lakh in 1995.

There has been a revolution in air travel in India in the last decade. Ever since the government launched its open sky policy and allowed private players to enter the arena there has been a sea change in the airline industry in India. Air travel has become cheaper and more affordable and the number of people traveling by air has gone up drastically. Consequently, Indian Airports too have changed for the better. Airports in India have become more swanky and passenger friendly.

In the recent past Indian civil aviation sector has grown manifold. The rapid growth of Indian economy has resulted in a spillover effect on the airline industry in India. Several new players have entered the industry and many more are about to enter the arena. The arrival of cheap airline carriers in India has spiced up the whole affair. Suddenly the air travel is no more the monopoly of the rich and the mighty.

Aviation Industry in India saw an important change in the year 2003, when budget flying was introduced by Air Deccan through the lowering down of fares to about 17 per cent in comparison to what the other airlines charged. Air Deccan was joined in this process by Go Airways, Spice Jet, and Kingfisher Air. Thus, new trends were introduced in the aviation market, by these budget airlines. Spice Jet, Go Air, IndiGo Airlines are some of the low cost carriers in India. Jet Airways, Kingfisher Airlines and Air India are not considered as the low cost carriers.

2.3 Overview of Major Players of Airline Industry in India

In India, many private airlines have entered the airline industry. Besides one public sector airline there are five privet airlines operating in India .The airline scenario totally changed because of the entry of low cost airlines. The various domestic airlines includes–

2.3.1 Air India

Air India was founded by J. R. D. Tata in July 1932 as Tata Airlines, a division of Tata Sons Ltd. (now Tata Group). It is the flag carrier airline of India and a part of the Government of India owned Air India Limited (AIL). The airline operates a fleet of Airbus and Boeing aircraft serving Asia, Australia, Europe and North America. Its corporate office is located at the Air India Building at Nariman Point in South Mumbai. Air India has two major domestic hubs at Indira Gandhi International Airport and Chhatrapati Shivaji International Airport.

Air India has the fourth largest share in India's domestic air travel market, behind Jet Airways, Kingfisher and IndiGo. Following its merger with Indian, Air India has faced multiple problems, including escalating financial losses and discontent among employees. The merger happened in. As part of the merger process, a new company called the National Aviation Company of India Limited (NACIL) was established, into which both Air India (along with Air India Express) and Indian Airlines (along with Alliance Air) will be merged.

On 27 February 2011, Air India and Indian Airlines merged along with their subsidiaries to form Air India Limited. Flying Returns is Air India's frequent flyer programme. The programme is also shared by all other Air India Limited carriers.

2.3.2 Go Air

Go Air was founded by Jehangir Wadia, currently the managing director of the airline. It launched commercial operations in November 2005. It is now wholly owned by the Wadia Group, Mumbai based and majority owners of Bombay Dyeing and Britannia Industries.

Go Air is an Indian low-fare airline based in Mumbai, Maharashtra. It operates domestic passenger services to 21 cities with 156 daily flights and approximately 1092 weekly flights. Its main base is Chhatrapati Shivaji International Airport, Mumbai. Being no-frills airlines, Go does not offer a complimentary meal service to its passengers. However, it does offer buy-on-board in-flight meals on Go Air.

2.3.3 Jet Airways

Jet Airways is the largest Indian airline based out of Mumbai, Maharashtra. It operates over 400 flights daily to 76 destinations worldwide. Its main hub is Mumbai, with secondary hubs at Delhi, Chennai, Cochin, Ahmedabad, Bengaluru and Kolkata. It has an international hub at Brussels Airport, Belgium. Jet Airways is owned by Naresh Goyal. Jet Airways is the largest Indian airline based out of Mumbai, Maharashtra. It operates over 400 flights daily to 76 destinations worldwide. Its main hub is Mumbai, with secondary hubs at Delhi, Chennai, Cochin, Ahmedabad, Bengaluru and Kolkata. It has an international hub at Brussels Airport, Belgium. Jet Airways is owned by Naresh Goyal. Jet Airway's head office is located in the Siroya Centre in Andheri, Mumbai. It was incorporated as an air taxi operator on 1 April 1992. It started commercial operations on 5 May 1993 with a fleet of four leased Boeing 737-300 aircraft.

On 12 April 2007 Jet Airways agreed to buy out Air Sahara for INR14.5 billion (US$340 million). Air Sahara was renamed Jet Lite, and was marketed between a low-cost carrier and a full service airline. In August 2008 Jet Airways announced its plans to completely integrate Jet Lite into Jet Airways. Jet Privilege is Jet Airways' frequent-flyer program.

2.3.4 Kingfisher

Kingfisher Airlines was established in 2003. It is owned by the Bengaluru based United Breweries Group. The airline is based in India. Its head office is Kingfisher House in Andheri (East), Mumbai. Kingfisher Airlines, through its parent company United Breweries Group, has a 50 per cent stake in low-cost carrier Kingfisher Red. The airline has been facing financial issues for many years.

Kingfisher Airlines is also the sponsor of F1 racing outfit, Force India, which Vijay Mallya also owns.The Frequent-flyer program of Kingfisher Airlines is called the King Club in which members earn King Miles every time they fly with Kingfisher or its partner airlines, hotels, car rental, finance and lifestyle businesses.

2.3.5 Spice Jet

SpiceJet is a low-cost airline headquartered in Chennai, India. It began service in May 2005 and by 2008, it was India's second-largest low-cost airline in terms of market share. Spice Jet operates over 243 flights daily to 31 Indian cities. The origins of Spice Jet track back to February 1993 when ModiLuft, one of India's first post-deregulation airlines that was launched by the Indian industrialist S K Modi, in technical partnership with the German flag carrier Lufthansa. The airline project was started in February, 1993 by S K Modi, Ashutosh Dayal Sharma It allows customers to earn reward points and cash back offers as they book using their Spice Jet State Bank of India Master Card which was recently introduced by Spice Jet in collaboration with the State Bank of India and Master card. They also provide Insurances Air Accident Insurance, Delayed Flight Insurance, and Lost Baggage Insurance. It has won CIO 100 Award for IT efforts for customer satisfaction and business growth (2007, 2008, 2009 and 2011)

2.3.6 IndiGo

IndiGo is a private, low-cost airline based in Gurgaon, Haryana, India. Since commencing operations in August 2006, it has established itself as one of India's leading airlines using its model of efficient, low-cost operations and by attracting customers with low fares. IndiGo has the second largest share in India's domestic air travel market, only behind Jet Airways and as of October 2011 it is the only airline in India making profit.

Former US Airways Executive vice-President and Marketing and Planning Bruce Ashby joined IndiGo as its Chief Executive Officer. IndiGo's domestic flights operating within India have no Business class or First class sections. It offers only Economy class seating.

2.4 Summary

This chapter describes the past history of the airlines of India. It also describes the present scenario of the domestic airlines undertaken for the study purposes which includes the year of starting, their present managing directors and the awards won by them. The next chapter presents the literature review that includes six broad heads; Service delivery and employees, Service quality in Airline industry, Antecedents and Consequences of FLSE commitment to service quality, FLSE behaviour, Management commitment to service quality and FLSE commitment towards service quality.

Chapter - 3

Literature Review

3.1 Introduction

This chapter presents an overview of current literature in the frame of the presented research problem. It presents the reviews of the studies already done and major findings that have come forth from those studies. The Sections 3.2 to 3.8 presents the literature related to

Service delivery and employees

Service quality in Airline industry

Antecedents and Consequences of FLSE commitment to service quality

FLSE behaviour

Management commitment to service quality

FLSE commitment towards service quality

Mediating role of job satisfaction

3.2 Service Delivery and Employees

The service employees' play an extremely important role on good service delivery. The company's profitability depends a lot on the way the services are delivered. Researchers have tried to establish a relationship between different variables and the delivery of service quality by employees. Vella (2009) tested empirically the relative influence of five ISFs (internal service factors) that interface with internal marketing strategies. Empirical data was collected from a sample (n=202) of super market employees across a large metropolitan city. The data analysis used bivariate correlations, step-wise regression, and structural equation modelling. The findings suggested that there are three main predictor variables, namely, service orientation, service role flexibility, and non-standardised scripted behaviour. The most important internal service quality predictor variable found was employees' service orientation attitude, followed by non-standardised scripted service behaviour and third by the organisational policy to adopt and change (flexible) service roles.

According to Getty M and Getty L(2000), customers naturally respond to better service and empathy from employees with their willingness to purchase the service. "Internal" customers, the employees, respond with their willingness to provide the service. Therefore, it was proposed that an organisation's effort to improve the financial bottom line must first focus on its internal customers before it can expect its external customers to respond. The utilisation of ergonomic precepts enhances the service delivery personnel/ customer interface and produces processes that result in satisfied customers.

Singh (2000) provides a conceptual distinction between frontline productivity and quality. Using data from 159 customer service and 147 bill collection representatives, the author examined proposed hypotheses through multiple-group path analysis. The results indicated support for the distinction between productivity and quality. Moreover, with increasing burnout levels, FLEs were found to maintain their productivity levels while their quality deteriorates directly. Relative to boss support, task control emerges as a more powerful resource in aiding FLEs in coping with role tension.

According to Haysa and Hill (2001), a learning organisation whose employees have a clear vision of the importance of service quality and are motivated to provide that quality will achieve superior service quality. A theoretical framework was developed and a cross-sectional empirical study was conducted to investigate the inter-relationships among the constructs. The results indicated that higher levels of both employees' motivation/vision and organisational learning positively affect perceived service quality. Additionally, employees' motivation/vision was found to mediate the relationship between organisational learning and perceived service quality. The results highlighted the importance of employees' motivation/vision in both the service process and the learning process.

Kivelä and Ha Chu (2001) explored and classified customer perceptions about specific service delivery dimensions. The methodology was underpinned by the critical incident technique (CIT). The findings allude to the linkages between customer feedback and employee performance and the possible integration of feedback into the overall management of service delivery. The resulting discussion highlighted the CIT's use in customer feedback analysis. The results of the survey undertaken suggested that the CIT might be sufficiently comprehensive to assess service delivery quality in restaurant operations.

Shipchandle (2001) in an article emphasised on the importance of delivery of service quality. According to the author, Quality service is becoming a critical weapon, even in developing countries, for maintaining and enhancing the competitive advantage of service firms. The globalisation of the service industry requires firms to assess their changing economic, competitive, legal and cultural environment and accelerate the development of strategies that include technology, coordinated systems, responsive employees and knowledgeable customers.

Vicky (2004) examined the service perception of the service delivery within the real estate industry using exploratory study, pre-test and survey. The study focussed on the gap that is existing in the literature related to the real estate industry. Four dimensions of service were identified SERVQUAL. Findings from the factor analysis showed that employees and clients have different perception of service. It was found that for the industry, increasing service delivery would ensure the industry gains a more professional image.

The increasing implementation of self-managing teams (SMTs) in service delivery suggests the importance of developing confidence beliefs about a team's collective competence. Jong *et. al.,* (2006) examined causality in the linkage between employee confidence beliefs and performance for boundary-spanning SMTs delivering financial services. The authors analysed employee and customer survey data as well as financial performance data from SMTs at two points in time using lagged analyses. The findings revealed divergent results for team efficacy and group potency, suggesting that team efficacy had reciprocal, causal relationships with service revenues and customer perceived service quality. In contrast, group potency had no causal relationship with service revenues.

Liu (2006) attempted to apply the concept of organisational vision to quantitative measures of service operation. According to the author, service organisations look at customer satisfaction ensuing from service quality delivery as a source of competitive advantage and to be able to contribute towards this end, vision must exert influence on the key variables job satisfaction and service effort of employees. The management, supervisory and tenured front-line personnel were surveyed. The hypotheses were tested using Linear Structural Relation (LISREL). Because of the nature of the major constructs, structural equation modelling (SEM) was selected .The results showed that organisational vision positively contributes to job satisfaction and service efforts of the participants working in the organisation.

Punjaisri and Wilson (2007) examined the employee role in delivering the service as promised by the brand. The study aimed to reveal their perceptions towards their role and the techniques that enable them to fulfil the brand promise. A case-study approach was adopted using a mixture of qualitative and quantitative methodologies. The findings from a survey of respondents demonstrated positive relationships among internal branding instruments and their brand promise delivery. It was found that internal branding not only directly influences the extent to which employees perform their role in relation to the brand promise, but also influences the attitudes employees have towards the brand, which in turn affects employee performance.

Wangenheim (2007) study analyses the link between employee and customer satisfaction in detail. Based on three different theories that prior research has used, it investigated whether or not the level of customer contact is a determinant of the existence or the intensity of the employee–customer satisfaction link. Analysis of dyadic data from customers and employees across different outlets showed that employee job satisfaction affects customer satisfaction even for employee groups that are not in direct interaction with customers, although effects seem to be slightly stronger for high interaction groups.

Choand Larry (2010) study offers a provider-based framework identifying four overarching types of online interactions useful for advancing understanding on the design and delivery of quality e-service encounters. The framework allowed for examination of the amount of service intervention, the degree of user participation, and the type of user connection underlying online interactions for both Web 1.0 and Web 2.0 applications and platforms. The article discussed how the quality of each e-service encounter type—informational, self-directive, intervenient, and intensive— requires, from a systems quality and operational standpoint, the management of three elements (i.e., target market, concept, and delivery system) underlying the firm's e-service operations strategy. The article proposed promising areas in e-service encounter quality research where further investigation of design and delivery issues is urgently needed.

Some of the authors have suggested that the employee's customer handling competencies should be evaluated. According to Potluri and Zeleke (2009), competent employees are the key to deliver excellent quality services. The study mainly focused on evaluation of customer handling competencies of the employees' which is an imperative to maximise customer satisfaction. The collected data was analysed using SPSS software package and the result showed that most employees working at the front desk service areas did not demonstrate most of the basic marketing competency indicators. As a result, most customers were not satisfied with the service provided by the organisation and ranked its service quality as poor.

Mishra (2010) in her study have discussed the importance of the concept Internal marketing which is based on the notion of communicating with internal markets and treating employees like customers. According to her, implementing an internal marketing plan helps in educating, stimulating, guiding and leading workforce to higher levels of performance and gratification and it is a promising area of study in the marketing and organisational behaviour literature. The study contributes to the understanding of what IM is and focuses on importance of employees in service encounters.

Ramseook *et. al.,* (2010) in their study tried to have a better understanding of the extent to which service quality is delivered by drawing on front-line employees (FLE) and customer perceptions of service quality. They investigated how closely customer expectations of service and FLE perceptions of customer expectations match. The survey captured customers' expectations of an excellent public service and compared these with their perceptions of the service delivered by a particular public service department. They also studied the parallel SERVQUAL survey of FLE to examine how well they understand their customers' expectations and how well its internal processes support the delivery of top quality public services. The findings revealed that while there was a significant shortfall in meeting customer expectations, the FLE appeared to have a good understanding of what these expectations actually were.

Ye and Liang (2010) in their case study suggested the human resource strategies for improving the employees' quality and quantity, and thereby tried to compare the differences in service delivery through people. In order to examine the validity of previous relevant theories hence put forward the developed theory of service quality delivery chain through collecting and analysing data from telephone interview with managers and survey employees through questionnaires in two hotels. They concluded that organisations should highlight that the service employees' play an extremely important role on good service delivery as well as specially emphasise on the service quality delivery through integrating the service culture and human resource strategies into the organisation.

In order to deliver good quality of services to the customers, the employees should have the knowledge of the customer's service expectations from them. Gaspari and Taga(2011) in their study examined that in order to satisfy the customers, the employees should be aware of the customers service expectations The authors investigated the correspondence between operational quality which was linked to the performer of the service, and perceived quality which was linked to consumer of the service respectively. The role of triangle marketing in improvement of tourist quality service was studied. Factor analysis was applied to the data. Hypothesis was tested and it was concluded that the Triangle marketing directly and indirectly served to narrow the gaps in service quality. It was found out that the delivery of quality service requires cooperation from employees, management and customers.

Rahim *et. al.,* (2011) focused on instrumental and integrative orientations of employees in taking service training. Findings of the study showed that the employees are both instrumentally and interactively oriented towards service training. The study also provided additional insights in better identifying motivational challenges and taking more realistic perspectives about the service training as an instrument of internal marketing.

Malhotra, *et. al.,* (2012) study compares the top performers in service quality in relation to three components of organisational commitment and their demographics by applying a profile deviation analysis. The results showed that the profile deviation for face-to-face employees is significantly negative, while for call center employees non-significant. Although the study finds no significant differences in the three components of commitment, significant differences exist in the total experience and age of the best performers. Also, affective commitment dominates the profile of high performers, while poor service providers seem to exhibit a higher level of continuance commitment.

Luk *et. al.,* (2013) study was specifically designed to accomplish two objectives: to validate the SERV*OR scale in an emerging oriental market; and to test empirically the effect of service orientation on front-line employees' service performance in various service skill areas. The whole research involved a triangulation process, which involved in-depth interviews, pilot test, and survey interviews, to collect both qualitative and quantitative information to validate the measurement scales and test the hypotheses. The major objective was to validate the measurement scales and test the relationship between service orientation and front-line service employees' performance in various skill areas. The results from measurement scale development show that service orientation was represented by service leadership, service contact, human resources management, and service system, whereas service skills were embodied by functional skills and technical skills. Results from structural equation model (SEM) analysis show that various dimensions of the service orientation have differential positive effects on different types of the service skills.

Psomas *et. al.,* (2013) in their study defined and subjectively measure ISO 9001 effectiveness as the achievement of the standard's objectives and determine its impact on the performance dimensions of service companies related to product/service quality, operational and financial performance. An empirical study was carried out using a sample of 100 ISO 9001:2008 certified service companies. Data were obtained from the quality managers of the companies through a structured questionnaire. Exploratory factor analyses are applied to extract the latent factors of the indicators of ISO 9001 objectives and performance dimensions. Multiple linear regression analyses are also applied in order to determine the impact of ISO 9001 effectiveness on the performance dimensions of service companies. The findings of the study confirmed the dimensionality of the ISO 9001 effectiveness (evaluated by the degree of achievement of the standard's objectives, namely prevention of nonconformities, continuous improvement and customer satisfaction focus) and reveal its significant contribution to the performance of the service companies. The product/service quality and operational performance of the service companies are directly and significantly influenced by ISO 9001 effectiveness. However, the financial performance is directly influenced only by operational performance, while the impact of ISO 9001 effectiveness is indirect through its significant correlation.

3.3 Management Commitment to Service Quality

Ahmed and Parasuraman (1994) defined management commitment to service as "the conscious choice of quality initiatives as operational and strategic options for the firm and engaging in activities such as providing visible quality leadership and resources for the adoption and implementation of quality initiatives" (p. 89). Hartline and Ferrell (1996) defined management commitment to service as "the manager's affective desire to improve his or her unit's service quality" (p. 53). Babakus *et. al.* (2003) asserted that management desires and good intentions do not mean much unless employees perceive them as such and defined management commitment to service as "employees' appraisal of an organisation's commitment to nurture, develop, support, and reward its employees to achieve service excellence" (p. 275).

Table 3.1: MCSQ Definitions

Ahmed and Parasuraman (1994)	"The conscious choice of quality initiatives as operational and strategic options for the firm and engaging in activities such as providing visible quality leadership and resources for the adoption and implementation of quality initiatives" (p. 89).
Hartline and Ferrell (1996)	"The manager's affective desire to improve his or her unit's service quality" (p. 53).
Babakus *et. al.* (2003)	"Employees' appraisal of an organisation's commitment to nurture, develop, support, and reward its employees to achieve service excellence" (p. 275).
Alexandrov *et. al.,* 2007; Hartline and Ferrell, 1996). Babakus *et. al.* (2003, p. 3)	"Employees' appraisals of an organisation's commitment to nurture, develop, support and reward its employees to achieve service excellence."

A number of studies have been conducted regarding the impact of management commitment to service on employee performance from the managers' perspective (Ahmed & Parasuraman, 1994; Hartline & Ferrell, 1996). Gronross (1983) found that when managers treat their employees well, employees in turn treat their customers well. Workers are more likely to commit themselves to the company when they feel that the company is committed to them (Fuller, Barnett, Hester, & Relyea, 2003).

Hartline and Ferrell (1996) developed and tested a model of service employee management that examined the attitudinal and behavioural responses of customer-contact employees that can influence customers' perceptions of service quality, the relationships among these responses, and three formal managerial control mechanisms (empowerment, behaviour-based employee evaluation, and management commitment to service quality). The findings indicated that managers who were committed to service quality are more likely to empower their employees and use behaviour-based evaluation.

Many researchers have tried to establish relationship between MCSQ and the employee job satisfaction. Tavitiyaman (1996) tried to establish a relationship between management commitment to service quality and employee job satisfaction; and between employee job satisfaction and pro-social service behaviours .To test the hypotheses, the data was analysed by using the Statistical Package for Social Sciences (SPSS version 12.0) and LISREL version 8.52 The findings of the Factor analysis and structural equation modelling confirmed the effect of management commitment to service quality on job satisfaction and prosocial service behaviours among frontline employees. The more confident employees are in their management, the more satisfied they are with their jobs, and the better service they provide to customers and co-workers.

Natalisa and Subrato (2003) studied the effect of management commitment to service quality on the customers level of satisfaction. The result showed that a majority of the customers were not satisfied with the service provided. The five dimensions of service quality positively affected the customer's level of satisfaction and among those dimensions, assurance had the strongest effect on the level of customer satisfaction. The customer's level of satisfaction and dissatisfaction was not differentiated by price and personal variables, but rather by other variables like the customer perception of service quality, the appropriation between the service quality and the external communication and the situational variables. The situational variable proved to be the differentiating variable in the level of satisfaction or dissatisfaction for business segment customers.

A model of service recovery performance was also investigated to study how factors characterising management commitment to service quality (MCSQ) affect their service recovery efforts. Ashill *et. al.,* (2006) did a cross-sectional survey and the results suggested that the influence of MCSQ is mediated by frontline employees' affective commitment to their organisation. Ashill *et. al.,* (2008) again tried to establish a relationship between MCSQ and the service recovery performance and the turnover intentions and tested a model of behavioural job outcomes grounded in Bagozzi's (1992) reformulation of attitude theory in the important and novel context of a former public sector government department that had undergone corporatisation. Data obtained from the FLEs was analysed using the SEM-based Partial Least Squares (PLS) methodology. Results suggested that there was a significant influence of MCSQ on job attitudes, which in turn influences service recovery performance and turnover intentions.

Elmadag *et. al.,* (2008) examined approaches for improving frontline service employee commitment to service quality in business-to-business contexts. Using a sample of frontline service employees from the logistics service provider industry, the effects of alternative developmental and reward-based antecedents and affective and behavioural consequences of frontline service employee commitment to service quality was examined. The findings indicated that managerial coaching had the strongest influence on frontline service employee commitment to service quality. The results also showed that frontline service employee commitment to service quality improved job-related outcomes.

Kim *et. al.* (2009) focused on the effect of four management-commitment-to-service factors (i.e., organisational support, rewards, empowerment, and training) on employees' job satisfaction and service behaviours. The structural equation model using Thai hotel workers indicated that rewards, empowerment, and training are positively related to job satisfaction but did not support a path from organisational support to job satisfaction. The positive impact of empowerment on employees' job satisfaction in a high-power-distance culture such as Thailand was an unexpected finding. It may result from proper training and reward systems offered to young Thai frontline employees who are familiar with and favour U.S. (Western) culture. Furthermore, job satisfaction was found to have a significant influence on Thai employees' extra-role customer service behaviours and cooperation. In summary, this study shows that job satisfaction serves as a mediator between three management service initiatives (rewards, empowerment, and training) and employees' service behaviours toward customers and coworkers.

Cheung and M. To, (2010) explored the mediating role of effective employee involvement in the links between management commitment to service quality, employees' job satisfaction, and customer perceptions of service performance. Based on a review of the literature on service management, the authors identified the role of effective employee involvement in the relationships between management commitment to service quality and employees' job satisfaction and between management commitment to service quality and customer perceptions of service performance. Using a random sampling method, the authors obtained 143 matched frontline employee-customer dyads. The results of the structural equations analysis showed that effective employee involvement fully mediates the positive effects of management commitment to service quality on employees' job satisfaction and customer perceptions of service performance.

Dolatabadi and Safa (2010) investigated the effect of directive and participative leadership styles on employees' role clarity, shared customer oriented values and employees' commitment to service quality (ECSQ) Data was collected from banks. To analyse the data, structural equation modeling (SEM) was used. The results of the structural equations analysis showed that leadership style of manager can influence on employees' responses. Directive leadership had negative effect on Shared values and ECSQ, and positive influence on employees' role clarity. The results also indicated that, participative leadership directly influenced Shared values and ECSQ but the leadership style did not influence on employees' role clarity.

The management commitment to service quality was also studied in the context of private as well as the public sector. Rod and Ashill (2010) did a cross-sectional survey in which frontline hospital employees (FHEs) were asked about how MCSQ impacted on their service recovery performance in both the public and private sectors. The results of the study suggested that the relationship between MCSQ and service recovery performance is mediated by organisational commitment. With the exception of the relationship between MCSQ and organisational commitment, no differences were found between FHEs in the private and public sectors.

Clark *et. al.* (2009) examined the role that individual unit management plays in the process of service delivery by looking at how a manager's commitment to service quality and that person's leadership style affected the way frontline employees do their job. The fundamental implication of the study was that managers who were committed to service quality and employed an empowering leadership style created a transformational climate that conveyed their commitment to quality service to their frontline employees. That led to employees who were more likely to share the organisation's values, who understood their role in the organisation, who were more satisfied with their jobs, and who performed at a higher level of quality in serving services.

Ghorbani (2013) study aims to investigate the relationship between management commitment to service quality (MCSQ) and services receiving performance in public and private hospitals of Mashhad. The studywas a descriptive research based on survey method which its statistical population selected according to two stage cluster sampling and comprised of 15000 people of all doctors, administrative and nursing personnel of public and private hospitals. Some tables such as frequency and percentage, mean and standard deviation were used in descriptive statistics and regression test and Pearson correlative test were used for testing the research hypotheses in inferential statistics. In addition, software of Ver 16.0 Spss/pc++ applied for the purpose of calculations. As shown by results of testing four hypotheses, it was confirmed that there is significant relationship between "giving proper reward to personnel", "training personnel regarding customer-oriented services", "transferring more authorities to personnel", "providing customer-oriented services" with therapeutic service quality. As shown by results, holding training courses in hospitals and granting proper rewards to personnel are effective on service quality.

3.4 FLSE Behaviour

Brady *et. al.,* (2011) study dealtwith the service sweet-hearting, an illicit behaviour that costs firms billions of dollars annually in lost revenues which occurs when frontline workers give unauthorised free or discounted goods and services to customer conspirators. They gathered dyadic data from service employees and their customers. Results from the employee data reveal that a variety of job, social, and remuneration factors motivate sweethearting behaviour and several measurable employee traits suppress its frequency. Results from the customer data indicated that although sweethearting inflates a firm's satisfaction, loyalty, and positive word-of-mouth scores by as much as 9 per cent, satisfaction with the confederate employee fully mediates these effects. So any benefits for customer satisfaction or loyalty initiatives are tied to a frontline worker that the firm would rather not employ.

Babin and Boles (1996) addressed key aspects of a retail employee's work environment, or 'climate,' and how these perceptions influence work-related outcomes. A causal modelling approach tested relationships among front-line service providers. Results suggested that employee perceptions of co-worker involvement and supervisory support can reduce stress and increase job satisfaction. Other results indicated a positive relationship between role conflict and job performance, a positive relationship between job performance and job satisfaction, and that job performance mediates effects of role stress on satisfaction.

Bansal *et. al.* (2001) emphasised on the internal customer well-being as it is a means to attract and retain external customer patronage. Based on the literature in marketing and human resource (HR) management, they proposed a model that relates six key internal marketing practices to external customer satisfaction and loyalty, mediated by internal customer attitudes (i.e., loyalty to the firm, job satisfaction, trust in management) leading to extra role behaviours directed at external customers.

According to Harris and Ogbonna (2002), the attitudes and behaviours of frontline, customer-contact service providers are a significant factor in customers' perceptions and interpretations of service encounters. The aims of the study were first to explore, describe, and classify such behaviours and second to model the antecedents and consequences of such actions. Existing studies and field interviews were used to forward the notion of "service sabotage", denoting organisational member behaviours that are intentionally designed negatively to affect service. Data reveal that more than 90 per cent of all informants accept that service sabotage is an everyday occurrence in their organisation. A typology of service sabotage behaviours is forwarded and a range of antecedents and consequences proposed

Managerial coaching has been positively associated with frontline employee job satisfaction and performance in industrial service contexts (Ellinger *et. al.,* (2003) The survey study integrates the perceptions of supervisors and their respective employees to examine supervisory coaching behaviour in an industrial context and to assess its association with employee job satisfaction and performance. Findings suggested that supervisory coaching behaviour is positively associated with employees' job satisfaction and performance.

The employees in-role and extra-role behaviour have also been studied. Vandaele and Gemmel (2006) have analytically studied both in role and the extra role behaviour of the employee and how it influences employee performed productivity and quality in business security services. For analyses structural equation modelling was used and the results indicated that performance quality is directly influenced by in-role employee behaviour oriented towards customers, while performance productivity is influenced by both in-role and extra-role employee behaviour oriented towards employees and customers.

Singh (2000) tried to understand mechanisms that govern the productivity and quality of frontline employees (FLEs), and provided a conceptual distinction between frontline productivity and quality, proposed an extended role theory-based model for mapping the influence of key antecedents and consequences of FLE productivity and quality, and also examined the effects of coping resources-boss support and task control-in helping employees cope with the inherent productivity-quality tension in frontline jobs. Using data from customer service and bill collection representatives, the author examined proposed hypotheses through multiple-group path analysis. The results indicated support for the distinction between productivity and quality. Moreover, with increasing burnout levels, FLEs are found to maintain their productivity levels while their quality deteriorates directly. Relative to boss support, task control emerges as a more powerful resource in aiding FLEs in coping with role tension.

Noelker *et. al.,* (2009) examined the effects of frontline workers' background characteristics, personal stressors, job-related stressors, and workplace support on satisfaction with supervision. Survey data was collected from 644 workers. Regression analysis was used to determine the effects of worker level and then Hierarchical Linear Modeling (HLM) and organisational factors on the outcome. Although all four variable categories made significant contributions to explaining satisfaction with supervision, the most powerful were personal stressors and job-related stressors. Results from HLM analysis showed frontline workers in nursing homes and those employed in for-profit organisations had lower levels of satisfaction with supervision.

Luria *et. al.* (2009) presented the concept of service workers' willingness to report service complaints (WRC) and examined frontline workers' discretion about reporting customer com-plaints in two qualitative studies and a quantitative study. The qualitative studies conceptualise WRC based on a critical incident technique and interviews with service providers and reveal that service providers practice much discretion in their decision to report both informal and formal complaints, weighing cost/ benefit considerations, customer motivation and complaint justification, and numerous organisational and other factors. The quantitative study examines a preliminary WRC scale and its relationship with several correlates and shows that WRC levels are associated with measures of organisational citizenship behaviour, service climate, and empowerment.

Clark *et. al.,* (2009) examined the role that individual unit management plays in the process by looking at how a manager's commitment to service quality and that person's leadership style affect the way frontline employees do their job. The fundamental implication of this study is that managers who were committed to service quality and employ an empowering leadership style could create a transformational climate that conveys their commitment to quality service to their frontline employees. This led to employees who were more likely to share the organisation's values, who understood their role in the organisation, who were more satisfied with their jobs, and who performed at a higher level of quality in serving customers.

Coelho and Augusto (2010) study tested a model with employees from a service setting and showed that consideration of the effects of job characteristic had an explanatory power beyond that of job complexity. Furthermore, the results showed that job characteristics interact with each other to affect creativity. Finally, the results also indicated that the componentwise approach is useful for managers for prioritising efforts. In particular, the results indicated that to promote creative behaviours, service managers should consider increasing employee job autonomy, variety, feedback, and identity. However, the interactions between job characteristics also reveal that to build an environment that stimulates creative performance, it is important to find the right balance between job characteristics.

Gudergan and Lings (2010) study looks at the decision-making process that determines the amount of effort frontline service employees will expend in delivering a service in a business-to-business context. Using theories in behavioural economics and interactional and social psychology, the paper develops and presents a model of employee decision-making. Managerial implications, which have the potential to enhance the marketing of business-to-business services and directions for future research in this area, are indicated.

Some of the studies are related to the FLSE willingness to engage in customer oriented behaviour. Pimpakorn and Patterson (2010) examined the need for front-line employees to be both willing (engaged) and able (confidence in their ability) in order to deliver high-quality customer service. The research hypotheses were tested using self-report data collected from front-line employees in service industries, covering both medium and high-contact settings. The results supported the notion that to deliver excellent customer service, employees must be both willing (engaged, positive attitude) and able (possess the capability, or at least the confidence, to do so). In addition, service climate (an organisation environment factor), employee demographics, and industry type were found to be significant. Finally, the interaction effects of being willing and able are significant in explaining customer-oriented behaviour of front-line employees.

Samad (2011) examined the relationship between organisational justice (procedural and distributive justice), demographic variables and employee willingness to engage with customer oriented behaviour. Consequently, the study examined the influence of demographic variables and organisational justice as predictor of employee willingness to engage with customer oriented behaviour. The stratified random sampling consisted of 292 respondents was taken analysed using SPSS version 16. The results indicated that there was a significant and positive relationship between organisational justice components, demographic variables and employee willingness to engage with customer oriented behaviour. The study found that all of the organisational justice components and demographic variables had a significant influence on employee willingness to engage with customer oriented behaviour. These variables therefore serve as predictors of employee willingness to engage with customer oriented behaviour. The study also revealed that procedural justice has more effect on employee willingness to engage with customer oriented behaviour as compared to distributive justice. Finally, the findings indicated that procedural justice emerged as the most influential predictor of employee willingness to engage with customer oriented behaviour.

Slatten *et. al.* (2011) explained the relationships between empowering leadership and a humorous work climate; and service employees' creativity and innovative behaviour in frontline service jobs. A model of causal relationships was presented, along with formulated hypotheses. The data were collected with a survey answered by frontline service employees in hotels. The findings indicated a strong relationship between frontline cognitive creativity production of novel ideas and the behavioural implementation of these ideas into their respective work role. The empirical findings indicated that both empowering leadership and a humorous work climate are able to trigger frontline service employees' creativity. In addition service employees' creativity appeared to be a mediating variable in the relationship between empowering leadership, a humorous work climate, and the service employees' innovative behaviour.

Some of the studies examined frontline service employees' understanding of good customer service, and explored potential gender differences. Mathies and Burford (2011) found out that males have a more functional outcome-oriented interpretation of customer service, while females focused on the emotional outcomes and actual service interaction. That added another dimension to the understanding of gender effects in service encounters, where gender is already known to influence customers' quality perceptions and the behaviour of frontline service employees.

Yavas *et. al.,* (2011) examined the nature of relationships among interrole conflicts and frontline service employees' in-role and extra-role performances in the hospitality sector. A related objective of the study was to uncover whether these relationships were moderated by two personality traits customer orientation (CO) and job resourcefulness. Results of the study revealed that interrole conflicts were significantly related to frontline employees' in-role and extra-role performances. Furthermore, results indicated that both CO and job resourcefulness moderate the relationships among interrole conflicts and employees' in-role and extra-role performances.

Karatepe (2011) investigated core self-evaluations (CSE) as a moderator of the effect of exhaustion on in-role performance and job satisfaction. The study also examined the effect of exhaustion on the aforementioned job outcomes. Full-time frontline employees in several four and five-star hotels served as the study setting. The study relationships were tested using LISREL 8.30 via path analysis. The results indicated that exhaustion influenced in-role performance and job satisfaction deleteriously. However, CSE reduced these detrimental effects.

Prentice and King (2011) investigated the effectiveness of two marketing approaches, namely customer orientation and adaptability. The paper explored how these approaches influence the performance of frontline employees operating in the casino high-end market. The questionnaire focused on the issues of customer orientation, adaptability and service performance. Various statistical analyses including multiple regressions were deployed to analyse the data generated by the 152 valid responses. It was concluded that relationship-oriented selling behaviours are significant predictors of service performance. The predictive capacity of adaptability was particularly strong in terms of the criterion variable.

Chih *et. al.,* (2009) examined customer orientation behaviour of frontline employees in which frontline employees of six life insurance companies were investigated. The relationsips among job satisfaction, job involvement, job stress and customer orientation behaviours was tried to be established.. The findings showed that job satisfaction and job involvement positively influence customer orientation behaviours, and job stress negatively influences customer orientation behaviours. It was also found that the emotional intelligence moderates the relationship between job stress and customer orientation behaviours. Some authors suggested the businesses to focus more on customer loyalty to differentiate themselves from their competitors.

Kwong *et. al.,* (2013) examined consumer attitudes and purchase intentions toward three major retail types within China-department stores, independent specialty stores, and franchising/chain specialty stores. Of particular interest is perceived risk of purchase, the relative importance of frontline sales staff, trust, and the relationships among satisfaction, trust, and customers' commitment to the salesperson. Personal interviews were conducted in four urban cities, each in a different region of China. Two measures of trust were studied – affective trust and cognitive trust.It was found that there was a difference in perceived risk in purchasing from the different types of stores, but the importance of the frontline salesperson's influence on consumers did not differ. Increased satisfaction by consumers with the salesperson leads to a higher level of both cognitive and affective trust. Intention to maintain a relationship with the salesperson is positively related to both types of trust.

Karatepe (2013) proposed and tested a research model that investigates work engagement as a mediator of the effects of perceptions of organisational politics on affective organisational commitment, extra-role performance, and turnover intentions. Data were gathered from a sample of 231 full-time frontline employee-supervisor dyads in Iran. The relationships in the model were tested using LISREL 8.30 through structural equation modeling.The results showed that the fully-mediated model provides a better fit to the data than does the partially mediated model and further indicate that work engagement acts as a full mediator of the impacts of perceptions of organisational politics on affective organisational commitment, extra-role performance, and turnover intentions.

3.5 Antecedents and Consequences of FLSE commitment to service quality

Slatten *et. al.* (2011) tested a selection of hypothesised relationships between: (i) employees perceived service quality, (ii) employees turnover intentions, (iii) role clarity, and (iv) empowerment and coaching. Drawing from theory, the article developed a set of hypothesised relationships. The data collection was based upon a survey with a sample of frontline employees in service organisations. The findings showed that there were indications that employees perceived service quality has a direct negative effect on employee's turnover intentions. The effect of empowerment, coaching, and role clarity on turnover intention appeared to be mediated through employees perceived service quality.

Chebat and Kollias (1992) conducted a study to test a hierarchical model in which empowerment of contact personnel was presented as an antecedent condition to role conflict, role ambiguity, adaptability, self-efficacy, and job satisfaction. The latter were, in turn, presented as antecedents to helping behaviours directed at customers. The model was structured on three interfaces: employee-manager, employee-role, and employee-customer. Results revealed that empowerment is a very efficacious managerial control tool in that it significantly affects the behaviour and attitudinal dispositions of boundary-spanning service employees. Specifically, role ambiguity emerged as the most influential variable in the employee-role interface, and employee adaptability was a highly determining factor for the delivery of effective role-prescribed and extra-role performances.

Borucki and Burke (1999) tested path models relating importance of service to management, service climate variables, sales personnel service performance, and store financial performance. At the store-level of analysis, the results indicated that: (a) importance of service to management does relate positively to service climate variables, (b) service climate variables are predictive of sales personnel service performance, and (c) sales personnel service performance in turn is predictive of store financial performance.

Lee (1999) in his study explained the link between customer satisfaction and loyalty in which switching costs plays an important role. If the market is competitive and switching costs are high, only satisfied customers repurchase products and services because of competition, which results in small number of false loyal customers who are dissatisfied but obliged to be loyal. The purposes of the paper was: (1) to examine heterogeneity in the customer satisfaction-loyalty link, (2) to identify customer segments with asymmetric levels of satisfaction and loyalty, and (3) to analyse the role of switching costs among different types of the satisfaction-loyalty link.

Singh (2000) provided a conceptual distinction between frontline productivity and quality and proposed an extended role theory-based model for mapping the influence of key antecedents and consequences of FLE productivity and quality. The author examined proposed hypotheses through multiple-group path analysis. The results indicated support for the distinction between productivity and quality. Moreover, with increasing burnout levels, FLEs are found to maintain their productivity levels while their quality deteriorates directly.

Babakus *et. al.,* (2003) proposed a model of service recovery performance [derived from Bagozzi's (1992) reformulation of attitude theory] and tested with data from frontline bank employees. The empirical results suggested that top management commitment to service quality, as manifested by frontline employees' appraisal of training, empowerment, and rewards, has a significant effect on their perceptions of service recovery performance. The influence of management commitment to service quality on service recovery performance is mediated by frontline employees' affective commitment to their organisation and job satisfaction.

Lin, C. and Yu Lin (2005) tested nine hypothesised relationships tested by structural equation modelling. The result showed that employee inner emotion, work group mood, and service environment all have a positive influence on employee affective delivery, which, in turn, positively influences customer emotion and service outcomes.

Service sabotage too has been tested in the service literature. Harris and Ogbonna (2006) tested a model of service sabotage dynamics that incorporates both the antecedents and the consequences of such behaviours. Using a survey-based approach, the authors found out that the findings largely supported the hypothesised antecedents of service sabotage and showed that a range of individual characteristics, management control efforts, and perceived labour market conditions are linked with service sabotage.

Yi and Gong (2006) too tested empirically the antecedents and consequences of customer extra-role behaviour (i.e., customer citizenship behaviour and badness behaviour). The model was tested in an exercise class context of participants at sports center. Results from the empirical test indicated that managing customer extra-role behaviour is as important as that of employee and also found that the organisation have to manage the negative affect of customers to prevent customer badness behaviour, and perceived justice and commitment to increase customer citizenship behaviour.

Many researchers took reward based activities as antecedent and studied its effect on FLSE commitment to service quality. Elmadag *et. al.,* (2008) studied the effects of alternative developmental and reward-based antecedents and affective and behavioural consequences of frontline service employee commitment to service quality. Their findings indicated that managerial coaching has the strongest influence on frontline service employee commitment to service quality. The results also showed that frontline service employee commitment to service quality improves job-related outcomes.

Shamdasini (2008) empirically tested a comprehensive model that captures the antecedents and consequences of perceived service quality to predict continued customer interaction in the technology-based self-service context of Internet banking. Important service evaluation constructs like perceived risk, perceived value and perceived satisfaction are modelled in this framework. The results showed that perceived control has the strongest influence on service quality evaluations. Perceived speed of delivery, reliability and enjoyment also have a significant impact on service quality perceptions. The study also found that even though perceived service quality, perceived risk and satisfaction are important predictors of continued interaction, perceived customer value plays a pivotal role in influencing continued interaction.

Aziz (2008) study contributes to the current body of work in the service marketing area by investigating four major constructs; Empowerment, Emotional Dissonance, Service quality and Customer satisfaction and their relationships.. The data was collected using a qualitative interview technique from the hotel employees. Findings indicated that empowerment has a relationship with emotional dissonance and empowerment may also have significant influence in managing employees' emotions at a workplace. Results also revealed that there is a positive relationship between empowerment, service quality and customer satisfaction.

Ashill *et. al.* (2008) established a relationship between MCSQ and the service recovery performance and the turnover intentions and tested a model of behavioural job outcomes grounded in Bagozzi's (1992) reformulation of attitude theory in the important and novel context of a former public sector government department that had undergone corporatisation. Data obtained from the FLEs was analysed using the SEM-based Partial Least Squares (PLS) methodology. Results suggested that there was a significant influence of MCSQ on job attitudes, which in turn influences service recovery performance and turnover intentions.

Kim *et. al.,* (2009) focused on the effect of four management-commitment-to-service factors (i.e., organisational support, rewards, empowerment, and training) on employees' job satisfaction and service behaviours. The structural equation model was used and the findings indicated that rewards, empowerment, and training are positively related to job satisfaction but did not support a path from organisational support to job satisfaction. Job satisfaction was found to have a significant influence on employees' extra-role customer service behaviours and cooperation.

Dolatabadi (2010) investigated the effect of directive and participative leadership styles on employees' role clarity, shared customer oriented values and employees' commitment to service quality (ECSQ). Data was collected from Iranian banks and questionnaires distributed between managers and employees that have directly contact to customer. The survey asked managers about their leadership styles, while frontline employees were asked about their shared values, role clarity, and commitment to service quality. To analysis the data used, structural equation modeling (SEM). The results of the structural equations analysis showed that leadership style of manager can influence on employees' responses. Directive leadership has negative effect on Shared values and ECSQ, and positive influence on employees' role clarity. The results also indicated that, participative leadership has directly influenced on Shared values and ECSQ but this leadership style did not influence on Employees' role clarity. Also in this study direct, indirect, and total effects of variable have been perused too. The study demonstrated the importance effects of leadership styles of manager in service climate on employees' responses.

The service culture too is linked by many authors to the customer service quality. Hoang *et. al.,* (2010) proposed a conceptual framework of the influence of service culture on customer service quality via the mediation of employee attitudes. It also conceptualises the role of potential moderators such as cultural differences, personal relationships towards service employee attitudes and customer service quality.

Masdek *et al.,* (2011) opined that customers often form their opinions on service quality of the firm based on how well the frontline employees perform. They explored two dimensions, the perceived managerial attitude dimension and the perceived work environment dimension. Managerial attitude was represented by two different constructs which include the customer service orientation of the firm and its willingness to reward their employees for service excellence. The working environment that may have an influence towards their performance include training, empowerment, teamwork, \role ambiguity, organisational commitment, trait competitiveness and motivation. A Croanbach alpha method was used to check the reliability. The findings showed that the employees' service recovery performance was associated with several variables under the headings of perceived managerial attitudes and perceived work factors (training, empowerment, teamwork, \role ambiguity, organisational commitment, trait competitiveness and motivation).

Brady and Robertson (2001) study employed a cross-cultural perspective to explore the antecedent role of service quality and satisfaction in the development of service customers' behavioural intentions. They examined the extent to which the causal order of service quality and satisfaction is robust across national borders. The overriding objective was to determine whether the effects of service quality and satisfaction on such behavioural outcomes as repurchase intentions, loyalty, and word of mouth are context-specific or uniform across varying service environments. Competing theories were tested and the results indicated that the effect of service quality on behavioural intentions is mediated by a consumer's level of satisfaction and that this relationship is consistent across cultures.

Gera (2011) tried to identify and discuss the key conceptual and empirical inter-relationships between service encounter variables of perceived agent service quality, overall customer satisfaction and perceived value and their relationships with behavioural outcomes of repurchase, recommendation and complaint intentions. A total of 258 valid responses were generated from existing customers of life insurance services on the selected variables. The relationships were tested by structural equation modeling using AMOS version 4.0. The initial hypothesised model was rejected and a model was modified till acceptable fit was achieved.The results provided an empirical support for the comprehensive nature of direct and indirect effects of service quality, value perceptions and overall satisfaction on future behavioural intentions (BI). The study identified the key agent service quality attributes of product knowledge, empathyand trust as important antecedents of favourable behavioural outcomes. Agent service quality, satisfaction and value perceptions have significant effect on recommendation intentions.

Whiting (2011) did two studies and investigated the immediate and long-term effects of job stressors on frontline service employees (FSEs). Using cognitive appraisal theory, they developed and tested a conceptual model of two job stressors (crowding and emotional labour) that affect coping strategies and job outcomes. Study 1, which was a field experiment, investigates the immediate effects of crowding in a single firm. Study 2 extended the findings of Study 1 and investigated the long-term effects of emotional labour and crowding on FSEs across multiple firms. The results showed that crowding has a negative impact on coping strategies and job-related outcomes. In addition, emotional labour can lead to long-term negative outcomes, such as emotional exhaustion and decreased job retention, for some FSEs. Consequently, service organisations should consider strategies or tactics that prevent high levels of customer crowding and help FSEs deal with emotional labour.

Coelho *et. al.,* (2011) suggested the creativity of FLSE to be crucial in organisational performance. The research applied Role Theory to enlighten the issue. After a preliminary data analysis, confirmatory factor analysis was used to assess the psychometric properties of the job characteristics of FLSE. The findings revealed that: role conflict and role ambiguity have opposing effects on creativity.The results underscored the need to reconceptualise the mechanisms which contextual factors influence creativity, and suggest how managers can promote creativity through the work environment.

Sun *et. al.,* (2012) study integrated value congruence and person–environment fit theories into a validation of the effects of developmental and reward-based interventions on frontline service employees' commitment to service quality (FLSE CSQ). Based on a dyad survey, the results reveal that formal training, coaching and rewards have positive relationships with FLSE CSQ. Moreover, FLSE CSQ was found to be positively related to job satisfaction, commitment to the organisation, job performance and organisational citizenship behaviours (OCBs). The associations of development interventions and rewards with FLSE CSQ and the relationships of FLSE CSQ with job performance and OCBs were significantly stronger when the consistency of CSQ is high.

Elinger *et. al.,* (2012) utilises social capital theory and the theory of reasoned action to propose and test a model that examines relationships between organisational investments in social capital and service employees' work-related attitudes, norms, and behaviours. Results from a field study of customer-facing employees from multiple service organisations suggested that making organisational investments in social capital favourably influences service employees' commitment, job performance, and organisational citizenship behaviour.

Brady *et. al.* (2011) research is the first to examine service sweethearting, which occurs when frontline workers give unauthorised free or discounted goods and services to customer conspirators. They gathered dyadic data from service employees and their customers. Results from the employee data revealed that a variety of job, social, and remuneration factors motivate sweet heartingbehaviour and several measurable employee traits suppress its frequency. Results from the customer data indicated that although sweethearting inflates a firm's satisfaction, loyalty, and positive word-of-mouth scores by as much as 9 per cent, satisfaction with the confederate employee fully mediates these effects. Thus, any benefits for customer satisfaction or loyalty initiatives are tied to a frontline worker that the firm would rather not employ.

Slatten *et. al.* (2011) tested a selection of hypothesised relationships between: (i) employees perceived service quality,

(ii) employees turnover intentions, (iii) role clarity, and (iv) empowerment and coaching. Drawing from theory, the article developed a set of hypothesised relationships. The data collection was based upon a survey with a sample of frontline employees in service organisations. Findings showed that employees perceived service quality had a direct negative effect on employee's turnover intentions. The effect of empowerment, coaching, and role clarity on turnover intention appeared to be mediated through employees perceived service quality.

Hashim and Mahmood (2011) argued that excellent service quality performance is one of the key factors in building niche and having competitive edge that separates one from its competitors nationally and globally. The result of the study revealed that there is a significant relationship between transformational leadership style and commitment to service quality. The study implied to the policy makers and academic leaders at the universities that they can focus in developing their academic staff, by tapping their potentials, inspiring them, promoting collaboration, motivating and reinforcing positive attitudes towards commitment to service quality.

Elinger *et. al.,* (2010) study integrated conceptual and empirical research on managerial coaching to develop a more comprehensive understanding of how managers as coaches can engage with their employees and facilitate their learning. Attention to factors that promote or may inhibit such coaching practice is given so that frontline supervisors, managers, and leaders can absorb this increasingly important role willingly and effectively.

Table 3.2: Summary of literature of antecedents and consequences

Author	*Antecedents*	*Consequences*
Coelho *et. al.*, (2011)	Job complexity and relationships at work (Mediating variables: Role stress and intrinsic Motivation)	FLSE Creativity
Masdek *et. al.*, (2011)	Perceived managerial attitude (customer service orientation of the firm and its willingness to reward their employees) and perceived work environment (training, empowerment, teamwork, \role ambiguity, organisational commitment, trait competitiveness and motivation).	Frontline Employees' Service Recovery Performance
Hoang *et. al.*, (2010)	Cultural differences (Mediating variable: Employee attitude)	Customer service quality
Brady *et. al.*, (2011)	Service sweat hearting	Firm's satisfaction, loyalty, and positive word-of-mouth
Sun *et. al.*, (2012)	Developmental and reward-based interventions	Frontline service employees' commitment to service quality (FLSE CSQ)
Gera (2011)	Service encounter variables of perceived agent service quality, overall customer satisfaction and perceived value	Behavioural outcomes of repurchase, recommendation and complaint intentions

3.6 Service Quality in Airline Industry

An airline can lead the market only if it offers superior quality service relatively to the competitors. Some recent studies show the different way of approaching to airline service quality. Many of the authors have tried to establish relationship between dimensions of service quality and the passengers' satisfaction.

Ariffin *et. al.*, (2010) examined some dimensions of service quality for low cost carrier and subsequently to determine the relationships between the dimensions of service quality and passengers' satisfaction on the airline services. The results of the factor analysis revealed that "caring and tangible" was the most important dimension of service quality for low cost carriers, followed by "reliability", "responsiveness", "affordability" and "visual attractiveness".

Efforts have also been made to examine the relationship between competition and airline service quality by regressing on-time performance on market structure. Greenfield (2012) in his study, addressed the endogeneity of market structure and for this two distinct instrumental variables were employed i.e. the lagged market structure and exploited a global airline merger that induced differential variations in market structure across hundreds of airport-pair markets. It was found that the effect of competition on airline delays was three times stronger than previous studies suggested.

Finklea II and Kegel (2005) described whether or not changes in the competitive landscape of the aviation industry are related to the movement of economy class prices. A literature study coupled with a comparative analysis was also done and the findings indicated that the competition is increasing not only between companies but between two competing business models and it is leading to better on-time performance but at the same time to the lower in-flight and ground service quality.

Ostrowski (1993) examined issues related to service quality and customer loyalty in the commercial airline industry. The results of an empirical study, using data collected on two air carriers, indicated that current levels of perceived service quality were below potential and that customer loyalty to airlines is low. A significant relationship was found to exist between service quality (carrier image) and retained preference, a measure of customer loyalty.

Bejou and Edvardsson (1996) presented the results of empirical studies of critical incidents in airline services. The main aim was to describe and analyse service break downs and thus create a basis for crisis management. The aim was also to compare Sweden, a monopoly market, with the United States, a market with keen competition in airline services. The discussion was based on personal interviews with customers and airline employees in Sweden and United States. The study focused on negative critical incidents in the relations between the service provider and business passengers.

Gilbert *et. al.,* (2001) study has contributed to the identification of a market segment attracted by low air fares and efficient airline service. The study is based upon qualitative research with marketers in the UK no-frills sector. The results indicated differences in the marketing approach and also the way the market place has responded, with the more traditional airlines embarking upon cost-cutting and alliance strategies.

Law and Leung, (2001) study examined airlines' Web-based online reservation services. Thirty airlines from three regions were assessed to determine whether there was any significant difference between the three regions, in terms of the Web site attributes and services provided to travellers. In this research, the attributes selected for examination included: (1) components of online reservation services, (2) provision of extra benefits, (3) factors affecting reservation time, and (4) provision of additional services/facilities. Empirical results indicated that some airlines did not provide all components in the chosen attributes and that airlines in these three regions differed significantly in certain dimensions of the chosen attributes. In particular, airlines in North America were found to have the most comprehensive Web-based reservation services.

According to the Singh (2003) study, organisations must become more strategic if they are to survive and succeed in the current business environment. Functional and unit strategies must be aligned with overall firm strategy to enhance organisational effectiveness. In this respect, strategic compensation systems are vital to ensuring desired employee behaviours and enhanced firm performance. This article reviews strategic reward systems and examines rewards at Southwest Airlines. It outlines the firm's strategic compensation and recognition programs and discusses implications for management.

According to Gupta and Kumar (2009) there has been considerable managerial interest in defining, measuring and developing customer satisfaction to meet the competitive challenge among industries. Airlines are also suffering from such competition. Airlines must understand that customer satisfaction is what guarantees the future of these companies and it is achievable by an adoption of a comparative tool to minimise discrepancies between their services and passenger's needs. Various researches are available which clearly depict the satisfaction among customers. In India, Low cost airline industry is going through an interesting phase of competition. Layoffs, shut downs and industry consolidation have battered employee morale – and that shows up the negative influence on the satisfaction level of the customers.

Venkatesh and Nargundkar (2006) examined the service quality delivered by four major airlines in India on the backdrop of stiff competition in the airline service sector. The process of travelling on a domestic airline was divided into pre-flight, in-flight and post-flight experiences. A survey was conducted to find out the perceived service quality of frequent fliers on each of the four airlines across a series of service performance variables. The airline brands were positioned in a perceptual space, where the perceived service attributes were also mapped. Clear differences emerged among the airlines, with two of them perceived as being similar to each other, and the other two differing in many respects.

Prince and Simon (2009) examined the relationship between multimarket contact and service quality. Two hypotheses: (1) multimarket contact negatively affects service quality and (2) multimarket contacts in less competitive markets more negatively affect service quality were developed and tested using U.S. airline on-time performance data to measure service quality. The findings showed that multimarket contact increases delays and that this effect is greater for contacts on more concentrated routes, although the effect diminishes on very highly concentrated routes.

Woo Park (2005) investigated how individual dimensions of airline service quality determine airline image and passengers' future behavioural intentions. To investigate the effects of individual dimensions of airline service quality, Structural Equation Modeling using a maximum likelihood estimator, was applied to data collected from Australian international air passengers. It was found that there were significant relationships between the variables except one path. The dimension of in-flight service and the dimension of convenience and accessibility were each found to have a positive effect on airline image, which was directly related to Australian international air passengers' future behavioural intentions.

Bhat (1995) study examined service quality using canonical correlation analysis. The service quality variables were denoted by the complaint rates, delays, and involuntary denials of boarding; and operating and financial variables by market share, revenue per passenger mile, revenue growth rate, debt-to-capital ratio, current ratio, load factor, employees per departure and operating revenue per employee. The analysis indicated that airline delays were directly related to load factors, and complaint rates to debt to capital ratios.

Huang (2009) tested a conceptual model that considered service value, airline service quality, satisfaction, perceived sacrifice, and behavioural intentions. A linear structural equations modeling system was applied to incorporate the service quality of airline companies into the passengers' airline choice models to enhance the models' performance and the forecasting ability. Two modeling approaches were applied in the research: the structural equation modeling (SEM) and the importance-performance analysis (IPA). The SEM results of the study showed that the service value is the major factor that can influence the behavioural intention.

Sim (2010) study on the airline industry covered the period from 1990 to 2006 and found that "complaints" is a leading indicator of future financial performance as measured by return on sales (ROS) one-quarter ahead. Results also indicated that the effect persisted into longer-term future performance (i.e., the average of one-quarter and two-quarter-ahead) as measured by return on assets (ROA) and ROS. Findings also indicated that service recovery effort in reducing mishandled baggage, was associated with higher future financial performance as measured by one-quarter-ahead ROA. Similarly, service recovery efforts, in reducing mishandled baggage and complaints, was found to be associated with both short-term and long-term future financial performance as measured by ROA or ROS.

Mitra (2010) study found out the passengers' perception regarding the service quality in public and private (low cost) Airlines for which passengers from different regions of India were taken as respondents. The study focused on identifying the most important factors in passenger service both in public as well as in private low cost airlines, to compare and contrast the services on the basis of collected data and to suggest some adequate measures to improve their passenger services. The significantly and positively influencing factors related to passenger's satisfaction and image of both the airlines' are identified with the help of factor analysis.

Lindberg and Löfgren (2009) tried to explore the importance of different attributes that passengers perceive to be important in the services of airlines. Respondents were asked to give their opinions of interaction with the airline when traveling by air – from the booking step to disembarking of the aircraft. The respondents were asked about what different attributes they thought were important in every step, and in relation how their real experience really was. By comparing these two factors, the differences between desired and perceived levels of service quality, regarding the interaction with airlines was found out. Six hypotheses were developed and regression analysis was done to prove that hypothesis. Friendliness in interaction was found to be the most important attribute that the passengers preferred.

Subagyo (2002) found out that there were twelve critical success factors of quality practices in the operations function, which should be managed differently depending on the airlines' organisational contexts, in order to keep their operational effectiveness and efficiency at the required level. The findings configured a model that provides airlines' executives or managers with guidelines, which they can consult in their decision-making process when conducting quality improvement for their organisation. They may well be used by other airlines as well.

Mazzeo (2003) study explored potential connections between the two airlines by examining whether the lack of competition on a particular route results in worse on-time performance. Analysis of data from the U.S. Bureau of Transportation Statistics in 2000 indicated that both the prevalence and duration of flight delays are significantly greater on routes where only one airline provides direct service. Additional competition is correlated with better on-time performance. Weather, congestion, and scheduling decisions also contribute significantly to explaining flight delays.

Hur *et. al.,* (2013) examined whether and how the perceived organisational support (POS) influences emotional labor and the relationship between emotional labor and flight attendants' outcomes. Structural equation modeling analysis provided support for the hypotheses from a sample of 256 flight attendants in South Korea. The results showed that POS has a positive effect on deep acting. Furthermore, it was found that surface acting has a positive influence on emotional exhaustion, whereas deep acting has a negative influence on emotional exhaustion. In addition, emotional exhaustion has a negative influence on organisational commitment, while organisational commitment has a negative influence on turnover intention. Furthermore, POS moderated the relationship between deep acting or surface acting and emotional exhaustion.

3.7 FLSE commitment to service delivery

Hashimand Mahmood (2011) discussed the relationship between leadership style of transformational and the state of commitment to service quality among academic staffs in selected six public and private Malaysian Universities. Total useable questionnaires were 387 with a response rate of 36 per cent from both private and public universities. The result revealed that there is a significant relationship between transformational leadership style and commitment to service quality among academic staff at the Malaysian universities. This study implies to the policy makers and academic leaders at the universities that they can focus in developing their academic staff, by tapping their potentials, inspiring them, promoting collaboration, motivating and reinforcing positive attitudes towards commitment to service quality.

Dolatabadi and Safạ (2010) study investigated the Effect of directive and participative leadership styles on employees' role clarity, shared customer oriented values and employees' commitment to service quality (ECSQ). Data was collected from banks and questionnaires distributed between managers and employees that have directly contact to customer. The survey asked managers about their leadership styles, while frontline employees were asked about their shared values, role clarity, and commitment to service quality. To analysis the data used, structural equation modeling (SEM). The results of the structural equations analysis showed that leadership style of manager can influence on employees' responses. Directive leadership had negative effect on Shared values and ECSQ, and positive influence on employees' role clarity. However, the results indicated that, participative leadership has directly influenced on Shared values and ECSQ but this leadership style did not influence on Employees' role clarity.

Elinger *et. al.,* (2012) study assesses the influence of an organisational human resource developmental initiative on service employees. The authors utilise social capital theory and the theory of reasoned action to propose and test a model that examines relationships between organisational investments in social capital and service employees' work-related attitudes, norms, and behaviours. Results from a field study of customer-facing employees from multiple service organisations suggested that making organisational investments in social capital favourably influences service employees' commitment, job performance, and organisational citizenship behaviour.

Sun *et. al.,* (2012) research integrated value congruence and person–environment fit theories into a validation of the effects of developmental and reward-based interventions on frontline service employees' commitment to service quality (FLSE CSQ). Based on a dyad survey, the results revealed that formal training, coaching and rewards have positive relationships with FLSE CSQ. Moreover, FLSE CSQ is positively related to job satisfaction, commitment to the organisation, job performance and organisational citizenship behaviours (OCBs). The associations of development interventions and rewards with FLSE CSQ and the relationships of FLSE CSQ with job performance and OCBs are significantly stronger when the consistency of CSQ is high.

Paulin *et. al.,* (2006) study tested a model comparing overall and customer-linked antecedents and consequences of employee affective organisational commitment. The study determined: (a) how service climate variables influence both overall and customer linked job satisfaction, (b) the contribution of both job satisfaction measures to commitment, (c) the relationship between commitment and both overall citizenship behaviours and customer-linked behaviours, and (d) the influence of commitment with regard to employee intentions to recommend the organisation to prospective employees and customers. Co-worker support and the perception of fair treatment were found to be precursors of customer-linked job satisfaction (not overall job satisfaction). Customer-linked job satisfaction was more related to organisational commitment than was overall job satisfaction. Organisational commitment influenced overall citizenship behaviours and customer-linked behaviours as well as intentions to recommend the organisation.

According to Loveman (1998), capable employees who are committed to service quality increase customer satisfaction. Authors have identified various variables and tried to establish relationship between these variables and the FLSE commitment to the delivery of services.

Mathieu (2003) addressed the issue of implementing a service offering strategy within the manufacturing sector. The author developed a model hypothesising links between key antecedents of employee commitment to the implementation of a service offering strategy. Amos 4 was used to analyse the data. It was found that the employees' commitment to their implementation role is related to their commitment to the service offering strategy and their understanding of the role they have to play in the service offering strategy implementation.

Hanson *et. al.,* (2003) presented a model for understanding the role of customers' commitment to service employees and their intention to stay with the firm. The model consisted of two kinds of commitment—calculative and affective—to both the service employee and the service firm. The model was tested with a sample of bank customers. The findings supported the direct effect of commitment to service employees on commitment to the service firm and the indirect effect on intention to stay.

Dean (2007) study investigated employees' views on the organisational factors that affect their ability to deliver service quality to customers. For this, data from of frontline employees was subjected to content analysis. Nine major factors were identified. The findings indicated that various factors from prior work need to be integrated in the special environment of the organisation. The study suggested that to deliver high levels of service quality, managers need to rethink their approaches to productivity and performance management, and hiring the 'right' service staff.

Ottenbacher and Gnoth (2005) identified nine factors that promote successful service innovations. The study found that the nature of the innovation is far less important than the effectiveness of a human resources management and employee training, empowerment, and commitment to the service. Ensuring that the innovation was matched to the targeted market was important, but such factors as effective marketing communication and public relations did not support innovations' success. Also important is the tangible nature of the service, but having innovative technology was not a significant factor in new-service development for these hoteliers.

Schwepker Jr. and Hartline (2005) tested a model that examined factors (code enforcement, ethical discussions, and punishment for ethical violations) involved in the internalisation of ethical codes by customer-contact service employees. The authors argued that code internalisation and perceived ethical climate serve as social and cultural control mechanisms that enhance the attitudinal responses (role stress, job satisfaction, and commitment to service quality) of service employees. The findings suggested that enforcing ethical codes and discussing ethical issues on the job enhance code internalisation, which in turn enhances perceptions of the ethical climate, reduces role conflict, and increases commitment to service quality. Ethical climate increases job satisfaction and indirectly affects commitment to service quality by reducing role conflict.

Implications for controlling code internalisation and managing the firm's ethical climate are provided, along with suggested avenues for future research.

Alexandrov *et. al.,* (2007) developed and tested a turnover intentions model, which examined the effects of frontline employees' perceptions of management concern for employees and customers on turnover intentions, mediated by job satisfaction and affective organisational commitment. The authors explored the role of employment status (full-time vs. part-time) as a moderator of the aforementioned relationships. The result indicated that perceived management concern for employees and customers had significant effects on employees' turnover intentions. Employment status moderated the relationships between perceived management concern for employees and affective organisational commitment, perceived management concern for customers and job satisfaction, and affective organisational commitment and turnover intentions.

In the same way, Farzad *et. al.* (2008) investigated the effects of internal marketing criteria on organisational commitment of employees A questionnaire survey of managers established that "inter-functional coordination and integration", training and motivation have positive effects on organisational commitment of employees. It was recommended that more attention be directed toward enhancing organisational commitment among personnel, with a focus on the effective criteria of internal marketing.

Kim *et. al.,* (2011) examined the mediating role of management trustworthiness in the relationship between empowerment and commitment, based on a survey of 330 employees A test of the model in the study finds that management trustworthiness fully mediates the relationship between influence, a dimension of empowerment, and organisational commitment while it partially mediates between attitude, another dimension of empowerment, and commitment.

Parish *et. al.*, (2008) considered the effects of three elements of the servicescape (pleasantness, safety, and convenience) upon service workers' job stress and job satisfaction and, subsequently, their commitment to the organisation and referral intentions. The authors developed a model to embody these processes and tested this model by conducting a quasi-experiment with longitudinal data from nurses working in a hospital that added a new wing to its existing facility. Their analysis of responses supported the model, and they suggested implications for service firms in managing the servicescape.

Ping he (2008) focused on the antecedents and the consequences of affective commitment. Data was collected from 400 employees. Results from the statistical analysis indicated that affective commitment was positively related to its antecedents and consequence: organisational commitment to employees, perceived organisational support, job satisfaction, and employee perceived service quality. In addition, organisational support to employees was found to have a positive effect on employee perceived service quality. The expected relationship between employee empowerment and affective commitment was not statistically significant, neither was the expected relationship between employee empowerment and employee perceived service quality.

Customer-firm and customer-employee relationships was explained by Mende and Bolton, (2011), using attachment theory. It provided theoretical and empirical evidence that customers with low levels of attachment anxiety and low levels of attachment avoidance perceive a service firm and service employee more positively—in terms of satisfaction, trust, and affective commitment—than customers with high levels. Since a service firm and service employee are separate attachment targets, the study also tested whether customers have a similar propensity to bond with both. Insecurely attached customers who find interpersonal bonds with employees deficient, compensate for this deficiency by being more likely to bond with the service firm. Companies that measure customer attachment styles can better segment markets, manage customer relationships, and allocate resources more effectively.

Chiang and Jang (2008) investigated the extent to which the level of psychological empowerment (meaning, competence, self-determination, and impact) was perceived by employees; to examine whether leadership, trust, and organisational culture function as the antecedents of empowerment; and to look into whether empowerment influences job satisfaction and organisational commitment. Using structural equation modeling, the study supported the conclusion that leadership had a positive, direct effect on trust and organisational culture, which are important antecedents related positively to psychological empowerment constructs. The study also suggested that self-determination in psychological empowerment had a significant effect on job satisfaction and was related to organisational commitment.

Tsai and Wang Wu (2011) examined the structural relationships among internal marketing, organisational commitment and service quality. The results of the survey were evaluated using equation models and one way ANOVA. The findings revealed that the internal marketing plays a critical role in explaining employee perceptions of organisational commitment and service quality. Organisational commitment is the mediator between internal marketing and service quality.

Pi Chuan (2012) integrated value congruence and person–environment fit theories into a validation of the effects of developmental and reward-based interventions on frontline service employees' commitment to service quality (FLSE CSQ). Based on a dyad survey the results revealed that formal training, coaching and rewards have positive relationships with FLSE CSQ. Moreover, FLSE CSQ was found to be positively related to job satisfaction, commitment to the organisation, job performance and organisational citizenship behaviours (OCBs).The associations of development interventions and rewards with FLSE CSQ and the relationships of FLSE CSQ with job performance and OCBs were significantly stronger when the consistency of CSQ was high.

Hmeidan (2013) study aimed to explore the potential effect of perceived working environment (training, empowerment, motivation, supportive management, and service technology) on frontline employees' service recovery performance. A total of 400 frontline employees were chosen with simple random sampling method from 20 hotels in Amman, the capital of Jordan. Respondents were asked to complete the questionnaire in a self-administered manner. 330 usable questionnaires were retrieved for a response rate of 82.5 per cent. Structural Equations Model was used to verify the reliability and validity of the scale and to test the proposed model. The results showed that dimensions of working environment such as training, empowerment, motivation, supportive management, and service technology significantly predict frontline employees' service recovery performance. Specifically, among the dimension of working environment, the most significant predictor of frontline employees' service recovery performance was service technology and empowerment. This study implies that managers of four and five star hotels in Jordan should come forward and try their best to present a better work environment for frontline employees to enhance service recovery performance to maintain customers' satisfaction.

3.8 Mediating role of job satisfaction

Faruk (2012) examined the mediating role of the facets of job satisfaction on the relationship between ethical climate and the dimensions of organisational commitment (affective and continuance). The sample data are derived from a questionnaire survey of 199 in a group of companies in Istanbul in Turkey. The results indicated that perception of positive ethical climate is positively associated with some facets of job satisfaction and affective and continuance dimensions of organisational commitment. The results also showed that some facets of job satisfaction mediate the relationship between ethical climate and dimensions of affective commitment and continuance commitment.

Carrière *et. al.,* (2009) study was related to the relationship between internal communication practices, communication satisfaction, job satisfaction, and organisational commitment. It was centred in the emergency services sector, and on land ambulance services in particular. In total, 91 (32.5 per cent) of the organisation's 280 paramedics participated. Data was collected using a questionnaire comprising pre-existing work-related psychometric measures. The measures included the Communication Audit Survey, the Communication Satisfaction Questionnaire, the Minnesota Satisfaction Questionnaire and the Affective Organisational Commitment Scale. Only quantitative data was collected.The data showed that internal communication practices explained 49.8 per cent of the variation in communication satisfaction, 23.4 per cent of the variation in job satisfaction, and 17.5 per cent of the variation in affective organisational commitment.These effects were fully mediated by communication satisfaction when job satisfaction and affective organisational commitment were regressed against both internal communication practices and communication satisfaction.

Malik *et. al.,* (2010) study aimed at exploring the mediating effects of job satisfaction on role stressors namely, role overload and role conflict as sources of stress, on one hand, and affective commitment, on the other. Using a self-administered questionnaire, 151 branch managers of private sector commercial banks in Pakistan were randomly selected and surveyed to examine the mediating role of job satisfaction. Results revealed that role overload and role conflict directly and negatively influence job satisfaction. It was also found that role overload and role conflict directly and negatively influence affective commitment. The causal steps method along with correlation tests revealed that job satisfaction partially mediated the effects of role overload and role conflict on affective commitment.

Güleryüz (2008) investigated the effect of emotional intelligence and its dimensions on job satisfaction and organisational commitment of nurses.The relations among emotional intelligence, job satisfaction and organisational commitment of nurses and the mediating effect of job satisfaction between emotional intelligence and organisational commitment has been studied.. The results showed that emotional intelligence was significantly and positively related to job satisfaction and organisational commitment. The positive relation between job satisfaction and organisational commitment was also significant. Job satisfaction was found to be related with "regulation of emotion (ROE) and "use of emotion (UOE) but not with other dimensions of emotional intelligence. "Other's emotional appraisal" did not have any relations with job satisfaction or organisational commitment and "self-emotional appraisal (SEA)" was found to be a suppressor. It was found that job satisfaction is a mediator between emotional intelligence and organisational commitment. The other finding of the study was that "SEA" and "UOE" have direct effects on organisational commitment whereas job satisfaction is a mediator between "regulation of emotion" and organisational commitment.

Cherati (2013) study investigated the mediating role of job satisfaction between spiritual intelligence and organisational commitment. The present study was conducted in a public bank in Iran. There were 1834 employees in the bank. According to Krejcie and Morgan (1970), the minimum number of sample size was determined as 320 employees. A total of 500 questionnaires were distributed among employees and 323 usable questionnaires were returned. The findings indicate that spiritual intelligence has a positive influence on job satisfaction; and organisational commitment has a positive influence on job satisfaction. Furthermore, no significant direct relationship was found between spiritual intelligenceand organisational commitment. But an indirect relationship between spiritual intelligence and organisational commitment with job satisfaction acting as a mediator was established. As a result, the effect of spiritual intelligence on organisational commitment is mediated by job satisfaction.

Kimura (2012) investigated the causal relationship among transformational leadership, perceptions of organisational politics, market orientation, and work-related outcome. In this study, he assumed that organisation-level perceptions of organisational politics and market orientation mediate the relationship between top management's transformational leadership and employees' work-related outcomes and that perceptions of organisational politics diminish market orientation. Data were collected from a sample of 200 employees working in Japanese companies. To test the hypothesised correlations, structural equation modelling using AMOS 16.0 was used. Results showed that both perceptions of politics and market orientation mediated the relationship between transformational leadership and employees' job satisfaction. However, perceptions of organisational politics were not significantly correlated with market orientation.

3.9 Research Gap

Frontline employees play a very crucial role in service organisations. They span the boundary between the firm and its customers and are directly responsible for service quality, customer satisfaction, and ultimately the overall performance of the firm (Hartline and Ferrell 1996).They are more committed to the firm only when their behaviour is responsible enough. Some of the researchers have found out that workers that are committed (i.e. identify and involve themselves) to their organisations perform to a higher standard (Meyer *et. al.,* 1989; Mowday *et. al.,* 1979) and with higher perceived service quality (Malhotra and Mukherjee, 2004). There have been a number of valuable studies of employee commitment towards service quality (Elmadag *et. al.,* 2008; Dolatabadi and Safa, 2010; Elinger E *et. al.,* 2012; Hmeidan, 2013), all of which present evidence. However, very few of these studies provides a picture of the changes over the last decade. Studies have been done mostly on the variables like caring, tangible, reliability", "responsiveness", "affordability" and "visual attractiveness". (Ariffin *et. al.,* 2010) Convenience and Accessibility (Park *et. al.* 2006) Customer loyalty (Ostrowski 1993) management commitment to service quality (Ashill *et. al.* 2008).

It is only recently that attention has been paid to the factors that are responsible for the changes in the concept of commitment to service quality. However these studies provide an effective evidence, it remains a matter of serious concern that there are few research-based models designed for their evaluation. Inspite of a very important role played by FLSE in the airline industry of India, few researchers have studied their behaviour and the reasons for such behaviour. While there has been some research on the general impact of service quality on the airline industry (Ariffin *et. al.,* 2010; Hur *et. al.,* 2013), little has been written on the effect of these variables on FLSE commitment to service quality. Using an exploratory study, this research seeks to address these knowledge gaps by exploring the antecedents and the consequences of FLSE commitment towards service quality. The research focuses on the different variables that constitute the antecedents and the consequences and also explains the role of job satisfaction as a mediator of the antecedents and the consequences. A framework that has been developed can guide future research aimed at explaining and predicting service employees' behaviour and that can also be managerially useful. This research is a small step in that direction, and one that hopefully, will encourage additional exploration in this area.

Major research gaps identified are –

- Lack of relevant studies regarding FLSE commitment to service quality in Indian context.
- There is lack of literature on the Antecedents and the consequences of FLSE commitment especially in Indian Context.

- The majority of studies were conducted in the context of a Western culture because the concepts of most management initiatives to improve service quality were developed from Western organisations.

3.10 Factors and their variants

Table 3.3 describes some of the factors and their variants studied in the literature review:

Table 3.3: Factors and their variants

Factors	*Variants*
1. Service delivery and employees	Organisational commitment (**Pittman F.** *et. al.*, **1995**) Employees' motivation/vision and organisational learning **(Haysa, M.,** Hill, V., 2001)customer's participation, satisfaction, and repurchase intentions **(John D.** 2003) organisational vision (**liu 2006)** cooperation from employees, management and customers (**Gaspari and Taga** 2011) Affective commitment (**Malhotra, N., 2012)**
2. Service quality in Airline industry	Caring, tangible, reliability", "responsiveness", "affordability and "visual attractiveness". **(Ariffin *et. al.,* 2010)** Convenience and Accessibility **(Park *et. al.* 2006)** Customer loyalty **(Ostrowski 1993)** Service value, airline service quality, satisfaction, perceived sacrifice, and behavioural intentions **(Huang 2009).**
3. Antecedents and Consequences of FLSE commitment to service quality	Effect of empowerment, coaching, and role clarity on turnover intention **(Slatten *et. al.* 2011)** Customer satisfaction and loyalty **(Jonathan Lee** 1999). Frontline productivity and quality (**Singh 2000)** Supervisory coaching behaviour and Employees' job satisfaction and performance **(Ellinger, Ellinger, and Keller 2003; Hannah 200**4). Top management commitment to service quality and employees perceptions of service recovery performance **(Babakus *et. al.* 2003)**

(Contd...)

	Developmental and reward-based interventions and frontline service employees' commitment to service quality **(Chuan Sun *et. al.* 2012).**
4. FLSE behaviour	Service sabotage behaviours (**Harris and Ogbonna 2002**) Supervisory coaching behaviour and employees' job satisfaction and performance **(Ellinger, *et. al.* 2003)** Employees in role and the extra role behaviour and productivity and service quality**(Vandaele and Gemmel 2006)** Management-commitment-to-service and employees' job satisfaction and service behaviours (**Kim** *et. al.* **2009**). Autonomy and self-efficacy **(Sousa M P *et. al.* 2012).**
5. Management commitment to service quality	Empowerment **Hartline & Ferrell 1996)** Job attitudes, which in turn influences service recovery Performance and turnover intentions (**Ashill *et. al.* 2008**) Employees' job satisfaction and service behaviours. (**Kim *et. al.* 2009)** Organisational commitment (**Rod. and Ashill** 2010) Service recovery performance **(Babakus, *et. al.* (2012)**
6. FLSE commitment towards service quality	Citizenship behaviours and customer-linked behaviours (**Paulin *et. al.* (2006)** Code enforcement, ethical discussions, and punishment for ethical violations **(Schwepker Jr. and. Hartline 200**5) Transformational leadership style (**Hashim A and Mahmood**) Directive and participative leadership styles (**Dolatabadi R, Safa M 2010)** Formal training, coaching and rewards **(Sun P, *et. al.* 2012)**
7. Mediating role of job satisfaction	Internal communication practices, communication satisfaction, job satisfaction, and organisational commitment (**Carrière *et. al.* (2009)** Job satisfaction, spiritual intelligence and

(Contd...)

	organisational commitment **(Cherati H 2013)** Job satisfaction, ethical climate and the dimensions of organisational commitment (affective and continuance). (**Faruk O 2012**)

3.9 Summary

This chapter presents the reviews of the studies already done. The sections presents the literature related to Service delivery and employees, Service quality in Airline industry, Antecedents and Consequences of FLSE commitment to service quality, FLSE behaviour, Management commitment to service quality, FLSE commitment towards service quality and the mediating role of job satisfaction. The definitions given by some of the researchers have also been stated. The next chapter deals with the conceptual framework and the hypothesis drawn from it.

Chapter - 4

Conceptual Framework and Hypotheses Development

4.1 Introduction

This chapter describes the conceptual framework tested in the study. The constructs indicated in the model are defined. Based on the literature review of empirical and theoretical studies on FLSE commitment in general and airline industry in specific, 55 hypotheses have been formulated. Section 4.2 describes the conceptual framework derived from Bagozzi's attitude theory and the development of these hypotheses on the basis of conceptual framework. Section 4.3 and section 4.4 summarises the hypothesised relationship and presents them in a table.

4.2 Conceptual Framework

The framework is derived from Bagozzi's (1992) reformulation of attitude theory and proposes a self-regulating process, where individuals appraise various past, present and future outcomes. These outcomes produce particular emotions that lead to various coping responses (behaviours).This framework of the Antecedents (Development and reward based activities) and the consequences (Affective and the behavioral outcomes) is developed keeping in mind the various important variables. Accordingly, in response to calls for research on the development of customer-facing people (Peccei and Rosenthal 2001; Rust 2004; Schultz 2002), and based on the premise that a firm's employee development practices ultimately influence customers' service experiences (Bowen, Gilliland, and Folger 1999; Schneider and Bowen 1993), a conceptual framework that examines the effects of alternative

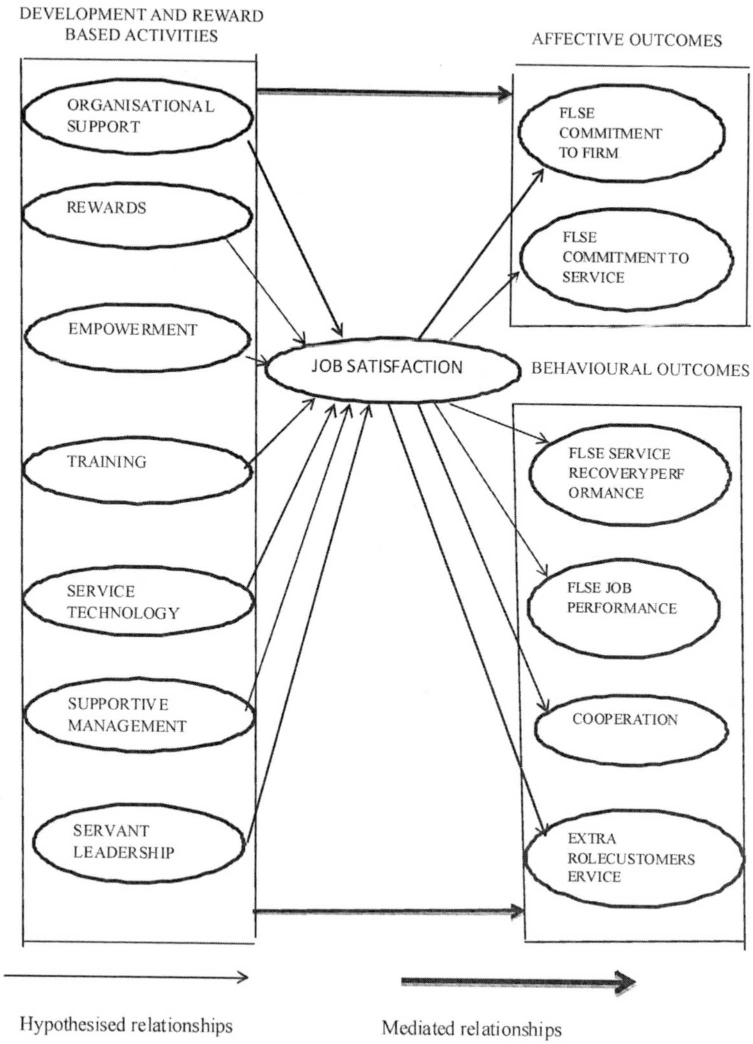

Fig. 4.1: Conceptual Model.

developmental and reward-based antecedents and affective and behavioural consequences of FLSE CSQ is proposed and tested. Figure 4.1 shows the conceptual framework used for the study.

4.2.1 Organisational support

Organisational support is the extent to which employees perceive that the organisation is concerned about their well-being (Eisenberger, Huntington, Hutchison, and Sowa, 1986) and encourages, respects, and recognises those who outperform (Scott and Bruce, 1994). Research has shown that organisational support is positively related to job satisfaction (Kim, Leong, and Lee, 2005; Randall, Cropanzano, Bormann, and Birjulin, 1999; Susskind, Borchgrevink, Kacmar, and Brymer, 2000). Susskind *et. al.* (2000) emphasised the importance of organisational support particularly in service organisations. The authors argued that when problems arise, employees with high levels of organisational support believe that the company supports and appreciates their work. This psychological process helps build trust between service workers and the organisation. Trust invokes high levels of affective commitment to the company on the part of the employees, thereby increasing work effort (Eisenberger *et. al.,* 1986), extra-role customer service behaviours and job satisfaction. (Polly, 2002).

Hypothesis 1a- There is a positive relationship between Organisational support and job satisfaction.

4.2.2. Rewards

The organisation's reward system also influences job satisfaction (Bowen, Gilliland, and Folger, 1999; Brown and Peterson, 1993; Farrell and Rusbult, 1981). Heskett, Jones, Loveman, asser, and Schlesinger *et. al.,* (1994) found that the perception of appropriate levels of pay and other compensation have a significant impact on frontline employees' job satisfaction and loyalty to their organisation. Babakus *et. al.* (2003) argued that management trying to build a strong service climate should establish and consistently implement rewards for exceptional service performance; such practices can be perceived by frontline employees as genuine commitments on the part of management, thereby creating a positive affective response from employees. Similarly, other researchers pointed out the significance of appropriate reward policies to encourage frontline employees to deliver high-quality services (Berry and Parasuraman, 1991; Parasuraman, 1987).

Hypothesis 1b-There is a positive relationship between rewards and job satisfaction.

4.2.3 Empowerment

Empowerment means enhancing a person's ability and motivation to develop and make the most constructive use of their talents and experience (Chebat and Kollias, 2002; Forrester, 2000). By empowering employees, management relinquish control over many aspects of the service delivery (Hartline and Ferrell, 1996) to frontline employees who, because of their boundary spanning roles, can provide quick and appropriate responses to dissatisfied customers (Boshoff and Allen, 2000). Upenieks (2003) found that job-related empowerment significantly impacted employee job satisfaction and work effectiveness. Other studies in the healthcare environment have also shown empowerment to be a significant predictor of job satisfaction (Laschinger *et. al.,* 2001; Manojlovich and Spence Laschinger, 2002; and organisational commitment (Laschinger *et. al.,* 2001; Kuokkanen, 2003).

Hypothesis 1c- Empowerment is positively related to job satisfaction.

4.2.4 Training

Training is a systematic development of the knowledge, skills, and expertise required by a person to effectively perform a given task or job (Patrick, 2000) Poorly trained employees fail to provide a high level of service quality and deal poorly with customer complaints (Bettercourt and Gwinner, 1996; Yavas *et. al.,* 2003). It is not only important to have the right employees for the right jobs but also necessary to train these employees to deal with problems and situations that arise (Boshoff and Allen, 2000). Research shows that customer service training positively impacts upon job satisfaction as it helps employees to develop the skills to handle the service failures effectively (Babakus *et. al.,* 2003; Benoy, 1996; Schneider and Bowen, 1995).

Hypothesis 1d- Training is positively related to Job satisfaction.

4.2.5 Service technology

The utilisation of technology is critical to creating a service system for the delivery of service quality excellence (Heskett *et. al.,* 1997; Dabholkar, 2000). Technology is considered an important asset in assessment of quality and skill provided in organisations (Johnson and Ventura, 2004). Today customers are demanding faster responses to service and the information they seek (Mahmoud and Rice, 1998). Service technology may elicit positive attitudinal and behavioural responses by frontline employees because information technology has the potential to streamline processes, make procedures more accurate and efficient, and reduce the risk of human error (Johnson and Ventura, 2004).

Hypothesis 1e- There is a positive relationship between service technology and job satisfaction.

4.2.6 Supportive management

Supportive management may also lead to positive attitudinal and behavioural responses by frontline employees. Supportive management characterises management concerns and support for employee work and represents the degree to which they create a facilitative climate of support, trust and helpfulness (Beck and Beck, 1986; Hartline *et. al.,* 2000). As frontline employees perceive greater support and authority from management, their sense of obligation to reciprocate with greater effort will increase. Singh (2000) found that a supportive management environment builds organisational commitment and job satisfaction, reduces turnover intentions and enhances employee performance.

Hypothesis 1f- There is a positive relationship between supportive management and job satisfaction.

4.2.7 Servant leadership

Servant leadership may also elicit affective reactions from frontline employees. Servant leadership is a practical philosophy, which supports people who choose to serve first, and then lead as a way of expanding service to individuals and institutions (Greenleaf, 1991). Servant–leaders therefore, set service standards by their own behaviour and management styles (Frick, 1997; Lytle *et. al.,* 1998). They actively engage in helping, assisting and meeting the needs of employees within the work setting (Schneider, 1990; Berry *et. al.,* 1994; Heskett *et. al.,* 1997). Servant leadership may impact on frontline employees' job satisfaction and organisational commitment because of its role in creating an environment conducive to delivering high quality service and handling customer complaints effectively.

Hypothesis 1g- There is a positive relationship between servant leadership and job satisfaction.

4.2.8 Job satisfaction and FLSE Commitment to Firm

Martin and Bennet (1996) mentioned the four alternative models of the job satisfaction-organisational commitment relationship. First, Job satisfaction is antecedent to organisational commitment (Porter *et. al.,* 1974; Poznanski and Bline, 1997; Yang and Chang, 2007). Second, organisational commitment is antecedent to job satisfaction (Curry *et. al.,* 1986; Lu *et. al.,* 2007). Third, organisational commitment and job satisfaction are reciprocally related (Martin and Bennet, 1996). Fourth, organisational commitment and job satisfaction are independent

(Martin and Bennet, 1996). Meta-analytic findings based on 59 empirical studies indicated that "organisational commitment is primarily a consequence, rather than an antecedent, of job satisfaction" (Brown and Peterson, 1993). The topic of job satisfaction and organisational commitment are important issues because of both reflecting a positive evaluation of the job (Udo *et. al.,* 1997). Many past studies reported a positive relationship between job satisfaction and organisational commitment (Fu *et. al.,* 2009; Van Dam, 2005; Johnston *et. al.,* 1990).The hypotheses is proposed as follows:

Hypothesis- 1h: There is a positive relationship between the job satisfaction and the FLSE commitment towards the firm.

4.2.9 Job satisfaction and FLSE Commitment to service quality

Job satisfaction is a product of the evaluation of the job, taking into account all aspects of the job such as pay, benefits, supervisor style, communication and discretion [Burke, 1989; Brown and Peterson, 1993 Most industry observers and practitioners agree that frontline employees who are satisfied with and committed to their jobs share the firm's customer-oriented values, exhibit low levels of role stress, and deliver the highest level of service quality (Hartline, Maxham, and McKee 2000; Singh 2000)].

Hypothesis 1i- There is a positive relationship between the job satisfaction and the FLSE commitment towards the service quality.

4.2.10 Job satisfaction and FLSE Service Recovery Performance

There is also evidence suggesting that being effective in performing a job is positively related to job satisfaction (Rust *et. al.,* 1996). In service-based industries, employee job satisfaction is widely cited as an antecedent of customer-orientated behaviour, for example, people who are happy in their work are more likely to be altruistic, helpful and considerate towards others (Rogers *et. al.,* 1994; Hartline and Ferrell, 1996; Yoon *et. al.,* 2001; Geralis and Terziovski, 2003). Schneider and Bowen (1985) attribute the positive relationship between employee satisfaction and customer satisfaction to a 'spill over effect', whereby employees need to feel that management is meeting their needs before they can fully focus on the needs of customers. In light of the above, we suggest that frontline hospital employees that have higher levels of job satisfaction are more likely to be in a positive mood are behave sensitively and considerately towards others. Therefore

Hypothesis 1j- There is a positive relationship between the FLSE service recovery performance and the job satisfaction.

4.2.11 Job satisfaction and FLSE job performance

In the recent years, many studies have measured job satisfaction as both an independent and dependent variables (Wanous and Lawler, 1972) Fitzgerald (1972) stated that employee job satisfaction relates to job performance. Satisfied employees perform better than dissatisfy employees (Boshoff and Allen, 2000). The individual employee's perceptions are correlated with their behaviors to customers (Schneider and Bowen, 1985). When employees feel that their contributions such as dealing with customers are important, they will feel like they are an essential part of the success of the organisation. These results, in turn, bring satisfaction in the organisation (Zerbe, Dobni, and Harel, 1998). The job satisfaction increases such positive employee behaviors as providing good service to customers, cooperating with coworkers, and commitment to the organisation and thereby improving their performance (Arnett, Laverie, and McLane, 2002).

Hypothesis 1k- There is a positive relationship between Job satisfaction and FLSE job performance.

4.2.12 Job satisfaction and cooperation

Research indicates that job satisfaction is positively related to the decision to help others as operationalised by organisational citizenship behaviour (OCB) (Bateman and Organ, 1983; Becker and Billings, 1993; Farh, Podsakoff and Organ, 1990; McNeely and Meglino, 1994; Motowidlo, 1984; Organ and Ryan, 1995; Scholl, Cooper and McKenna, 1987). Berkowitz (1972) explained this relationship by suggesting that people who were in a good mood are more likely to engage in prosocial behaviour. Subsequent research has supported this contention (Puffer, 1987; Smith, Organ and Near, 1983). Another explanation for this relationship is social exchange theory (Blau, 1964), which predicts that individuals will attempt to reciprocate those who benefit them. Thus, it would seem that more satisfied employees will be more likely to be supportive of other employees than less satisfied employees. By similar reasoning, we believe that those who are more satisfied with their jobs would be more willing to cooperate with others in performing their jobs.

Hypothesis 1l-There is a positive relationship between job satisfaction and cooperation.

4.2.13 Job satisfaction and extra role customer service behaviour

Extra-role customer service behaviours refer to desirable behaviours performed by contact employees to serve customers that are in addition to their official role requirements (Brief and Motowidlo, 1986). Service behaviours that go beyond customer expectation provide a competitive advantage for the organisation. The recent marketing literature emphasises the importance of extra-role service behaviours during service encounters (Bettencourt and Brown, 1997; Kelly and Hoffman, 1997). Bettencourt and Brown (1997) found that job satisfaction is positively correlated with extra-role customer services.

Hypothesis 1m- There is a positive relationship between job satisfaction and extra role customer service behaviour.

4.2.14 Mediating impact of job satisfaction

Job satisfaction will mediate the impact of the seven antecedent variables –organisational support, rewards, empowerment, training, service technology, supportive management and servant leadership – on consequences i.e. FLSE commitment to firm, FLSE commitment towards service quality, FLSE service recovery performance, FLSE job performance, cooperation and extra role customer service behaviour.

4.3 Summary of Hypothesised relationship between antecedents and their consequences

The summary of the hypothesised relationship between development and reward based activities, job satisfaction, affective and behavioural outcome is shown in Table 4.1.

Table 4.1: Summary of Hypothesised relationships between antecedents and their consequences

H1a	There is a positive relationship between Organizational support and Job satisfaction
H1b	There is a positive relationship between Rewards and Job satisfaction
H1c	There is a positive relationship between Empowerment and Job satisfaction
H1d	There is a positive relationship between Training and Job satisfaction
H1e	There is a positive relationship between Service technology and Job satisfaction
H1f	There is a positive relationship between Supportive management and Job satisfaction
H1g	There is a positive relationship between servant leadership and job satisfaction
H1h	There is a positive relationship between Job satisfaction and FLSE commitment to firm
H1i	There is a positive relationship between Job satisfaction and FLSE commitment towards service quality
H1j	There is a positive relationship between Job satisfaction and FLSE service recovery performance

(Contd...)

H1k	There is a positive relationship between Job satisfaction and FLSE job performance
H1l	There is a positive relationship between Job satisfaction and cooperation
H1m	There is a positive relationship between Job satisfaction and extra role customer service behavior

4.4 Summary of Mediated relationships

The summary of the mediated relationship of job satisfaction with the developmental and reward based activities and affective and behavioral outcomes is depicted in Table 4.2.

Table 4.2: Summary of mediated relationship

H2a	Job satisfaction will mediate the relationship between Organisational support and FLSE Commitment to firm
H2b	Job satisfaction will mediate the relationship between Organisational support and FLSE Commitment to service quality
H2c	Job satisfaction will mediate the relationship between Organisational support and FLSE Commitment service recovery
H2d	Job satisfaction will mediate the relationship between Organisational support and FLSE job performance
H2e	Job satisfaction will mediate the relationship between Organisational support and cooperation
H2f	Job satisfaction will mediate the relationship between Organisational support and Extra role customer service
H3a	Job satisfaction will mediate the relationship between Reward and FLSE Commitment to firm
H3b	Job satisfaction will mediate the relationship between Rewards and FLSE Commitment to Service quality
H3c	Job satisfaction will mediate the relationship between Reward and FLSE Service recovery

(Contd...)

H3d	Job satisfaction will mediate the relationship between Reward and FLSE job performance
H3e	Job satisfaction will mediate the relationship between Reward and cooperation
H3f	Job satisfaction will mediate the relationship between Reward and Extra role customer service
H4a	Job satisfaction will mediate the relationship between Empowerment and FLSE Commitment to firm
H4b	Job satisfaction will mediate the relationship between Empowerment and FLSE Commitment to Service quality
H4c	Job satisfaction will mediate the relationship between Empowerment and FLSE Service recovery
H4d	Job satisfaction will mediate the relationship between Empowerment and FLSE job performance
H4e	Job satisfaction will mediate the relationship between Empowerment and cooperation
H4f	Job satisfaction will mediate the relationship between Empowerment and Extra role customer service
H5a	Job satisfaction will mediate the relationship between Training and FLSE Commitment to firm
H5b	Job satisfaction will mediate the relationship between Training and FLSE Commitment to Service quality
H5c	Job satisfaction will mediate the relationship between Training and FLSE Service recovery
H5d	Job satisfaction will mediate the relationship between Training and FLSE job performance
H5e	Job satisfaction will mediate the relationship between Training and cooperation
H5f	Job satisfaction will mediate the relationship between Training and Extra role customer service
H6a	Job satisfaction will mediate the relationship between Service technology and FLSE Commitment to firm
H6b	Job satisfaction will mediate the relationship between Service technology and FLSE Commitment to Service quality

(*Contd...*)

H6c	Job satisfaction will mediate the relationship between Service technology and FLSE Service recovery
H6d	Job satisfaction will mediate the relationship between service technology and FLSE job performance
H6e	Job satisfaction will mediate the relationship between service technology and cooperation
H6f	Job satisfaction will mediate the relationship between Service technology and Extra role customer service
H7a	Job satisfaction will mediate the relationship between Supportive management and FLSE Commitment to firm
H7b	Job satisfaction will mediate the relationship Supportive management and FLSE Commitment to Service quality
H7c	Job satisfaction will mediate the relationship between Supportive management and FLSE Service recovery
H7d	Job satisfaction will mediate the relationship between Supportive management and FLSE job performance
H7e	Job satisfaction will mediate the relationship between Supportive management and cooperation
H7f	Job satisfaction will mediate the relationship between Supportive management and Extra role customer service
H8a	Job satisfaction will mediate the relationship between Servant leadership and FLSE Commitment to firm
H8b	Job satisfaction will mediate the relationship Servant leadership and FLSE Commitment to Service quality
H8c	Job satisfaction will mediate the relationship between Servant leadership and FLSE Service recovery
H8d	Job satisfaction will mediate the relationship between Servant leadership and FLSE job performance
H8e	Job satisfaction will mediate the relationship between Servant leadership and cooperation
H8f	Job satisfaction will mediate the relationship between Servant leadership and Extra role customer service

4.5 Summary

This chapter develops hypotheses on the basis of the conceptual framework which has been developed on the Bagozzi's (1992) reformulation of attitude theory. Thirteen Hypotheses has been developed on the basis of the relationship between the antecedents and the consequences. Further to find out the mediating effect of job satisfaction on antecedents and consequences, 42 more Hypotheses were developed. Finally all the hypotheses were shown in tables. The next chapter presents the research methodology which includes sampling process, data collection sources and questionnaire designing.

Chapter - 5

Research Methodology

5.1 Introduction

The concept of research methodology is very extensive. It can be classified as a tool for problem solving or a way to conduct and gather new knowledge. Everything that can contribute to this is research methodology (Olle Strömgren 2007). However, all methods are not as bearable or suitable for its purpose.The methods to be used depends upon the formulation of problem. Section 5.2 presents the statement of the problem. Section 5.3 describes the research design. Section 5.4 deals with the research approach. Section 5.5 presents research frames I, II and III. Section 5.6 describes the adaption of various measures. Section 5.7 and 5.8 deals with the Questionnaire Development and the data collection which describes data collection methods and the duration for the collection. Section 5.9 presents the sampling design. Section 5.10 describes the analysis procedure and Section 5.11 summarises the chapter.

5.2 Problem Statement

After the liberalisation policy of government of India, many private airlines have entered into the airline industry and this has resulted in a tough competition. Especially the low cost airlines like Indigo which has become a major competitor to public sector airlines as well as some major private airlines. Also the general belief is that the aviation industry services quality in India is far behind the international standards. The service delivery in the Indian Aviation industry has been mainly product-oriented and also not much emphasis has been given to the delivery of the service quality by the FLSE. In service organisations, contact employees have undoubtedly one of the most difficult yet rewarding jobs in the service organisations. The role of FLSE has been given importance these days as they works on the boundary of the organisation and performs boundary spanning roles (Friedman and Podolny, 1992), and the organisation has high stakes on how the service employee behaves in service encounters. These service employees are faced with multiple challenges on a daily basis ranging from technical faults to badly behaved customers. It is the manner in which these challenges are dealt with and the degree to which one can cope with the strain of boundary spanning roles, which distinguishes excellent service providers. There are certain factors which directly or indirectly affects the procedure adopted by them to deal with these challenges. It is also very important to see how committed the FLSE are to the organisation in delivering services to the customers. Lack of commitment from employees can be harmful to an organisation, resulting in poorer performance arising from inferior service offerings and higher costs. (Caruana, A. P. Calleya, 1998.) Although commitment to service quality (CSQ) has been recognised as a critical determinant of service quality (Ahmed and Parasuraman 1994; Babakus *et. al.* 2003; Hartline and Ferrell 1996), and despite contentions that effective HRD enhances employee attitudes and performance (Goleman 2000; Guzzo, Jette, and Katzell 1985; Huselid 1995), relatively little is known about service firms' utilisation of developmental and motivational approaches for improving FLSE CSQ. So for these particular problems the study on the factors affecting the commitment of the FLSE has been undertaken.

5.3 Research Questions and objectives

The study comprises of below stated research questions and objectives.

5.3.1 Research Questions

In order to study the effect of different variables on FLSE commitment to service quality, the following research questions require answering-

1. What are the antecedents of Job satisfaction of FLSE?
2. What are the consequences of FLSE commitment to service quality?
3. What are the effects of antecedents on job satisfaction of FLSE?
4. What are the effects of consequences on FLSE commitment to service quality?
5. What is the role played by the job satisfaction as a mediator between antecedents and consequences?

5.3.2 Research objectives

In order to address the research questions as outlined in preceding section, the study was designed to accomplish the different research objectives, presented as under:–

5.3.2.1 General objective

The general objective of this study was to analyse the effect of antecedents and the consequences on the services delivered by FLSE.

5.3.2.2 Specific objectives

- To identify the antecedents of Job satisfaction of FLSE.
- To identify the consequences of FLSE commitment to service quality.
- To analyse the effect of antecedents on job satisfaction of FLSE.
- To analyse the effect of consequences on FLSE commitment to service quality.
- To study the role of job satisfaction as a mediator between antecedents and consequences.

5.4 Scope of the study

The study covers the following categories of airlines–

Full Service Carriers–Public Sector which includes Air India (Domestic)

Full Service Carriers–Private Sector which includes Jet Airways and Kingfisher

Low cost Carriers-Spice jet, Indigo and Go airlines

5.5 Research Hypotheses

Based on the extant literature and objectives of the study,hypotheses were framred and they have been placed under two groups. The first group of hypotheses(1a-1m) were developed to measure the relationship between development and reward based activities, job satisfaction, affective and behavioural outcome The second group of hypotheses (2a-8f) are related to the effect of mediator (job satisfaction) on antecedents (development and reward based activities) and consequences (affective and behavioural outcome).The null hypotheses considered for the study are listed below–

Table 5.1: Hypotheses (Group 1)

Group 1:

H1a	There is a positive relationship between Organisational support and Job satisfaction
H1b	There is a positive relationship between Rewards and Job satisfaction
H1c	There is a positive relationship between Empowerment and Job satisfaction
H1d	There is a positive relationship between Training and Job satisfaction
H1e	There is a positive relationship between Service technology and Job satisfaction
H1f	There is a positive relationship between Supportive management and Job satisfaction

(Contd...)

H1g	There is a positive relationship between servant leadership and job satisfaction
H1h	There is a positive relationship between Job satisfaction and FLSE commitment to firm
H1i	There is a positive relationship between Job satisfaction and FLSE commitment towards service quality
H1j	There is a positive relationship between Job satisfaction and FLSE service recovery performance
H1k	There is a positive relationship between Job satisfaction and FLSE job performance
H1l	There is a positive relationship between Job satisfaction and cooperation
H1m	There is a positive relationship between Job satisfaction and extra role customer service behavior

Table 5.2: Hypotheses (Group 2)

Group 2:

H2a	Job satisfaction will mediate the relationship between Organisational support and FLSE Commitment to firm
H2b	Job satisfaction will mediate the relationship between Organisational support and FLSE Commitment to service quality
H2c	Job satisfaction will mediate the relationship between Organisational support and FLSE Commitment service recovery
H2d	Job satisfaction will mediate the relationship between Organisational support and FLSE job performance
H2e	Job satisfaction will mediate the relationship between Organisational support and cooperation
H2f	Job satisfaction will mediate the relationship between Organisational support and Extra role customer service
H3a	Job satisfaction will mediate the relationship between Reward and FLSE Commitment to firm
H3b	Job satisfaction will mediate the relationship between Rewards and FLSE Commitment to Service quality

(Contd...)

H3c	Job satisfaction will mediate the relationship between Reward and FLSE Service recovery
H3d	Job satisfaction will mediate the relationship between Reward and FLSE job performance
H3e	Job satisfaction will mediate the relationship between Reward and cooperation
H3f	Job satisfaction will mediate the relationship between Reward and Extra role customer service
H4a	Job satisfaction will mediate the relationship between Empowerment and FLSE Commitment to firm
H4b	Job satisfaction will mediate the relationship between Empowerment and FLSE Commitment to Service quality
H4c	Job satisfaction will mediate the relationship between Empowerment and FLSE Service recovery
H4d	Job satisfaction will mediate the relationship between Empowerment and FLSE job performance
H4e	Job satisfaction will mediate the relationship between Empowerment and cooperation
H4f	Job satisfaction will mediate the relationship between Empowerment and Extra role customer service
H5a	Job satisfaction will mediate the relationship between Training and FLSE Commitment to firm
H5b	Job satisfaction will mediate the relationship between Training and FLSE Commitment to Service quality
H5c	Job satisfaction will mediate the relationship between Training and FLSE Service recovery
H5d	Job satisfaction will mediate the relationship between Training and FLSE job performance
H5e	Job satisfaction will mediate the relationship between Training and cooperation
H5f	Job satisfaction will mediate the relationship between Training and Extra role customer service
H6a	Job satisfaction will mediate the relationship between Service technology and FLSE Commitment to firm
H6b	Job satisfaction will mediate the relationship between Service technology and FLSE Commitment to Service quality
H6c	Job satisfaction will mediate the relationship between Service technology and FLSE Service recovery

(*Contd...*)

H6d	Job satisfaction will mediate the relationship between service technology and FLSE job performance
H6e	Job satisfaction will mediate the relationship between service technology and cooperation
H6f	Job satisfaction will mediate the relationship between Service technology and Extra role customer service
H7a	Job satisfaction will mediate the relationship between Supportive management and FLSE Commitment to firm
H7b	Job satisfaction will mediate the relationship Supportive management and FLSE Commitment to Service quality
H7c	Job satisfaction will mediate the relationship between Supportive management and FLSE Service recovery
H7d	Job satisfaction will mediate the relationship between Supportive management and FLSE job performance
H7e	Job satisfaction will mediate the relationship between Supportive management and cooperation
H7f	Job satisfaction will mediate the relationship between Supportive management and Extra role customer service
H8a	Job satisfaction will mediate the relationship between Servant leadership and FLSE Commitment to firm
H8b	Job satisfaction will mediate the relationship Servant leadership and FLSE Commitment to Service quality
H8c	Job satisfaction will mediate the relationship between Servant leadership and FLSE Service recovery
H8d	Job satisfaction will mediate the relationship between Servant leadership and FLSE job performance
H8e	Job satisfaction will mediate the relationship between Servant leadership and cooperation
H8f	Job satisfaction will mediate the relationship between Servant leadership and Extra role customer service

5.6 Research Design

A research design is the structure designed to answer the research question. According to Allison *et. al.* (2000: 4) a research design includes the planning ofthe research procedure as well as the procedure for data collection and analysis.

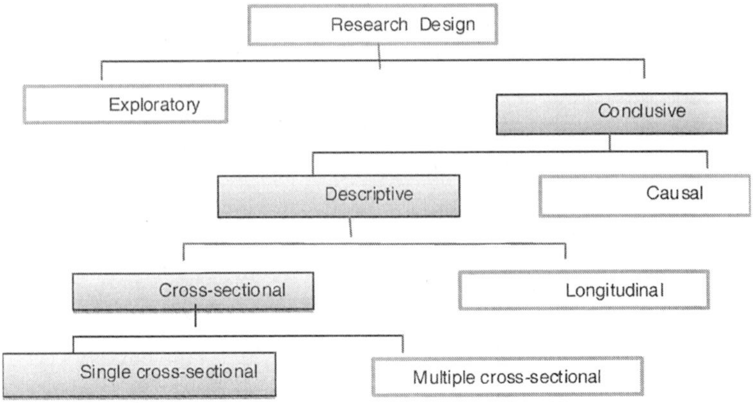

Conclusive Research: Information needed is clearly defined and the research process is formal and structured. Sample is representative and data analysis is quantitative.

Descriptive Research: It describes the relation between independent and dependent variable. It has a structured research design conducted normally through surveys.

Cross-sectional Design: It involves the collection of information from any given sample of population elements only once.

Source: Adapted from Malhotra, N. K. (2007), Marketing Research –An applied orientation, 5th Edition, Prentice Hall of India.

Fig. 5.1: Research design of the study.

Sekaran (2003) highlights the following elements of research design that are used in this thesis which includes:

Purpose of the study

Type of investigation

Extent of researcher interference with the study

Unit of analysis

Time horizon of study

5.6.1 Purpose of the Study

The main purpose of this study is basically to analyse the antecedents and the consequences of FLSE commitment towards delivery of services in domestic airlines andat New

Delhi International airport. It is basically a descriptive study. The descriptive research describes the relation between independent and the dependent variables. The current study has a structured research design conducted normally through surveys.

5.6.2 Type of Investigation

This thesis can be considered as a correlational type of study since it tries to explainrelationships among variables, and thus, hypotheses testing are undertaken to prove these relationships.

5.6.3 Extent of Researcher Interference

The extent of researcher interference in this study can be considered as minimalsince a correlational type of study is usually conducted in the natural environment of the companies without intrusion from the researcher.

5.6.4 Unit of Analysis

The unit of analysis in this study is Airline Industry of India.

5.6.5 Time Horizon

The time horizon of this study is one-shot or cross-sectional since the data are gathered just once, over a period of time from the starting of May 2011 to the end of October 2011. Due to the fact that no incentive was offered to the respondents, their decision to participate in the survey was of pure interest.

5.7 Research Approach

By performing a quantitative study, the results gained through the survey can be interpreted and analysed to view a broader picture of the problem that is researched (Bryman and Bell 2007:169).This was the reason the quantitative approach has been undertaken in order to complete the study as it was found to be the most suitable option for this specific research problem. It also helps the researcher to see the problem from a wider standpoint, where a more general perspective of the problem can be emphasised. As the study is of quantitative nature, the answers were coded numerically, which made this study positivistic.

5.8 Research Framework

There are three research frameworks that are used in this study. The framework scheme has been explained in Figure 5.1.

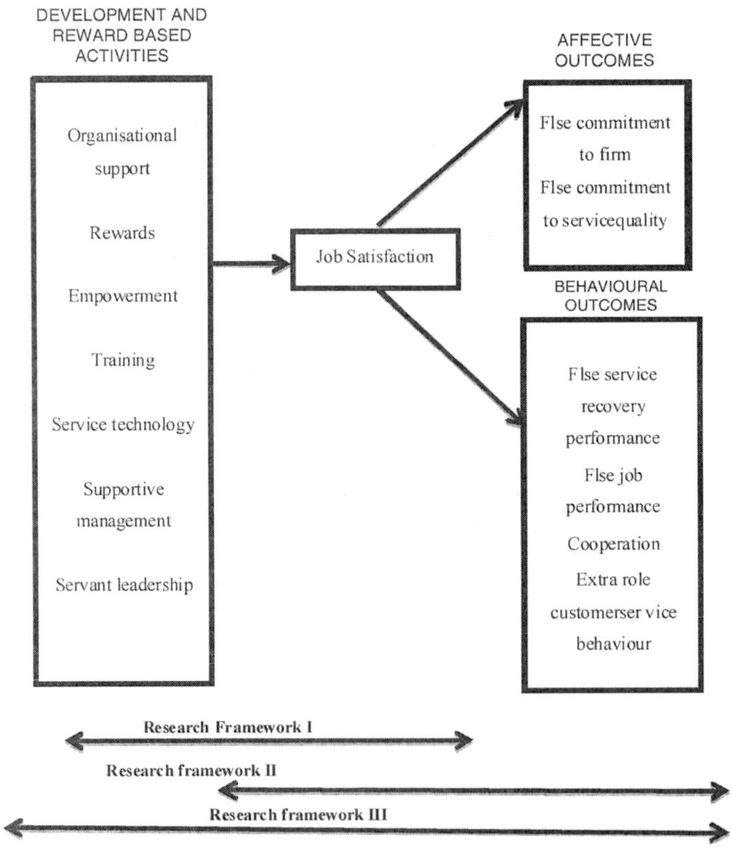

Fig. 5.2: Research framework.

The explanations of the independent and dependent variables that will betested in each framework are as follows:

5.8.1 Research Framework I

The first research framework is used to test hypothesis H1a, H1b, H1c, H1d, H1e, H1f and H1g. Hence, thevariables that are used in the first research framework are:

Independent Variables-

Independent variables are those variables that are manipulated by the researchers, in which the manipulation will cause an effect on the dependent variables. In this study the independent variables used for the research framework I are organisational support, reward, empowerment, training, service technology, supportive management, Servant leadership.

Dependent Variables-

Dependent variables can be defined as the variable that can be influenced by other variables. In this study, the dependent variable for research framework I is job satisfaction.

5.8.2 Research Framework II

Additionally, the second framework is used to test hypothesis H1h, H1i, H1j, H1k, H1l and H1m. The variables that are used in research framework II are:

Independent Variable-

The independent variable for the research framework II is job satisfaction.

Dependent Variable-

Subsequently, the dependent variable are FLSE commitment to firm, FLSE commitment to service quality, FLSE service recovery performance, FLSE job performance, cooperation, Extra role customer service behaviour.

5.8.3 Research framework III

For research framework III, the effect of a mediator i.e. job satisfaction, on the dependent and the independent variables has been examined for which mediation analysis (suggested by Hayes, 2009) is used. Mediation analysis consists of estimating the indirect effect of *X* on *Y* via an intervening variable called a mediator (*M*). Baron and Kenny (1986) suggested that a mediation model should not be tested unless there is a significant relationship between *X* and *Y*. In more recent treatments of mediation, it has been pointed out that in situations where one of the path coefficients is negative; there can be significant mediated effects even when *X*1 and *Y* are not significantly correlated (A. F. Hayes, 2009). Bootstrap procedures described by Preacher and Hayes (2008) were used for mediational analyses and is currently recommended as best practice with small sample sizes (e.g., Preacher and Hayes, 2008; Shrout and Bolger, 2002). Additionally, this method is preferred because it does not assume normality of the distribution of the indirect effects and therefore reduce Type II error, compared to procedures such as the Sobel test (Preacher and Hayes, 2008). The reported results are based upon bias corrected and accelerated confidence intervals which were set at 0.95 with 1000 resamples. If the values of the estimated effect sizes within the confidence interval include zero, this indicates a non-significant effect.

A single mediator model was used in which the effect of the mediator i.e. job satisfaction on different variables was measured. Researchers in organisational behaviour are placing increasing importance on single mediator models in which the effect of an antecedent is transmitted to a consequence through a mediator (James and Brett, 1984). Preacher and Hayes (2004) state that the simple relationship between X and Y is referred to as the total effect of X on Y denoted by c. However, when the relationship between X and Y is mediated by one variable (M) the effect of X on Y is referred to as the direct effect denoted by c′. The indirect effect of X on Y is defined as the product of X_M path (a) and the M_Y path (b), or ab (Figure 5.2, Panel A and B).

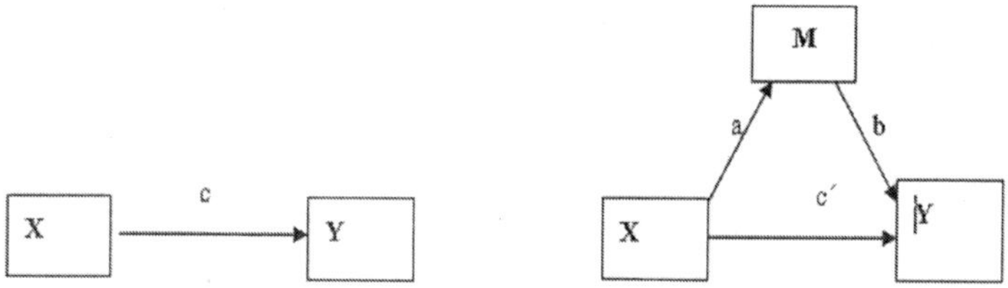

Panel A

(Illustration of Total Effect of X on Y)

Panel B

(Illustration of Mediated Effect of X on Y)

Fig. 5.3: Panel A and Panel B showing Total and Mediated effect of X on Y.

Panel B is the simplest of all intervening variable models, the simple mediation model. In this model, a is the coefficient for X in a model predicting M from X, and band c' are the coefficients in a model predicting Y from both M and X, respectively. In the language of path analysis, c' quantifies the direct effect of X, whereas the product of a and b quantifies the indirect effect of X on Y through M.1 If all three variables are observed, then c_c'_ab (in latent variable models or models of dichotomous outcomes, this will not always be true). Simple algebra shows that the indirect effect, ab, is just the difference between the total and direct effect of X: ab_c_c'. The indirect effect is interpreted as the amount by which two cases who differ by one uniton X are expected to differ on Y through X's effect on M, which in turn affects Y. The direct effect is interpreted as the part of the effect of X on Y that is independent of the path way through M. Hayes (2009).

5.9 Adaption of the variables

The questionnaire was divided into two parts: Part I and Part II. The first part of the questionnaire included six demographic questions related to gender, age, education, job position, length of employment and income. The second part of the questionnaire consisted of 64 questions pertaining to 14 variables (organisational support, rewards empowerment, training, employee job satisfaction,frontline employee commitment to firm, frontline commitment to service quality, frontline employee service recovery performance, frontline employees job performance, cooperation and extra role customer service behaviour).

5.9.1 Measuring variables

Specifically, empowerment was measured with three items from Hayes (1994); rewards (three items) and training (three items) scales were adapted from Boshoff and Allen (2000); organisational support (three items) came from Eisenberger *et. al.* (1986); four items of job satisfaction were selected from Lucas *et. al.* (1990); five items of FLSE commitment to firm were adapted from Jaworski and Kohli (1993) and five items of FLSE commitment to service quality were selected from Hartline and Ferrell (1996). For FLSE service recovery (four items) were selected from Ashill *et. al.,* (2006); FLSE performance (five items) were adapted from Bablin and Boles (1996); Cooperation (three items and Extra role customer service behaviours (two items were taken from Bettencourt and Brown (1997).The adaption of various items for the variables is shown in Table 5.1.

5.9.2 Measurement scale

Each FLSE appraised their commitment towards service quality thereby using a 7-point Likert scale (1 = strongly disagree; 7 = strongly agree) to indicate the level of agreement on each statement in their questionnaire. The coding of the Likert scale was made as (1=Strongly disagree), (2=Some what disagree), (3=Disagree), (4=Neither Agree nor Disagree), (5=Agree), (6=Somewhat Agree), (7=Strongly Agree). This format is appropriate as it allows for a wide range of responses from strongly disagreeing to strongly agreeing. The questionnaire was pilot tested to check the clarity of each item prior to survey distribution. To reduce non-response rate the

Table 5.3: Adaption of different variables

Measures	***Variables***	***Adapted from***	***Items***
Development and Reward based activities	Organisational support	Eisenberger *et. al.*, (1986)	3
	Rewards	Boshoff and Allen (2000)	6
	Empowerment	Hayes (1994)	4
	Training	Boshoff and Allen (2000)	4
	Service technology	Ashill *et. al.*, (2006)	4
	Supportive management	Ashill *et. al.*, (2006)	4
	Servant leadership	Ashill *et. al.*, (2006)	6
Mediating variable	Job satisfaction	Lucas *et. al.*, (1990), Dubinsky *et. al.*, (1986)	9
Affective Outcome	FLSE Commitment to the firm	Jaworski and Kohli (1993)	5
	FLSE commitment to service quality	Hartline and Ferrell (1996)	5
Behavioural Outcome	FLSE service recovery	Ashill *et. al.*, (2006)	4
	FLSE performance	Babin and Boles (1996)	5
	Cooperation	Bettencourt and Brown (1997)	3
	Extra role customer service behaviours	Bettencourt and Brown (1997	2

questionnaire was accompanied with a letter to describe the purpose of the survey. All these actions were taken to help increase the response rate.

5.9.3 Composition of Various Measures

Development and Reward based activities were comprised of seven variables i.e. organisational support, Rewards, Empower-ment, Training, Service technology, Supportive management and servant leadership.

5.9.3.1 Organisational support

It is the extent to which employees perceive that the organisation is concerned about their well-being (Eisenberger, Huntington, Hutchison, and Sowa, 1986) and encourages, respects, and recognises those who outperform (Scott and Bruce, 1994) The work of Eisenberger *et. al.* (1986) generated three items. Organisational support is a multi-item, endogenous construct, comprised of three variables:

1. Availably of help from the organisation when in problem
2. Designing of interesting and rewarding job by the organisation
3. Considering employees goals and values

5.9.3.2 Rewards

The organisation's reward system also influences job satisfaction (Bowen, Gilliland, and Folger, 1999; Brown and Peterson, 1993; Farrell and Rusbult, 1981). Heskett, Jones, Loveman, Sasser and Schlesinger (1994) found that the perception of appropriate levels of pay and other compensation have a significant impact on frontline employees' job satisfaction and loyalty to their organisation. Reward is also multi-item, endogenous constructs measured by "satisfying complaining passengers" as well as by other scales comprising of 6 variables that have been tested in the context of employee commitment.

4. Rewards in case of improvement in the level of service delivery

5. Rewards based on passenger's evaluation of service
6. Rewarding staff for dealing effectively with the passengers problems
7. Visible recognition in case of exceling in providing service to passengers
8. Reward for satisfying complaining passengers
9. Dependence of promotion on the delivery of service

5.9.3.3 Empowerment

Empowerment involves the responsibility and authority to make quick decisions and take actions (Forrester, 2000). It works well for frontline employees if the company creates the appropriate environment. Hayes (1994) generated four variables for this multi item, and endogenous construct.

10. Handling of passenger problems by the FLSE themselves.
11. No need to get managements approval before handling passenger's problems.
12. FLSE to do anything to solve passenger problems
13. FLSE having control over solving the passenger problems

5.9.3.4 Training

Job-related and behavioral training improves the ability to deal with customer needs (Bettencourt and Gwinner, 1996). Bitner, Booms, and Tetreault (1990) reported that more than 40 per cent of unsatisfactory service encounters come from service providers' unwillingness or inability to respond to service failures. Boshoff and Allen (2000) constructed four variarbles for this multi item, endogenous construct. The purpose of the variables is to measure the respondent's beliefs about the training on a positive to negative scale.

14. Receiving continuous training to provide good service
15. Receiving extensive passenger service training before coming into contact with passengers.

16. Receiving training on how to serve passengers better.
17. Trained to deal with passengers complaints.

5.9.3.5 Service Technology

Ashill *et. al.,* (2006) constructed four variables for this construct. The purpose behind it was to measure the effect of technology on the service delivery by the employees.

18. Having 'state of the art' technology to enhance service quality.
19. Allocation of sufficient money for technology to support FLSE efforts to deliver better service.
20. Having the necessary technology support to serve passengers better.
21. Hard work by the management to make the systems and processes more passenger friendly.

5.9.3.6 Supportive Management

Ashill *et. al.,* (2006) constructed four variables for the supportive management. The purpose was to measure the effect of management support on the efficiency of employees.

22. Flexibility of boss about how FLSE accomplishes his objectives.
23. Support of boss on the FLSE ideas and ways of getting things done.
24. Authority given to FLSE by the boss to do the job as he (FLSE) see fit.
25. Trust of the boss to back FLSE on the decisions he (FLSE) makes.

5.9.3.7 Servant leadership

Ashill *et. al.,* (2006) constructed six variables for the servant leadership and the purpose was to examine its effect on the process of service delivery.

26. Regular communication by the management on the importance of service quality.

27. Management regularly spending time 'on the floor' with passengers and frontline staff.
28. Management constantly measuring service quality.
29. Management providing leadership into creating quality service.
30. Management providing resources, not just 'lip service', to enhance FLSE ability to provide excellence service.
31. Management showing care about service by constantly giving of themselves.

5.9.3.8 Job satisfaction

Job satisfaction plays a role as a mediator between the Developmental and reward based activities and the affective and the behavioural. This is a multi item endogeneous construct. Lucas *et. al.* (1990), Dubinsky *et. al.* (1986) generated nine variables for this construct.

32. FLSE satisfaction with the job.
33. FLSE satisfaction with the kind of work he do in the job.
34. FLSE deep satisfactions from working for the company.
35. Getting positive feedback from customers.
36. FLSE well awarded financially for their work.
37. FLSE satisfaction with the amount of pay he receive for the job he do.
38. FLSE satisfactions with his working conditions.
39. FLSE not satisfied by the benefits provided by the airlines.
40. Feeling a sense of pride and accomplishment by the FLSE as a result of the work he do.

5.9.3.9 FLSE Commitment to firm

It is a useful predictor of employee turnover intentions and turnover (e.g., Tett and Meyer 1993). It is well associated with the job satisfaction. It is also a multi item endogeneous construct and has been given five variables by Jaworski and Kohli (1993).

41. FLSE feeling his future to be closely linked to that of the company.
42. FLSE committed to his company.
43. FLSE feeling proud to tell others about his being a part of the company.
44. FLSE caring about the fate of his company.
45. FLSE finding his values and those of his company to be very similar.

5.9.3.10 FLSE Commitment to service quality

Hartline and Ferrell (1996) developed five variables for this construct.

46. FLSE feeling strongly about improving the service his company provides to its customers.
47. FLSE gaining a sense of personal accomplishment in providing quality services to customers.
48. FLSE willingness to put in a great deal of effort to help his company deliver high-quality service to his customers.
49. FLSE caring about the quality of his company's services.
50. FLSE enjoying discussing quality-related issues with people in his company.

5.9.3.11 FLSE service recovery performance

Ashill *et. al.,* (2006) developed four variables for this construct. It includes

51. FLSE handling dissatisfied passengers quite well.
52. FLSE not minding dealing with complaining passengers.
53. FLSE resolving problems of all the passengers he deals with.
54. Satisfying complaining passengers is a great thrill to FLSE

5.9.3.12 FLSE job performance

Babin and Boles (1996) generated five variables for this multi item endogeneous construct. It includes FLSE effectively managing his work to other variables to know the effect of mediating variable job satisfaction on this construct.

55. FLSE satisfying his customers' service expectations.
56. FLSE managing his works time effectively.
57. FLSE knowledgeable about his company's services.
58. FLSE knowing expectation of the passengers.
59. FLSE good at his job.

5.9.3.13 Cooperation

Organ (1990) states that helping behaviours include extra work taken on by the employee, which is not in the job description. Cooperation can be related to either job or personal matters. Bettencourt and Brown (1997) gave three variables to this multiitem endogeneous behavioural outcome.

60. FLSE helping other employees who have excessive workloads.
61. FLSE always ready to lend a helping hand to co-workers around him.
62. FLSE helping orient new employees even though it is not required.

5.9.3.14 Extra-role customer service behaviours

Extra-role customer service behaviours refer to desirable behaviours performed by contact employees to serve customers that are in addition to their official role requirements (Brief and Motowidlo, 1986). Service behaviours that go beyond customer expectation provide a competitive advantage for the organisation. The work of Bettencourt and Brown (1997) generated the following two variables.

63. FLSE voluntarily assisting customers even if it means going beyond the job requirements.
64. FLSE frequently going out of his way to help customers

5.10 Questionnaire Development

A questionnaire was developed for the purpose of collecting data from the employees. Table:5.2 illustrates an example of the questionnaire that was developed togather necessary information in the empirical data collection.

Table 5.4: Format of the questionnaire

	1	2	3	4	5	6	7
	Strongly Disagree	*Some-what Disagree*	*Dis-agree*	*Neither Disagree nor Agree*	*Agree*	*Some-what Agree*	*Strongly Agree*
1. Help is available from my organisation when I have a problem							
2. The organisation tries to design my job as interesting and rewarding as possible							

The items in the questionnaire were measured on a seven-point scale ranging from "Strongly disagree to strongly agree". The questionnaire contained close ended 64 items. The questionnaire was in English. Non-probability sampling technique was used to collect the data. This technique is characterised by collecting data from first available individual of the population.

The test also provided a time estimate of 15 minutes to fully complete a questionnaire. Copy of the questionnaire is in (Annexure No- 1)

5.10.1 Question content and wording

The questions were designed to be short, simple and comprehensible. Care was taken to avoid ambiguous, vague, estimation based, generalisation type, leading double barrelled and presumptuous questions. (Boyed *et. al.,* 2003)

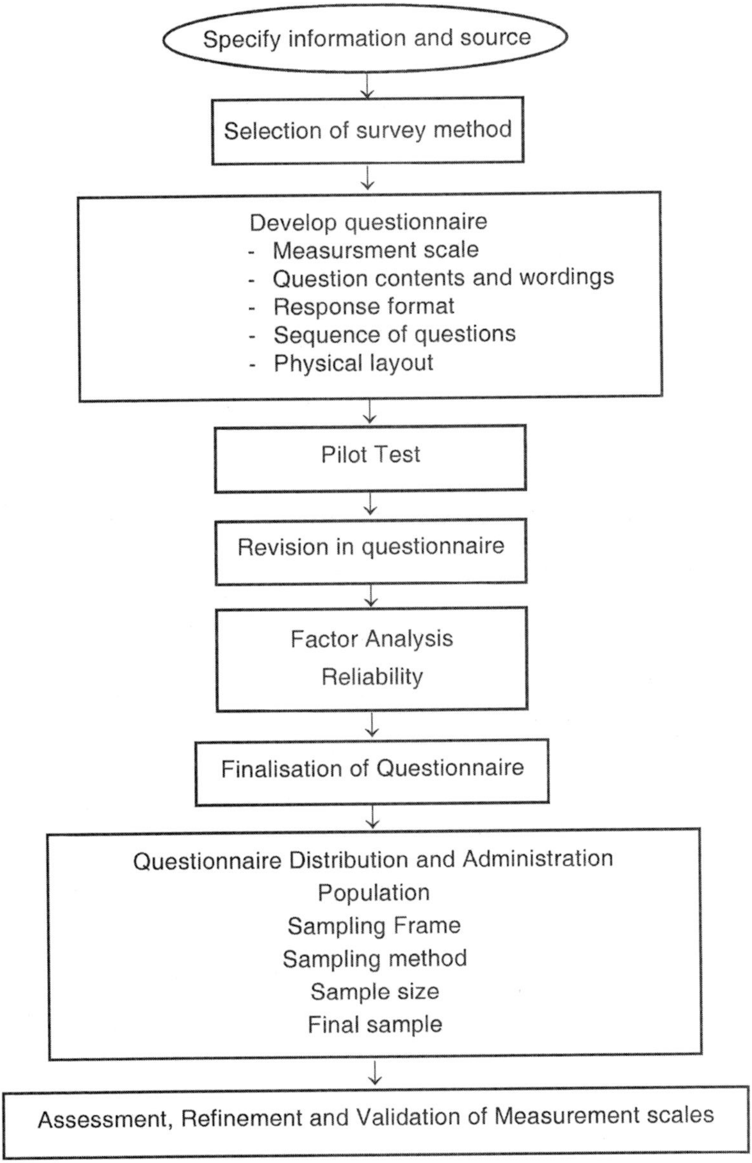

Fig. 5.4: Questionnaire Development.

5.10.2 Response format

The labelled scale response was used for its simplicity in administration. It is appropriate in marketing research as it allows the respondents to attitudinal questions in varying degrees that describes the dimensions being studied (Aaker *et. al., 2002;* Boyd *et. al.,* 2003) In relation to the number of scale points, there is no clear rule indicating an ideal number. However, many researchers acknowledge that opinions can be captured best with five to seven point scale (Aaker *et. al., 2002;* Malhotra, 2007). Keeping the same in mind, seven point Likert scale was used in this research.

5.10.3 Sequence of questions

The questionnaire began with lesscomplex and less sensitive questions. It was divided into two parts. Part A consisted of demographic information and Part B included the questions related to various variables undertaken for the study.

5.10.4 Pilot study

To test the questionnaire, a pilot test was implemented to a convenience sample of 50 employees at the airport.The aim was to ensure that the errors before the survey was carried out on a large scale (Zikmund, 2000; Burns *et. al.,*) Forty seven questionnaires were fully completed (n=47), without any detectable difficulties. Only three questionnaires were not sufficiently completed. Thus, the questionnaire was deemed to be satisfactory and ready for the full implementation.

5.10.5 Administration of Final questionnaire

The sampling process included several steps-

Step 1: Population

The population consisted of Frontline service employees who deal directly with customers on the daily basis. The choice for employees with customer facing role is borne out of the fact that they are believed to know the customers more since they have daily interactions with them. This included all the FLSE working in the selected six domestic airlines operating at the Indira Gandhi International Airport (Terminal 3) and the Domestic Airport (Terminal 1) New Delhi.

Step 2: Sampling frame

This included all the FLSE working in the selected six domestic airlines operating at the Indira Gandhi International Airport (Terminal 3) and the Domestic Airport (Terminal 1) New Delhi.

Step 3: Sampling method

Non-probability sampling method was used.

Step 4: Sample size

Sample consisted of 282 respondents working in six different airlines, one belonging to public sector and five belonging to private sector. A bird eye view of the sample distribution is as shown in the Table 5.3.

Table 5.5: No of respondents of different airlines.

Selected Airlines	*Air India*	*King-fisher*	*Jet airways*	*Spice jet*	*Indigo*	*Go*	*Total*
No. of Respondents	51	52	42	47	46	44	282

Step 5: Final Sample

In all 367 employees were randomly approached during the months of

Of these agreed to participate in the study. During editing phase of the questionnaire, it was observed that 11 responses were incomplete in various respects and thus has to be discarded. This resulted in a total of 282 samples. It included the members of cabin crew, CSA- ticketing, CSA-Check in and the Traffic control assistant.

It may be noted that the feedback received is still relevant as the airline scenario has not changed significantly since then.

Convenience sampling approach was used to collect the data from airlines staff. They were approached individually during their rest periods.

5.11 Assessment, Refinement and Validation of Measurement Scales

Prior to carrying out further analysis, the multi-item scales developed for the study have to be evaluated for their reliability and validity (Anderson and Gerbing, 1988; Sureshchander, Rajenderan and Anantharaman, 2002; SSI, 2007a). Before actual evaluation of the scale, it would be proper to understand these concepts from the point of view of present research.

5.11.1 Reliability

Reliability of scale refers to how consistent or stable the ratings generated by the scale are likely to be (Parasuraman *et. al.,* 1991; Malhotra, 2007; Warner, 2008). Internal consistency reliability was used to assess the reliability of the scales. The most common use approach to this method is the use of Cronbach alpha (Cronbach, 1951; Warner, 2008). The analysis yields a correlation coefficient that indicates the level of internal consistency. Cronbach's alpha is the average of all possible split-half coefficients resulting from different ways of splitting the scale items (Park *et. al.,* Malhotra, 2007). Cronbach alpha tends to be high if the scale items are highly correlated (Hair, Anderson, Tatham and Black, 1998, Hau, 2005). However, another test that must be undertaken before the reliability test is the test for unidimensionality of a measurement scale.

5.11.2 Validity

Validity of a measurement scale is the extent to which the scale fully capture all aspects of the construct to be measured (Parasuraman *et. al.,* 1991; Hayes, 1998; Garson, 2002). In a general sense, a measurement scale is considered to be valid if it measure what it is intended to measure. Among several types of validation procedures suggested in the literature, three types are considered as being appropriate to the current research. They are content validity, convergent validity and discriminant validity.

5.11.2.1 Content Validity

Content Validity (also known as face validity) is defined as the extent to which the content of measurement scale appears to tap all relevant facets of the construct it is attempting to measure (Parasuraman *et. al.,* 1991; Ding and Hershberger, 2002; Malhotra, 2007; Warner, 2008). It refers to the degree that the construct is represented by items that covers the domain of meaning for the construct (Garver *et. al.,* 1999; Malhotra 2007). Content validity is essentially a subjective agreement among concerned professionals (Parasuraman *et. al.,* 1991). Content validity of the scale used in the current research is established by their origins from the extant literature. The new items that are used for the time have been developed through a careful review of the extant literature on the practical manifestations of the respective construct, extensive discussions were held with airline executives, passengers and academicians who reviewed the questionnaire and confirmed that it (with minor change in words of few items) had face validity. After evaluation of the question, they judged that all these were appropriate for measuring employees commitment towards service quality in domestic airlines of India.

5.12 Data Collection

Data collection is simply the way information is gathered. Secondary Data and primary data collection are the two ways of collecting information.

5.12.1 Primary and Secondary data sources

Throughout the study, both primary and secondary data sources are used. The primary data, directly relating to the purpose, was collected through an empirical study. The empirical study was obtained through a questionnaire survey.The secondary data, indirectly relating to the study purpose, was collected through a theoretical study which comprised of books and articles that were not directly related to the study purpose. Certain websites were also used.

5.12.2 Procedure of data collection

A structured survey method was used in which a formal lists of questions was asked to all respondents in the same way. For this purpose a structured questionnaire was developed.

Data was collected from the FLSE of six domestic airlines in Delhi. Permission was asked from the airport manager and then after informal talks with the employees, the questionnaire was given to them.The respondents were frontline employees who possess an accurate and comprehensive perception of service quality practices employed and also they are the one who interacts the most with the passengers.

The estimated time for the completion of the questionnaire was kept to be 15 minutes. Also, it was necessary to collect the target of 5 surveys per day.The respondents were instructed to read the directions before filling the questionnaire. At the very outset they were assured of the confidentiality of their responses. Respondents were assured that they need not mention their names and also that the study was not commissioned by their management and their participation was entirely on voluntary basis. They were asked to answer all the statement as honestly and completely as possible and not to leave any items unanswered. Only after their doubts were clarified, the data collection began. The respondents were encouraged to complete a questionnaire by the researcher itself. Most were able to complete the questionnaire in 10 to 15 minutes. The exact numbers of refusals are difficult to track but it is estimated to be just less than half. The number of questionnaires collected was 282 out of 293, with only eleven incomplete questionnaires and thus excluded. Certain precautions were taken during the process of data collection. They are as given below:

(a) Following the ethics of data collection in research, it was made sure, that the respondents were willing to take the test.

(b) Rapport was established and maintained throughout the procedure of data collection.

(c) Respondents were made confident that their identities would not be disclosed in any case.

(d) To extent possible, an attempt was made to include people from departments which were in direct contact with the passengers.

(e) The respondents were told to give free and frank responses and the responses that came first to their mind.

5.13 Sample Design

Sekaran (2003) describes sampling as the process of selecting a sufficient number and the right type of elements for study from a certain population. As population is defined, the entire group of elements that the researcher is interested to investigate. An *element* on the other hand, is a single member of the population (Jankowicz, 1991). Sample is defined as a portion or subset of the population, the size of which is determined by the type and objective of the study, as well as time and financial constraints (Fink, 1995). Sampling therefore is the method of drawing the sample and it is a vital part of a research as it allows to the researcher to generalise findings, as it is impossible to examine the whole population (Frankfort-Nachmias and Nachmias, 1996).

5.13.1 Elements

The elements of the study were the members of cabin crew, CSA- ticketing, CSA-Check in and the Traffic control assistant, as they play a major role while interacting with the passengers.

5.13.2 Sample size

Figure 5.3 shows the bar diagram showing the number of respondents belonging to different airlines.

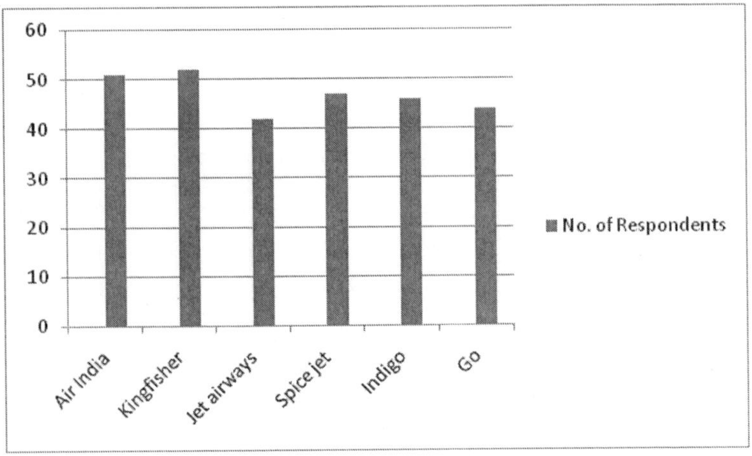

Fig. 5.5: Graph showing number of respondents of different airlines.

5.13.3 Area of the Study

The present study was conducted at Indira Gandhi International Airport (Terminal 3) and the Domestic Airport (Terminal 1) New Delhi. The three airlines i.e. Air India, Jet airways and Kingfisher operates from Terminal 3 and IndiGo, Go airlines and Spice jet operates from Terminal 2. As Delhi is the national capital as well as the city of twenty first century and also being a cosmopolitan city, it has a good representation of diversified culture. It has the entire major public sector as well as the private airlines.

5.13.4 Sampling technique

The non-probability sampling technique was used to collect the data. Non-probability sampling happens if there is no way of estimating the probability that each individual or element will be included in the sample; hence, probability of any particular member of the population being chosen is unknown. In this method, not all the sampling elements in the population are given a chance of being included in the sample. Convenience sampling method was used in which the researcher chooses units which come to hand or are convenient; selecting sample items that are close at hand or otherwise easy to obtain. As the method is inexpensive, and needs little time to administer, it is more economical than the other methods of non-probability technique.

5.14 Data Analysis

The analysis of data was carried out through the following steps:

(1) All the incomplete questions (11) were removed.

(2) Total 282 questionnaires were complete and were further processed for data analysis.

The data was coded and fed into computers for data analysis. Firstly, Demographic analysis was done.To test the hypotheses, the data was analysed by using the Statistical Package for Social Sciences (SPSS version 19.0). Descriptive statistics with mean, standard deviation, correlation and regression were used to explain the relationship among the different variables. Mediation analysis was done to see whether job satisfaction acts as a mediator for different antecedents and consequences undertaken for the study.

5.14.1 Data Analysis Strategy

After computation following statistical analysis was done for which descriptive and the inferential statistics was used.

5.14.1.1 Descriptive Analysis

Descriptive analysis is the term given to the analysis of data that helps describe, show or summarise data in a meaningful way which allows simpler interpretation of the data. Typically there are two general types of static that are used to describe data i.e. Measures of central tendency and Measures of spread. When we use descriptive statistics it is useful to summarise our group of data using a combination of tabulated description (i.e. Tables), graphical description (i.e. Graphs and charts) and statistical interpretation.

5.14.1.2 Inferential Analysis

Inferential analysis consists of the methods involved with the analysis and interpretation of data that will enable the statistician to develop meaningful inferences about the data. Both subfields are interrelated; while descriptive analysis organises the collected data in a systematic manner, inferential statistics analyses the data and enables one to produce significant inferences about it.

5.15 Summary

In this chapter, the details of research methodology and questionnaire designing are discussed. The problem has been formulated; Sample design of the study has been defined. It also defines the tools and techniques applied to measure the variables and their relationships. Besides this, questionnaire designing and statistical treatment of the data has also been explained. The next chapter 6 discusses the empirical analysis and the interpretation of the collected data.

Chapter - 6

Data Analysis and Interpretation

6.1 Introduction

In this chapter the results of the study are presented. The data was collected from six airlines out of which one was a public sector airline and the other five were private sector airlines. Total of 282 data was collected from the FLSE of these airlines by a standard questionnaire on their commitment towards the service quality. This information of the 282 questionnaire was fed in the computer and the data was analysed with the help of Statistical Package for Social Science version 19 (SPSS) software to do the required analysis. Section 6.2 presents the reliability and validity of different measures. Section 6.3 describes the demographic analysis done on the basis of designations of the respondents and the sample description of the employees. Section 6.4 deals with the descriptive analysis of the data. Section 6.5 deals with the inferential statistics which includes factor analysis, correlation, regression. Section 6.6 and 6.7 summarises the results.

6.2 Reliability and Validity of Measures

The purpose of the reliability analysis is to determine whether data are trustworthy or not. Testing reliability is to measure consistency in the data that is defined as "an assessment of the degree of consistency between multiple measurements of a variable" (Hair, Andersson, Tatham, Black and William, 1998). A commonly accepted type of measuring reliability is internal consistency, which applies to the consistency between the variables in a summated scale.

The concept for internal consistency is that the individual items or indicators of the scale should all be measuring the same construct and thus be highly correlated. Furthermore Hair *et. al.,* (1998) suggest that a series of diagnostic measures are to be used to assess internal consistency.

Validity of measurement scale is the extent to which the scale fully captures all the aspects of the construct to be measured (Parasuraman *et. al.,* 1991). In a general sense, a measurement scale is considered to be valid if it measures what it is intended to measure.

6.2.1 Reliability investigation through Cronbach's Alpha

It is the method that is frequently used that assessing the consistency of the entire scale.Table 6.1 shows the reliability of the variables. For this study, the Cronbach alpha was used and it showed the reliability to be .973 indicating that the instruments' items and subscales to be highly reliable.

Table 6.1: Reliability Statistics

Reliability Statistics	
Cronbach's Alpha	N of Items
.973	64

Table 6.2 shows the Item–Total Statistics for reliability between the variables. As can be seen in the reliability statistics table, the items shows the reliability to be between .7-1and so it ·seems to be contributing reasonably well to the scale's reliability and a deletion of any item does not reflect much on the Cronbach's alpha value (reliability).

Table 6.2: Item-Total Statistics for reliability

Item Statistics

	Mean	*Std. Deviation*	*N*
Q1	5.28	.974	282
Q2	5.25	.854	282
Q3	5.22	.854	282

(Contd...)

Q4	5.27	.843	282
Q5	5.24	.809	282
Q6	5.32	.915	282
Q7	5.32	.820	282
Q8	5.27	.868	282
Q9	5.30	.916	282
Q10	5.47	.861	282
Q11	5.44	.892	282
Q12	5.41	.801	282
Q13	5.79	.776	282
Q14	5.55	.759	282
Q15	5.62	.819	282
Q16	5.58	.862	282
Q17	5.52	.819	282
Q18	5.51	.836	282
Q19	5.47	.844	282
Q20	5.55	.826	282
Q21	5.29	.896	282
Q22	5.37	.892	282
Q23	5.33	.925	282
Q24	5.34	.892	282
Q25	5.31	.869	282
Q26	5.31	.844	282
Q27	5.34	.834	282
Q28	5.34	.875	282
Q29	5.30	.884	282
Q30	5.29	1.005	282
Q31	5.30	.900	282
Q32	5.41	1.006	282
Q33	5.40	.987	282
Q34	5.37	1.050	282
Q35	5.68	.842	282
Q36	5.28	.996	282
Q37	5.14	.994	282
Q38	5.29	.890	282
Q39	4.79	1.677	282
Q40	5.45	.843	282
Q41	5.30	.872	282

(Contd...)

Q42	5.46	.861	282
Q43	5.29	.928	282
Q44	5.41	.913	282
Q45	5.39	.930	282
Q46	5.58	.948	282
Q47	5.66	.904	282
Q48	5.71	.962	282
Q49	5.73	.912	282
Q50	5.57	.907	282
Q51	5.86	.801	282
Q52	5.84	.860	282
Q53	5.83	.807	282
Q54	5.84	.774	282
Q55	5.88	.794	282
Q56	5.99	.740	282
Q57	5.76	.818	282
Q58	5.80	.848	282
Q59	6.02	.787	282
Q60	5.81	.800	282
Q61	5.89	.799	282
Q62	5.82	.773	282
Q63	5.79	.779	282
Q64	5.91	.758	282

The content validity was measured in the current research which was established by their origins from the extant literature. Extensive discussions were held with airline employees and academicians who reviewed the questionnaire and confirmed that it had face validity. After evaluation of the questions, they judged that all of these were appropriate for measuring FLSE commitment towards service quality in domestic airlines of India.

6.3 Demographic Profile of the respondents

Demographic profile consisted of the general profile of the respondents of the six public and the private airlines.

6.3.1 Sample Description of employees (in percentage)

The sample consisted of 282 employees of the six domestic airlines operating at Indira Gandhi international airport in New Delhi. About 67.4 per cent of the respondents were males and 32.6 per cent of them were females. Sample demographics are shown below in a table 6.3. It shows the details of the demographic profile of the respondents.

Table 6.3: Sample Description of employees

Airlines	*Designation*	*Gender*	*Age*	*Income level*	*Qualifi-cation*	*Expe-rience*
Kingfisher airlines 18.4 per cent	Cabin crew 24.1 per cent	Male 67.4 per cent	18-25 77.0 per cent	0-20000 61.7 per cent	12th with Diploma 69.1 per cent	0-2 71.3 per cent
IndiGo 16.3 per cent	CSA-Ticketing 27.3 per cent	Female 32.6 per cent	26-35 21.6 per cent	20001-30000 36.9 per cent	Graduate 30.9 per cent	3-5 26.2 per cent
Jet airways 14.9 per cent	CSA-Check in 24.1 per cent	-	36-45 1.4 per cent	30001-40000 1.4 per cent	- -	6-8 2.1 per cent
Air India 18.1 per cent	Traffic control assistant 24.5 per cent	-	-	-	-	9-11 0.4 per cent
Go airlines 15.6 per cent	-	-	-	-	-	-
Spice jet 16.7 per cent	-	-	-	-	-	-

6.3.2 Demographic analysis on the basis of Airlines and Designation of the respondents

As can be seen from the Table 6.4 and Figure 6.1, 68 (24.1 per cent) constituted cabin crew; 77 (27.3 per cent) - CSA-Ticketing; 68 (24.1 per cent)-CSA-Check in and 69 (24.4 per cent) of the respondents were Traffic control assistant.

Table 6.4: Demographic analysis of the designation of respondents

Name of the airline	*Designation of candidate*				*Total*
	cabin crew	*CSA-Ticketing*	*CSA-Check in*	*Traffic control assistant*	
Kingfisher	13	13	13	13	52
IndiGo	12	13	9	12	46
Jet airways	9	12	11	10	42
Air India	13	15	12	11	51
Go airlines	9	12	13	10	44
Spice jet	12	12	10	13	47
Total	**68**	**77**	**68**	**69**	**282**

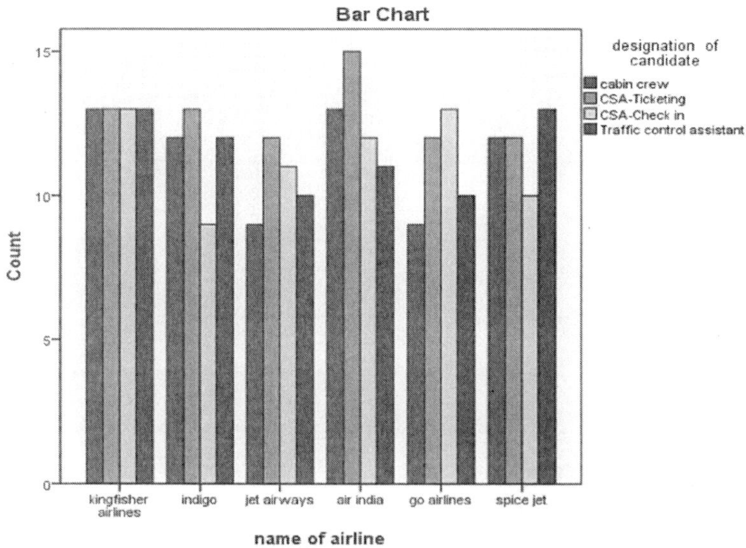

Fig. 6.1: Bar diagram showing Demographic analysis on the basis of Airlines and designation of the respondents.

6.3.3 Demographic analysis on the basis of Airlines and gender of the respondents

Table 6.5 presents the gender distribution in the study. A greater number of participants were male with a percentage of

190 (67.4 per cent) in comparison to 92 females, with a percentage of 32.6 per cent.

Table 6.5: Demographic analysis on the basis of gender of the respondents

Name of airline * gender of candidate Cross tabulation

Name of the Airline	*Gender of candidate*		*Total*
	Male	*Female*	
Kingfisher	39	13	52
IndiGo	26	20	46
Jet Airways	32	10	42
Air India	30	21	51
Go Airlines	34	10	44
Spice Jet	29	18	47
Total	**190**	**92**	**282**

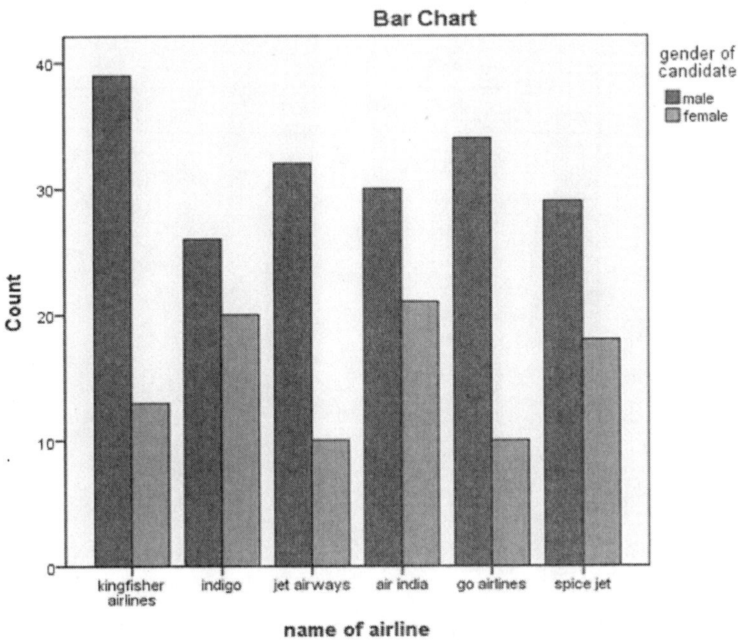

Fig. 6.2: Bar diagram showing Demographic analysis on the basis of Airlines and gender of the respondents.

6.3.4 Demographic analysis on the basis of Airlines and age of the respondents

Table 6.6 and Figure 6.3 shows the Demographic analysis of the respondents on the basis of the age of the respondents. The age group 18-25 has the largest amount of participants namely 61 (77 per cent), followed by the age group 26-35, with 61 (21.6 per cent).The smallest group consisted of age group 36-45 with four participants.

Table 6.6: Demographic analysis on the basis of Airlines and age of the respondents

Name of Airline * Age of Candidate Cross tabulation

Name of the Airline	*Age of Candidate*			*Total*
	18-25	*26-35*	*36-45*	
Kingfisher	42	10	0	52
IndiGo	37	9	0	46
Jet Airways	33	9	0	42
Air India	23	24	4	51
Go Airlines	42	2	0	44
Spice Jet	40	7	0	47
Total	**217**	**61**	**4**	**282**

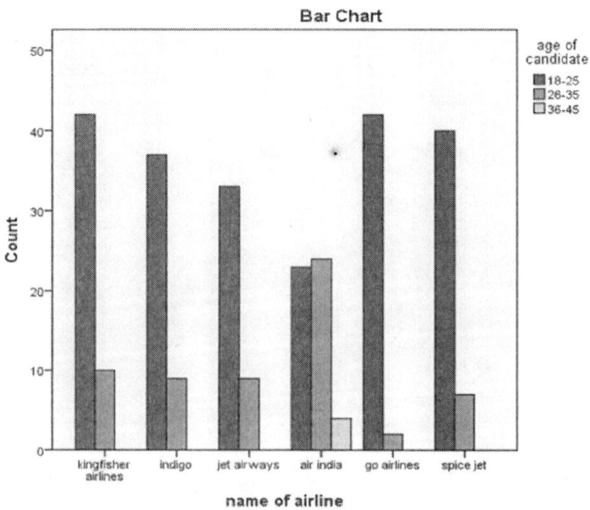

Fig. 6.3: Bar diagram showing Demographic analysis on the basis of Airlines and age of the respondents.

6.3.5 Demographic analysis on the basis of Airlines and qualifications of the respondents

Table 6.7 and the Figure 6.4 represent the different qualification possessed by the respondents of different airlines. The respondents possessing 12 standard and the graduation degree constituted 195 i.e. 69.1 per cent and 87 or 30.9 per cent.

Table 6.7: Demographic analysis on the basis of Airlines and qualifications of the respondents

Name of Airline * Qualification Cross-tabulation

Name of the Airline	*Qualification*		*Total*
	12th	*Graduate*	
Kingfisher	39	13	52
IndiGo	33	13	46
Jet Airways	34	8	42
Air India	18	33	51
Go Airlines	34	10	44
Spice Jet	37	10	47
Total	**195**	**87**	**282**

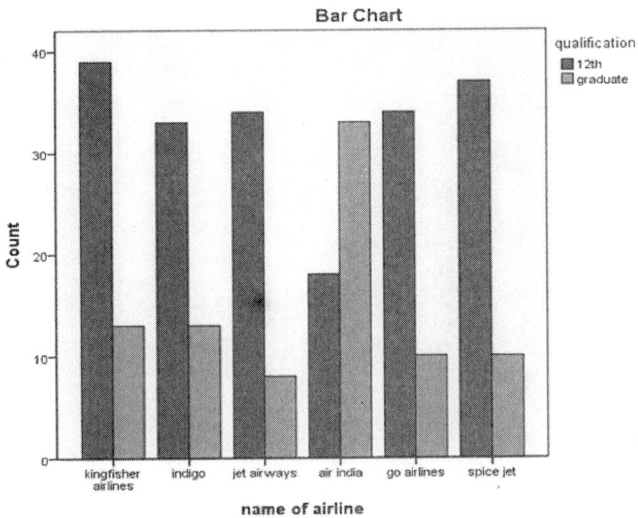

Fig. 6.4: Bar diagram showing Demographic analysis on the basis of Airlines and qualifications of the respondents.

6.3.6 Demographic analysis on the basis of Airlines and work experience of the respondents

The largest number of respondents have worked for the airlines for 0-2 years and they constitute 71.30 per cent followed by the next largest group having experience of 3-5 years i.e. 26.27 per cent.The respondents having experience between 6-8 and 9-11 constitutes 2.1 per cent and 0.4 per cent.

Table 6.8: Demographic analysis on the basis of Airlines and work experience of the respondents

Name of airline * no of years worked Cross tabulation

Name of the airline	*No of years worked*				
	0-2	*3-5*	*6-8*	*9-11*	*Total*
Kingfisher	42	10	0	0	52
IndiGo	34	12	0	0	46
Jet Airways	32	10	0	0	42
Air India	18	26	6	1	51
Go Airlines	39	5	0	0	44
Spice Jet	36	11	0	0	47
Total	**201**	**74**	**6**	**1**	**282**

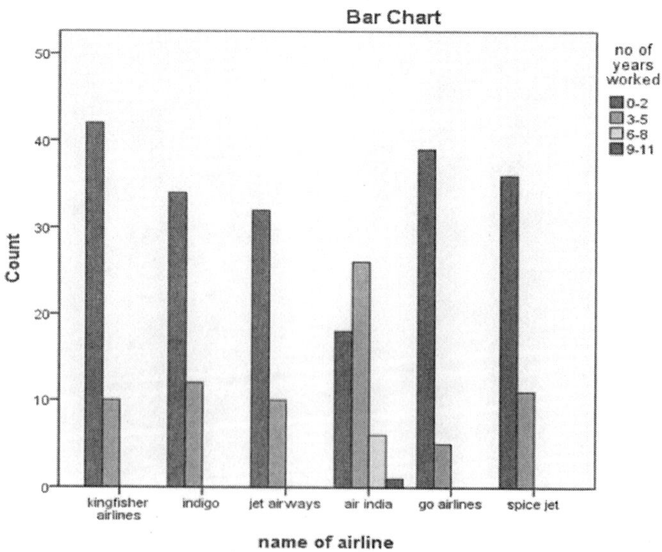

Fig. 6.5: Demographic analysis on the basis of Airlines and work experience of the respondents.

Table 6.9: Summary of different demographic results

The summary of demographic results are shown in Table 6.9.

Variables	Category	Air India	King-fisher	Jet airlines	Go airlines	IndiGo	Spice jet	Total
Gender	Male	30	39	32	34	26	29	190
	Female	21	13	10	10	20	18	92
Age	18-25	23	42	33	42	37	40	217
	26-35	24	10	9	2	9	7	61
	36-45	4	0	0	0	0	0	4
	46 & Above	0	0	0	0	0	0	0
Designation	Cabin crew	13	13	9	9	12	12	68
	CSA Ticketing	15	13	12	12	13	12	77
	CSA-Check in	12	13	11	13	9	10	68
	Traffic control assistants	11	13	10	10	12	13	69
Qualification	12th	18	39	34	34	33	37	195
	Graduate	33	13	8	10	13	10	87
	Post graduate	0	0	0	0	0	0	0
Income	0-20000	0	39	31	35	34	35	174
	20001-30000	47	13	11	9	12	12	104
	30001-40000	4	0	0	0	0	0	4
	40001-50000	0	0	0	0	0	0	0
	50001& Above	0	0	0	0	0	0	0
Experience	0-2	18	42	32	39	34	36	201
	3-5	26	10	10	5	12	11	74
	6-8	6	0	0	0	0	0	6
	9-11	1	0	0	0	0	0	1
	12-14	0	0	0	0	0	0	0
	15-17	0	0	0	0	0	0	0
	18 & Above	0	0	0	0	0	0	0

6.4 Descriptive Statistics

Descriptive analysis includes mean and standard deviation which are described as measures of central tendency and measures of variability or dispersion.

6.4.1 Mean and standard deviation of different variables

The respondents were asked to rate 64 questions related to antecedents and consequences which affect their service delivery commitment, to rate on a scale from 1 to 7, where 1=strongly disagree and 7= strongly agree. Table 6.10 and the Figure 6.6 show the Descriptive analysis of 14 variables that are undertaken for the study. The variable Flse_jp was rated as most important variable, with mean of 5.89 and SD of .589. The item with the lowest mean, rated as least important by FLSE was the supportive management with the means of 5.26 and SD of .751. Table 6.10 and Figure 6.6 shows the descriptive analysis of the respondents.

Table 6.10: Descriptive analysis of the variables

	Mean	*Std. Deviation*
Os	5.61	4.421
Re	5.28	.698
Emp	5.44	.767
Trg	5.46	.731
St	5.46	.695
Sm	5.26	.751
Sl	5.33	.727
Js	5.32	.799
fl_cf	5.37	.725
fl_sq	5.65	.751
fl_sr	5.84	.616
fl_jp	5.89	.589
co_p	5.85	.668
er_sb	5.85	.657

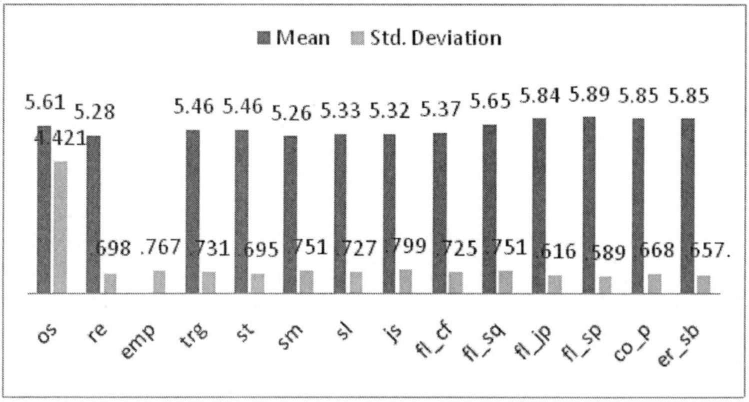

Figure 6.6: Bar diagram showing the Descriptive analysis of different Variables.

6.5 Inferential statistics

It includes the methods involved with the analysis and interpretation of data that will enable the statistician to develop meaningful inferences about the data.

6.5.1 Factor analysis of the data

Before using factor analysis the data adequacy was tested. Data adequacy shows KMO (Kaiser-Meyer and Bartlett's Test of Sphericity). KMO indicator varied from 0 to 1. In case the indicator is closer to 1, data adequacy is higher. The criterion of Bartlett's Test of Sphericity is Chi-Square value is 11760.887 with 2016 degree of freedom at the 0.05 level of significance.

KMO indicator .952 shows that data is adequate near to 1 and also Bartlett's Test of Sphericity shows that significant is valued perfectly because of the significance $p<0.05$. It was decided the appropriateness of factor analysis and also suggested further investigation using principles components analysis method.

Table 6.11: KMO and Bartlett's Test

Kaiser-Meyer-Olkin Measure of Sampling Adequacy.		.952
Bartlett's Test of Sphericity	Approx. Chi-Square	11760.887
	Df	2016
	Sig.	.000

The results from the survey were coded and entered for statistical analysis. The data obtained for the study were analysed by using "Factor Analysis" for identification of the "key factors" preferred by the respondents. Principal component factor analysis with rotated factor loadings was performed on the survey data. Principal Component Analysis (PCA) is the commonly used method for grouping the variables under few unrelated factors. Variables with a factor loading of higher than 0.5 are grouped under a factor.

The analysis of the sixty four variables yielded fourteen indicators. As none of the dimensions were found to less than 0.05, hence all the 64 items were retained. The result of the factor analysis is presented in Table 6.12. Further, the communalities of the variables constituted the factors are found very strong which indicates strong relationships among the variables.

Table 6.12: Rotated Factors Structure of the Variables Used in the Study

	Variables	*Factor loadings*	*Factors*
1.	Help is available from my organisation when I have a problem	.678	1
2.	The organisation tries to design my job as interesting and rewarding as possible.	.765	1
3.	My organisation strongly considers my goals and values	.645	1
4.	If I improve the level of service, I offer passengers; I will be rewarded by my employer.	.713	2
5.	The rewards I receive are based on passenger's evaluations of service.	.755	2

(Contd...)

6.	Staff of this airline is rewarded for dealing effectively with passengers problems.	.856	2
7.	I am rewarded for satisfying complaining passengers.	.765	2
8.	I receive visible recognition when I excel in serving passengers.	.657	2
9.	My promotion depends on the quality of service I deliver.	.873	2
10.	I am encouraged to handle passenger problems by myself.	.762	3
11.	I do not have to get management's approval before I handle passenger problems	.625	3
12.	I am allowed to do almost anything to solve passenger problems.	.785	3
13.	I have control over how I solve passenger problems.	.634	3
14.	I receive training continuously to provide good service.	.847	4
15.	I receive extensive passenger service training before I come into contact with passengers.	.788	4
16.	I receive training on how to serve passengers better.	.870	4
17.	I am trained to deal with customer complaints	.859	4
18.	We have 'state of the art' technology to enhance our service quality.	.851	5
19.	Sufficient money is allocated for technology to support my efforts to deliver better service.	.746	5
20.	I have the necessary technology support to serve my passengers better.	.849	5
21.	Management works hard to make our systems and processes more passengers friendly.	.877	5
22.	My boss is flexible about how I accomplish my objectives.	.832	6
23.	My boss is supportive of my ideas and ways of getting things done.	.735	6
24.	My boss gives me the authority to do my job as I see fit.	.657	6
25.	I can trust by boss to back me up on decisions I make.	.847	6
26.	Management regularly communicates the importance of service quality.	.736	7
27.	Management regularly spends time 'on the floor' with passengers and frontline staff.	.836	7
28.	Management is constantly measuring service quality.	.635	7
29.	Management provide leadership into creating quality service.	.746	7
30.	Management provides resources, not just 'lip service', to enhance my ability to provide excellence service.	.847	7
31.	Management shows they care about service by constantly giving of themselves.	.856	7
32.	Generally speaking, I am very satisfied with my job.	.645	8
33.	I am generally satisfied with the kind of work I do in this job.	.746	8

(*Contd...*)

34.	I get a deep satisfaction from working for this company.	.837	8
35.	I get positive feedback from customers.	.736	8
36.	I am relatively well awarded financially for my work.	.728	8
37.	I am satisfied with the amount of pay I receive for the job I do.	.829	8
38.	I am satisfied with my working conditions.	.863	8
39.	The benefits provided by the airline are not satisfactory.	.783	8
40.	I feel a sense of pride and accomplishment as a result of the work I do.	.672	8
41.	I feel my future is closely linked to that of this company.	.827	9
42.	I feel very committed to this company.	.852	9
43.	I am proud to tell others that I am part of this company.	.723	9
44.	I really care about the fate of this company.	.637	9
45.	My values and those of this company are very similar.	.833	9
46.	I feel strongly about improving the service my company provides to its customers.	.716	10
47.	I gain a sense of personal accomplishment in providing quality services to customers.	.824	10
48.	I am willing to put in a great deal of effort to help my company deliver high-quality service to our customers.	.827	10
49.	I really care about the quality of my company's services.	.723	10
50.	I enjoy discussing quality-related issues with people in my company	.846	10
51.	Considering all the things I do, I handle dissatisfied passengers quite well.	.627	11
52.	I do not mind dealing with complaining passengers.	.778	11
53.	No passenger I deal with leaves with problems unresolved.	.842	11
54.	Satisfying complaining passengers is a great thrill to me.	.727	11
55.	I satisfy my customers' service expectations.	.893	12
56.	I manage my work time effectively.	.634	12
57.	I am knowledgeable about my company's services.	.817	12
58.	I know what my customers expect.	.617	12
59.	I am good at my job.	.811	12
60.	I help other employees who have excessive workloads	.716	13
61.	I am always ready to lend a helping hand to co-workers around me.	.892	13
62.	I help orient new employees even though it is not required.	.883	13
63.	I voluntarily assists customers even if it means going beyond my job requirements	.795	14
64.	I frequently go out of the way to help customers.	.832	14

Not a single factor has been dropped out under this circumstance. The values of factor loadings indicate the affiliation of the items to a factor. Generally, the factor is the natural affinity of an item for a group. The higher loading (factor) indicates the stronger affiliation of an item to a specific factor. The findings of this study indicate that each of the fourteen dimensions is homogeneously loaded to the different factors.

6.5.2 Correlation

The main result of a correlation is called the correlation coefficient (or "r"). It ranges from -1.0 to +1.0. The closer r is to +1 or -1, the more closely the two variables are related. If r is close to 0, it means there is no relationship between the variables. If r is positive, it means that as one variable gets larger the other gets larger. If r is negative it means that as one gets larger, the other gets smaller (often called an "inverse" correlation).

Table 6.13 shows the correlation between different variables It indicates that Organisational support was not significantly related to Empowerment (r=.045, p>.05), FI_jp (r=.094, p>.05) and er_sb (r=.061, p>.05). Organisational support showed very low correlation with most of the variables. The highest correlation is between service technology and organisational support (r=.224, p<.05).

As expected reward was moderately correlated with all the variables.The highest correlation was between reward and job satisfaction (r=.637, p<.05)and the lowest between reward and er_sb ((r=.200, p<.05).

Empowerment was not significantly related to fl_jp (r=.112, p>.05),co_p (r=.094, p>.05) and er_sb (r=.001, p>.05). The highest correlation was between employee empowerment and job satisfaction (r=.380, p<.05)and the lowest between employee empowerment and er_sb (r=.001, p>.05).

As expected training was significantly correlated with all the variables.The highest correlation was between training and service technology (r=.563, p<.05) and the lowest correlation was with er_sb (r=.253, p>.05).The same is the case with the service technology. It was positively and significantly correlated with all the variables. The highest correlation was between service technology and job satisfaction ($r=.666, p<.05$) and the lowest between service technology and er_sb ($r=.301, p>.05$). Supportive management was also found to be significantly related to other variables.The highest correlation with job satisfaction ($r=.652, p<.05$) and the lowest with the organisational support ($r=.140, p<.05$). Servant leadership was also found to significantly correlated to the other variables. Servant leadership was found to be highly correlated with the job satisfaction ($r=.770,p<.05$). The lowest correlation was between servant leadership and organisational support ($r=.170, p>.05$).

Job satisfaction was positively and significantly correlated with all the variables. Servant leadership and the job satisfaction showed the highest correlation ($r=.770, p<.05$).The lowest correlation was between organisational support and job satisfaction ($r=.216, p<.05$).Fl_cf was also significantly correlated with rest of the variables.The highest relationship in this case was between fl_cf and fl_sq ($r=.782, p<.05$).The lowest correlation was between fl_cf and organisational support ($r=.207, p<.05$).

The correlation matrix also indicated a significant correlation between fl_sq and the other variables.The highest correlation was between fl_sq and fl_cf($r=.782, p<.05$). as stated above.The lowest correlation was between organisational support ($r=.181, p<.05$). The variable fl_sr was also found to be significantly related to the other variables.In case of organisational support, it showed a very low correlation which was also the lowest among the other variables ($r=.142, p<.05$).The highest correlation in this case was between fl_sr and fl_sq ($r=.608, p<.05$).

The variable fl_jp showed insignificant relationship between fl_jp and organisational support ($r=.094, p>.05$) which was also the lowest correlation in this case and with employee empowerment ($r=.112, p>.05$). The highest correlation was between fl_jp and fl_sr ($r=.599, p<.05$). The variable co_p also showed insignificant relationship with empowerment (($r=.094, p>.05$). It was also the lowest correlation as far as the relationship

Table 6.13: Correlation matrix

Correlations														
	Os	Re	Emp	Trg	St	Sm	Sl	Js	fl_cf	fl_sq	fl_sr	fl_jp	co_p	er_sb
Os	1													
Re	.209**	1												
	.000													
Emp	.045	.420**	1											
	.450	.000												
Trg	.172**	.481**	.309**	1										
	.004	.000	.000											
St.224**	.569**	.358**	.563**	1										
	.000	.000	.000	.000										
Sm	.140*	.525**	.342**	.450**	.605**	1								
	.019	.000	.000	.000	.000									
Sl.170**	.552**	.289**	.454**	.597**	.615**	1								
	.004	.000	.000	.000	.000	.000								
Js.216**	.637**	.380**	.546**	.666**	.652**	.770**	1							
	.000	.000	.000	.000	.000	.000	.000							
fl_cf	.207**	.525**	.355**	.474**	.603**	.504**	.602**	.758**	1					
	.000	.000	.000	.000	.000	.000	.000	.000						
fl_sq	.181**	.431**	.310**	.460**	.568**	.465**	.535**	.702**	.782**	1				
	.002	.000	.000	.000	.000	.000	.000	.000	.000					
fl_sr	.142*	.384**	.224**	.324**	.423**	.318**	.361**	.520**	.467**	.608**	1			
	.017	.000	.000	.000	.000	.000	.000	.000	.000	.000				
fl_jp	.094	.286**	.112	.347**	.381**	.336**	.370**	.463**	.375**	.527**	.599**	1		
	.116	.000	.061	.000	.000	.000	.000	.000	.000	.000	.000			
co_p	.154**	.216**	.094	.306**	.400**	.266**	.392**	.411**	.359**	.408**	.426**	.475**	1	
	.010	.000	.114	.000	.000	.000	.000	.000	.000	.000	.000	.000		
er_sb	.061	.200**	.001	.253**	.301**	.271**	.339**	.349**	.313**	.343**	.362**	.449**	.535**	1
	.307	.001	.991	.000	.000	.000	.000	.000	.000	.000	.000	.000	.000	

**. Correlation is significant at the 0.01 level (2-tailed).

*. Correlation is significant at the 0.05 level (2-tailed).

of co_p with the other variables are concerned. The highest correlation was between co_p and er_sb (r=.535, p<.05).

The correlation matrix also showed insignificant correlation between organisational support(r=.061, p>.05) and empowerment (r=.001, p>.05) which was the lowest correlation in this case.The correlation between er_sb and co_p was found to be highest (r=.535, p<.05).

As far as the correlation among all the variables is concerned,fl_cf and fl_sq showed the highest correlation (r=.782, p<.05). The lowest correlation was among the variables empowerment and er_sb(r=.001, p>.05).

(os=organisational support; re=reward;;emp=empowerment; trg=training; sr=service technology; sm=supportive management; sl= servant leadership ; js=job satisfaction; flse_cf-frontline employee commitment to firm; flse_sq=frontline commitment to service quality; flse_sr=frontline employee commitment to service recovery performance; flse_jp=frontline commitment to job performance; co_p=cooperation; er_sb=extra role customer service behaviour.)

6.5.3 Regression

A regression analysis for research framework I,II and III was undertaken to predict job satisfaction from the combination of the dependent and independent variables.

6.5.3.1 Mediating effects of job satisfaction

The model for the study places job satisfaction as a mediator between the seven antecedents and six consequences. In order to test the degree to which job satisfaction acts as a mediator of the relationship between all possible antecedent consequences relationships, Mediation tests were conducted for all the direct, indirect and the total effects. The mediated approach followed the guidelines as outlined by (Preacher and Hayes, 2008). Using the SPSS script for the Indirect procedure, bootstrapping was performed; 1,000 samples were requested; a bias-corrected and accelerated confidence interval (CI) was created for *ab*. For this 95 per cent CI, the lower limit and the upper limit were also considered. The important concepts related to mediation test by Hayes are-

IV to Mediators== (a path)

Direct Effects of Mediators on DV=(b path)

Total Effect of IV on DV=(c path)

Direct Effect of IV on DV =(c-prime path)

BOOTSTRAP RESULTS FOR INDIRECT EFFECTS

Indirect Effects of IV on DV through Proposed Mediators= (ab paths)

Bias Corrected and Accelerated Confidence Intervals=Upper and Lower Limit

6.5.3.1.1 Mediation effect of OS – JS- FL_CF

Table 6.19 shows the direct, total and the indirect effect of mediation i.e. JS on OS and FL_CF.

Total and Direct effect output

a path (IV to Mediators) is not significant (p=.2881)

b path (Direct Effects of Mediators on DV) is significant (p=.0000)

c path (Total Effect of IV on DV) is not significant (p=.2300)

c prime path (Direct Effect of IV on DV) is also not significant (p=.4252)

Bootstrapped tests of the INDIRECT effects

A bias-corrected and accelerated confidence interval (CI) for *ab at* 95 per cent, the lower limit is -.0397 and the upper limit is .0408. In this case the true total indirect effect is 95 per cent likely to range from -.0395 to .0408. As zero occurs between the LL and the UL, it can be concluded that neither direct effect nor indirect effect is significant.

Table 6.14: Mediation between OS- JS- FL_CF

OS JS FL_CF				
	Coeff	*Se*	*T*	*P*
IV to Mediators (a path)	.0064	.0061	1.0644	.2881
Direct Effects of Mediators on DV(b path)	.5598	.0650	8.6120	.0000
Total Effect of IV on DV (c path)	.0088	.0073	1.2029	.2300
Direct Effect of IV on DV (c-prime path)	.0052	.0065	.7986	.4252
BOOTSTRAP RESULTS FOR INDIRECT EFFECTS	Data	Boot	Bias	SE
Indirect Effects of IV on DV through Proposed Mediators (ab paths)	.0036	.0144	.0108	.0191
Bias Corrected and Accelerated Confidence Intervals	Lower= -.0395		Upper=.0408	

6.5.3.1.2 Mediation effect of OS JS FL_SQ

Table 6.20 shows the direct, total and the indirect effect of mediation i.e. JS on OS and FL_SQ.

Total and Direct effect output

- a path (IV to Mediators) is not significant (p=.2881)
- b path (Direct Effects of Mediators on DV) is significant (p=.0000)
- c path (Total Effect of IV on DV) is not significant (p=.3802)
- c prime path (Direct Effect of IV on DV) is also not significant (p=.6481)

Bootstrapped tests of the INDIRECT effects

A bias-corrected and accelerated confidence interval (CI) for *ab at* 95 per cent, the lower limit is -.0377 and the upper limit is .0444. As zero occurs between the LL and the UL, it can be concluded that both direct and the indirect effect are not significant.

Table 6.15: Mediation effect between OS-JS-FL_SQ

OS JS FL_SQ

	Coeff	*Se*	*T*	*P*
IV to Mediators (a path)	.0064	.0061	1.0644	.2881
Direct Effects of Mediators on DV(b path)	.5921	.0734	8.0620	.0000
Total Effect of IV on DV(c path)	.0072	.0082	.8790	.3802
Direct Effect of IV on DV (c-prime path)	.0034	.0074	.4569	.6481
BOOTSTRAP RESULTS FOR INDIRECT EFFECTS	Data	Boot	Bias	SE
Indirect Effects of IV on DV through Proposed Mediators (ab paths)	.0038	.0159	.0121	.0215
Bias Corrected and Accelerated Confidence Intervals	Lower = -.0377		Upper =.0444	

6.5.3.1.3 Mediation effect of OS JS FL_SR

Table 6.21 shows the direct, total and the indirect effect of mediation i.e. JS on OS and FL_SR.

Total and Direct effect output

- a path (IV to Mediators) is not significant (p=.2881)
- b path (Direct Effects of Mediators on DV) is significant (p=.0000)
—c path (Total Effect of IV on DV) is not significant (p=.5730)
- c prime path (Direct Effect of IV on DV) is also not significant (p=.8018)

Bootstrapped tests of the INDIRECT effects

A bias-corrected and accelerated confidence interval (CI) for *ab at* 95 per cent, the lower limit is -.0241 and the upper limit is .0258. As zero occurs between the LL and the UL, it can be concluded that both direct and the total indirect effect are not significant.

Table 6.16: Mediation effect between OS JS FL_SR

OS JS FL_SR

	Coeff	*Se*	*T*	*P*
IV to Mediators (a path)	.0064	.0061	1.0644	.2881
Direct Effects of Mediators on DV(b path)	.3864	.0732	5.2817	.0000
Total Effect of IV on DV(c path)	.0043	.0077	.5643	.5730
Direct Effect of IV on DV (c-prime path)	.0018	.0073	.2512	.8018
BOOTSTRAP RESULTS FOR INDIRECT EFFECTS	Data	Boot	Bias	SE
Indirect Effects of IV on DV through Proposed Mediators (ab paths)	.0025	.0090	.0065	.0122
Bias Corrected and Accelerated Confidence Intervals	Lower= -.0241		Upper=.0258	

6.5.3.1.4 Mediation effect of OS JS FL_JP

Table 6.22 shows the direct, total and the indirect effect of mediation i.e. JS on OS and FL_JP.

Total and Direct effect output

- a path (IV to Mediators) is not significant (p=.2881)
- b path (Direct Effects of Mediators on DV) is significant (p=.0000)
—c path (Total Effect of IV on DV) is not significant (p=.8608)
- c prime path (Direct Effect of IV on DV) is also not significant (p=.6731)

Bootstrapped tests of the INDIRECT effects

A bias-corrected and accelerated confidence interval (CI) for *ab at* 95 per cent, the lower limit is -.0196 and the upper limit is .0176. As zero occurs between the LL and the UL, it can be concluded that both direct and the total indirect effect are not significant.

Table 6.17: Mediation effect between OS JS FL_JP

OS JS FL_JP				
	Coeff	*Se*	*T*	*P*
IV to Mediators (a path)	.0064	.0061	1.0644	.2881
Direct Effects of Mediators on DV(b path)	.2745	.0725	3.7860	.0002
Total Effect of IV on DV(c path)	-.0013	.0074	-.1756	.8608
Direct Effect of IV on DV (c-prime path)	-.0031	.0073	-.4224	.6731
BOOTSTRAP RESULTS FOR INDIRECT EFFECTS	Data	Boot	Bias	SE
Indirect Effects of IV on DV through Proposed Mediators (ab paths)	.0018	.0070	.0052	.0052
Bias Corrected and Accelerated Confidence Intervals	Lower= -.0196		Upper=.0176	

6.5.3.1.5 Mediation effect of OS JS CO_P.

Table 6.23 shows the direct, total and the indirect effect of mediation i.e. JS on OS and CO_P.

Total and Direct effect output

- a path (IV to Mediators) is not significant (p=.2881)
- b path (Direct Effects of Mediators on DV) is significant (p=.0185)
—c path (Total Effect of IV on DV) is not significant (p=.2845)
- c prime path (Direct Effect of IV on DV) is also not significant (p=.3547)

Bootstrapped tests of the INDIRECT effects

A bias-corrected and accelerated confidence interval (CI) for *ab at* 95 per cent, the lower limit is -.0119 and the upper limit is .0141. As zero occurs between the LL and the UL, it can be concluded that both direct and the total indirect effect are not significant.

Table 6.18: Mediation effect between OS JS CO_P

OS JS CO_P				
	Coeff	*Se*	*T*	*P*
IV to Mediators (a path)	.0064	.0061	1.0644	.2881
Direct Effects of Mediators on DV(b path)	.1960	.0827	2.3688	.0185
Total Effect of IV on DV(c path)	.0090	.0084	1.0723	.2845
Direct Effect of IV on DV (c-prime path)	.0077	.0083	.9270	.3547
BOOTSTRAP RESULTS FOR INDIRECT EFFECTS	Data	Boot	Bias	SE
Indirect Effects of IV on DV through Proposed Mediators (ab paths)	.0013	.0046	.0034	.0071
Bias Corrected and Accelerated Confidence Intervals	Lower= -.0119		Upper=.0141	

6.5.3.1.6 Mediation effect of OS JS ER_SB

Table 6.24 shows the direct, total and the indirect effect of mediation i.e. JS on OS and ER_SB

Total and Direct effect output

- a path (IV to Mediators) is not significant (p=.2881)
- b path (Direct Effects of Mediators on DV) is significant (p=.0500)
—c path (Total Effect of IV on DV) is not significant (p=.6623)
- c prime path (Direct Effect of IV on DV) is also not significant (p=.5726)

Bootstrapped tests of the INDIRECT effects

A bias-corrected and accelerated confidence interval (CI) for *ab at* 95 per cent, the lower limit is -.0166 and the upper limit is .0125. As zero occurs between the LL and the UL, it can be concluded that neither direct and nor indirect effect is significant.

Table 6.19: Mediation effect between OS JS ER_SB

OS JS ER_SB

	Coeff	*Se*	*T*	*P*
IV to Mediators (a path)	.0064	.0061	1.0644	.2881
Direct Effects of Mediators on DV(b path)	.1667	.0847	1.9686	.0500
Total Effect of IV on DV(c path)	-.0037	.0085	-.4372	.6623
Direct Effect of IV on DV (c-prime path)	-.0048	.0085	-.5649	.5726
BOOTSTRAP RESULTS FOR INDIRECT EFFECTS	Data	Boot	Bias	SE
Indirect Effects of IV on DV through Proposed Mediators (ab paths)	.0011	.0041	.0030	.0070
Bias Corrected and Accelerated Confidence Intervals	Lower= -.0166		Upper=.0125	

6.5.3.1.7 Mediation effect of RE JS FL_CF

Table 6.25 shows the direct, total and the indirect effect of mediation i.e. JS on RE and FL_CF

Total and Direct effect output

- a path (IV to Mediators) is not significant (p=.0004)
- b path (Direct Effects of Mediators on DV) is significant (p=.0000)
—c path (Total Effect of IV on DV) is not significant (p=.0716)
- c prime path (Direct Effect of IV on DV) is also not significant (p=.8646)

Bootstrapped tests of the INDIRECT effects

A bias-corrected and accelerated confidence interval (CI) for *ab at* 95 per cent, the lower limit is .0446 and the upper limit is .1791. The bootstrapped CI for *ab* does not includes zero. As zero does not occurs between the LL and the UL, it can be concluded that only indirect effect is significant.

Table 6.20: Mediation effect between RE JS FL_CF

RE JS FL_CF				
	Coeff	*Se*	*T*	*P*
IV to Mediators (a path)	.1814	.0507	3.5782	.0004
Direct Effects of Mediators on DV(b path)	.5598	.0650	8.6120	.0000
Total Effect of IV on DV(c path)	.1111	.0614	1.8090	.0716
Direct Effect of IV on DV (c-prime path)	.0095	.0558	.1706	.8646
BOOTSTRAP RESULTS FOR INDIRECT EFFECTS	Data	Boot	Bias	SE
Indirect Effects of IV on DV through Proposed Mediators (ab paths)	.1016	.0982	-.0034	.0329
Bias Corrected and Accelerated Confidence Intervals	Lower= .0446		Upper=.1791	

6.5.3.1.8 Mediation effect of RE JS FL_SQ

Table 6.26 shows the direct, total and the indirect effect of mediation i.e. JS on RE and FL_SQ

Total and Direct effect output

- a path (IV to Mediators) is significant (p=.0004)
- b path (Direct Effects of Mediators on DV) is not significant (p=3.5782)
—c path (Total Effect of IV on DV) is not significant (p=.9196)
- c prime path (Direct Effect of IV on DV) is also not significant (p=.1122)

Bootstrapped tests of the INDIRECT effects

A bias-corrected and accelerated confidence interval (CI) for *ab at* 95 per cent, the lower limit is .0511 and the upper limit is .2080.The bootstrapped CI for *ab* does not includes zero. As zero does not occurs between the LL and the UL, it can be concluded that the only indirect effect is significant.

Table 6.21: Mediation effect between RE JS FL_SQ

RE JS FL_SQ

	Coeff	*Se*	*T*	*P*
IV to Mediators (a path)	.1814	.0507	3.5782	.0004
Direct Effects of Mediators on DV(b path)	.5921	.0734	.80620	.0000
Total Effect of IV on DV(c path)	.0069	.0685	.1011	.9196
Direct Effect of IV on DV (c-prime path)	-.1005	.0631	-1.5937	.1122
BOOTSTRAP RESULTS FOR INDIRECT EFFECTS	Data	Boot	Bias	SE
Indirect Effects of IV on DV through Proposed Mediators (ab paths)	.1074	.1025	-.0049	.0361
Bias Corrected and Accelerated Confidence Intervals	Lower= .0481		Upper=.1974	

6.5.3.1.9 Mediation effect of RE JS FL_SR

Table 6.27 shows the direct, total and the indirect effect of mediation i.e. JS on RE and FL_SR

Total and Direct effect output

- a path (IV to Mediators) is significant (p=.0004)
- b path (Direct Effects of Mediators on DV) is significant (p=.0000)

—c path (Total Effect of IV on DV) is significant (p=.0396)

- c prime path (Direct Effect of IV on DV) is not significant (p=.3170)

Bootstrapped tests of the INDIRECT effects

A bias-corrected and accelerated confidence interval (CI) for *ab at* 95 per cent, the lower limit is .0314 and the upper limit is .1430. The bootstrapped CI for *ab* does not includes zero. As zero does not occurs between the LL and the UL, it can be concluded that the total indirect effect is significant.

Table 6.22: Mediation effect between RE JS FL_SR

RE JS FL_SR

	Coeff	*Se*	*T*	*P*
IV to Mediators (a path)	.1814	.0507	3.5782	.0004
Direct Effects of Mediators on DV(b path)	.3864	.0732	5.2817	.0000
Total Effect of IV on DV(c path)	.1331	.0643	2.0682	.0396
Direct Effect of IV on DV (c-prime path)	.0630	.0628	1.0025	.3170
BOOTSTRAP RESULTS FOR INDIRECT EFFECTS	Data	Boot	Bias	SE
Indirect Effects of IV on DV through Proposed Mediators (ab paths)	.0701	.0657	-.0044	.0259
Bias Corrected and Accelerated Confidence Intervals	Lower= .0314		Upper= .1430	

6.5.3.1.10 Mediation effect of RE JS FL_JP

Table 6.28 shows the direct, total and the indirect effect of mediation i.e. JS on RE and FL_JP

Total and Direct effect output

- a path (IV to Mediators) is significant (p=.0004)
- b path (Direct Effects of Mediators on DV) is significant (p=.0002)
—c path (Total Effect of IV on DV) is not significant (p=.8196)
- c prime path (Direct Effect of IV on DV) is not significant (p=.5682)

Bootstrapped tests of the INDIRECT effects

A bias-corrected and accelerated confidence interval (CI) for *ab at* 95 per cent, the lower limit is .0192 and the upper limit is .1075. The bootstrapped CI for *ab* does not includes zero. As zero does not occurs between the LL and the UL, it can be concluded that only total indirect effect is significant.

Table 6.23: Mediation effect between RE JS FL_JP

RE JS FL_JP

	Coeff	*Se*	*T*	*P*
IV to Mediators (a path)	.1814	.0507	3.5782	.0004
Direct Effects of Mediators on DV(b path)	.2745	.0725	3.7860	.0000
Total Effect of IV on DV(c path)	.0142	.0623	.2283	.8196
Direct Effect of IV on DV (c-prime path)	-.0356	.0623	-.5714	.5682
BOOTSTRAP RESULTS FOR INDIRECT EFFECTS	Data	Boot	Bias	SE
Indirect Effects of IV on DV through Proposed Mediators (ab paths)	.0498	.0480	-.0018	.0212
Bias Corrected and Accelerated Confidence Intervals	Lower= .0192		Upper=.1075	

6.5.3.1.11 Mediation effect of RE JS CO_OP

Table 6.29 shows the direct, total and the indirect effect of mediation i.e. JS on RE and CO_P

Total and Direct effect output

- a path (IV to Mediators) is significant (p=.0004)
- b path (Direct Effects of Mediators on DV) is significant (p=.0500)
- —c path (Total Effect of IV on DV) is not significant (p=.8198)
- c prime path (Direct Effect of IV on DV) is not significant (p=.5227)

Bootstrapped tests of the INDIRECT effects

A bias-corrected and accelerated confidence interval (CI) for *ab at* 95 per cent, the lower limit is .0085 and the upper limit is .0965. The bootstrapped CI for *ab* does not includes zero. As zero does not occurs between the LL and the UL, it can be concluded that the total indirect effect is significant.

Table 6.24: Mediation effect of RE JS CO_P

RE JS CO_P

	Coeff	*Se*	*T*	*P*
IV to Mediators (a path)	.1814	.0507	3.5782	.0004
Direct Effects of Mediators on DV(b path)	.1667	.0847	1.9686	.0500
Total Effect of IV on DV(c path)	-.0163	.0714	-.2280	.8198
Direct Effect of IV on DV (c-prime path)	-.0465	.0727	-.6400	.5227
BOOTSTRAP RESULTS FOR INDIRECT EFFECTS	Data	Boot	Bias	SE
Indirect Effects of IV on DV through Proposed Mediators (ab paths)	.0302	.0267	-.0035	.0172
Bias Corrected and Accelerated Confidence Intervals	Lower= .0085		Upper=.0965	

6.5.3.1.12 Mediation effect of RE JS ER_SB

Table 6.30 shows the direct, total and the indirect effect of mediation i.e. JS on RE and ER_SB

Total and Direct effect output

- a path (IV to Mediators) is significant (p=.0004)
- b path (Direct Effects of Mediators on DV) is significant (p=.0500)
—c path (Total Effect of IV on DV) is not significant (p=.8198)
- c prime path (Direct Effect of IV on DV) is not significant (p=.5227)

Bootstrapped tests of the INDIRECT effects

A bias-corrected and accelerated confidence interval (CI) for *ab at* 95 per cent, the lower limit is .0049 and the upper limit is .0869. The bootstrapped CI for *ab* does not includes zero. As zero does not occurs between the LL and the UL, it can be concluded that only the total indirect effect is significant.

Table 6.25: Mediation effect of RE JS ER_SB

RE JS ER_SB				
	Coeff	*Se*	*T*	*P*
IV to Mediators (a path)	.1814	.0507	3.5782	.0004
Direct Effects of Mediators on DV(b path)	.1667	.0847	1.9686	.0500
Total Effect of IV on DV(c path)	-.0163	.0714	-.2280	.8198
Direct Effect of IV on DV (c-prime path)	-.0465	.0727	-.6400	.5227
BOOTSTRAP RESULTS FOR INDIRECT EFFECTS	Data	Boot	Bias	SE
Indirect Effects of IV on DV through Proposed Mediators (ab paths)	.0302	.0269	-.0033	.0178
Bias Corrected and Accelerated Confidence Intervals	Lower= .0049		Upper=.0869	

6.5.3.1.13 Mediation effect of EMP JS FL_CF

Table 6.31 shows the direct, total and the indirect effect of mediation i.e. JS on EMP and FL_CF

Total and Direct effect output

- a path (IV to Mediators) is significant (p=.1481)
- b path (Direct Effects of Mediators on DV) is significant (p=.0000)
—c path (Total Effect of IV on DV) is not significant (p=.0582)
- c prime path (Direct Effect of IV on DV) is not significant (p=.1684)

Bootstrapped tests of the INDIRECT effects

A bias-corrected and accelerated confidence interval (CI) for *ab at* 95 per cent, the lower limit is -.0029 and the upper limit is .0754. As zero occurs between the LL and the UL, it can be concluded that neither direct nor indirect effect is significant.

Table 6.26: Mediation effect of EMP JS FL_CF

EMP JS FL_CF

	Coeff	*Se*	*T*	*P*
IV to Mediators (a path)	.0552	.0380	1.4504	.1481
Direct Effects of Mediators on DV(b path)	.5598	.0650	8.6120	.0000
Total Effect of IV on DV(c path)	.0876	.0460	1.9020	.0582
Direct Effect of IV on DV (c-prime path)	.0567	.0411	1.3810	.1684
BOOTSTRAP RESULTS FOR INDIRECT EFFECTS	Data	Boot	Bias	SE
Indirect Effects of IV on DV through Proposed Mediators (ab paths)	.0309	.0290	-.0019	.0193
Bias Corrected and Accelerated Confidence Intervals	Lower=-.0029		Upper=.0754	

6.5.3.1.14 Mediation effect of EMP JS FL_SQ

Table 6.32 shows the direct, total and the indirect effect of mediation i.e. JS on EMP and FL_SQ

Total and Direct effect output

- a path (IV to Mediators) is significant (p=.1481)
- b path (Direct Effects of Mediators on DV) is significant (p=.0000)
—c path (Total Effect of IV on DV) is not significant (p=.1425)
- c prime path (Direct Effect of IV on DV) is not significant (p=.3564)

Bootstrapped tests of the INDIRECT effects

A bias-corrected and accelerated confidence interval (CI) for *ab at* 95 per cent, the lower limit is -.0052 and the upper limit is .0788. As zero occurs between the LL and the UL, it can be concluded that both direct and the total indirect effect are not significant.

Table 6.27: Mediation effect of EMP JS FL_SQ

EMP JS FL_SQ				
	Coeff	*Se*	*T*	*P*
IV to Mediators (a path)	.0552	.0380	1.4504	.1481
Direct Effects of Mediators on DV(b path)	.5921	.0734	8.0620	.0000
Total Effect of IV on DV(c path)	.0755	.0513	1.4709	.1425
Direct Effect of IV on DV (c-prime path)	.0429	.0464	.9237	.3564
BOOTSTRAP RESULTS FOR INDIRECT EFFECTS	Data	Boot	Bias	SE
Indirect Effects of IV on DV through Proposed Mediators (ab paths)	.0327	.0311	-.0016	.0205
Bias Corrected and Accelerated Confidence Intervals	Lower= -.0052		Upper=.0788	

6.5.3.1.15 Mediation effect of EMP JS FL_SR

Table 6.33 shows the direct, total and the indirect effect of mediation i.e. JS on EMP and FL_SR

Total and Direct effect output

- a path (IV to Mediators) is significant (p=.1481)
- b path (Direct Effects of Mediators on DV) is significant (p=.0000)
—c path (Total Effect of IV on DV) is not significant (p=.6163)
- c prime path (Direct Effect of IV on DV) is not significant (p=.9501)

Bootstrapped tests of the INDIRECT effects

A bias-corrected and accelerated confidence interval (CI) for *ab at* 95 per cent, the lower limit is -.0028 and the upper limit is .0540. The bootstrapped CI for *ab* includes zero. As zero occurs between the LL and the UL, it can be concluded that both direct and the total indirect effect are is insignificant.

Table 6.28: Mediation effect of EMP JS FL_SR

EMP JS FL_SR

	Coeff	*Se*	*T*	*P*
IV to Mediators (a path)	.0552	.0380	1.4504	.1481
Direct Effects of Mediators on DV(b path)	.3864	.0732	5.2817	.0000
Total Effect of IV on DV(c path)	.0242	.0483	.5017	.6163
Direct Effect of IV on DV (c-prime path)	.0029	.0462	.0627	.9501
BOOTSTRAP RESULTS FOR INDIRECT EFFECTS	Data	Boot	Bias	SE
Indirect Effects of IV on DV through Proposed Mediators (ab paths)	.0213	.0194	-.0019	.0136
Bias Corrected and Accelerated Confidence Intervals	Lower= -.0028		Upper=.0540	

6.4.3.1.16 Mediation effect of EMP JS FL_JP

Table 6.34 shows the direct, total and the indirect effect of mediation i.e. JS on EMP and FL_JP

Total and Direct effect output

- a path (IV to Mediators) is significant (p=.1481)
- b path (Direct Effects of Mediators on DV) is significant (p=.0000)

—c path (Total Effect of IV on DV) is not significant (p=.1974)

- c prime path (Direct Effect of IV on DV) is not significant (p=.1004)

Bootstrapped tests of the INDIRECT effects

A bias-corrected and accelerated confidence interval (CI) for *ab at* 95 per cent, the lower limit is -.0005 and the upper limit is .0444. The bootstrapped CI for *ab* includes zero. As zero occurs between the LL and the UL, it can be concluded that neither direct nor the total indirect effect is insignificant.

Table 6.29: Mediation effect of EMP JS FL_JP

EMP JS FL_JP

	Coeff	*Se*	*T*	*P*
IV to Mediators (a path)	.0552	.0380	1.4504	.1481
Direct Effects of Mediators on DV (b path)	.2745	.0725	3.7860	.0002
Total Effect of IV on DV (c path)	-.0604	.0467	-1.2922	.1974
Direct Effect of IV on DV (c-prime path)	-.0755	.0458	-1.6487	.1004
BOOTSTRAP RESULTS FOR INDIRECT EFFECTS	Data	Boot	Bias	SE
Indirect Effects of IV on DV through Proposed Mediators (ab paths)	.0151	.0138	-.0013	.0101
Bias Corrected and Accelerated Confidence Intervals	Lower= -.0005		Upper=.0444	

6.5.3.1.17 Mediation effect of EMP JS CO_P

Table 6.35 shows the direct, total and the indirect effect of mediation i.e. JS on EMP and CO_P

Total and Direct effect output

- a path (IV to Mediators) is significant (p=.1481)
- b path (Direct Effects of Mediators on DV) is significant (p=.0000)
—c path (Total Effect of IV on DV) is not significant (p=.3409)
- c prime path (Direct Effect of IV on DV) is not significant (p=.2450)

Bootstrapped tests of the INDIRECT effects

A bias-corrected and accelerated confidence interval (CI) for *ab at* 95 per cent, the lower limit is -.0004 and the upper limit is .0352. The bootstrapped CI for *ab* includes zero. As zero occurs between the LL and the UL, it can be concluded that neither direct nor the total indirect effect is insignificant.

Table 6.30: Mediation effect of EMP JS CO_P

EMP JS CO_P

	Coeff	*Se*	*T*	*P*
IV to Mediators (a path)	.0552	.0380	1.4504	.1481
Direct Effects of Mediators on DV (b path)	.1960	.0827	2.3688	.0185
Total Effect of IV on DV (c path)	-.0501	0525	-.9540	.3409
Direct Effect of IV on DV (c-prime path)	-.0609	.0523	-1.1651	.2450
BOOTSTRAP RESULTS FOR INDIRECT EFFECTS	Data	Boot	Bias	SE
Indirect Effects of IV on DV through Proposed Mediators (ab paths)	.0108	.0100	-.0008	.0081
Bias Corrected and Accelerated Confidence Intervals	Lower= -.0004		Upper=.0352	

6.5.3.1.18 Mediation effect of EMP JS ER_SB

Table 6.36 shows the direct, total and the indirect effect of mediation i.e. JS on EMP and ER_SB

Total and Direct effect output

- a path (IV to Mediators) is significant (p=.1481)
- b path (Direct Effects of Mediators on DV) is significant (p=.0500)
—c path (Total Effect of IV on DV) is not significant (p=.0102)
- c prime path (Direct Effect of IV on DV) is not significant (p=.0061)

Bootstrapped tests of the INDIRECT effects

A bias-corrected and accelerated confidence interval (CI) for *ab at* 95 per cent, the lower limit is -.0001 and the upper limit is .0352. The bootstrapped CI for *ab* includes zero. As zero occurs between the LL and the UL, it can be concluded that the total indirect effect is insignificant. In this case, only the direct effect is significant.

Table 6.31: Mediation effect of EMP JS ER_SB

EMP JS ER_SB

	Coeff	*Se*	*T*	*P*
IV to Mediators (a path)	.0552	.0380	1.4504	.1481
Direct Effects of Mediators on DV (b path)	.1667	.0847	1.9686	.0500
Total Effect of IV on DV (c path)	-.1385	.0536	-2.5858	.0102
Direct Effect of IV on DV (c-prime path)	-.1477	.0535	-2.7613	.0061
BOOTSTRAP RESULTS FOR INDIRECT EFFECTS	Data	Boot	Bias	SE
Indirect Effects of IV on DV through Proposed Mediators (ab paths)	.0092	.0080	-.0012	.0077
Bias Corrected and Accelerated Confidence Intervals	Lower= -.0001		Upper=.0352	

6.5.3.1.19 Mediation effect of TRG JS FL_CF

Table 6.37 shows the direct, total and the indirect effect of mediation i.e. JS on TRG and FL_CF

Total and Direct effect output

- a path (IV to Mediators) is significant (p=.0113)
- b path (Direct Effects of Mediators on DV) is significant (p=.0000)
—c path (Total Effect of IV on DV) is not significant (p=.0731)
- c prime path (Direct Effect of IV on DV) is not significant (p=.4909)

Bootstrapped tests of the INDIRECT effects

A bias-corrected and accelerated confidence interval (CI) for *ab at* 95 per cent, the lower limit is .0104 and the upper limit is .1223. The bootstrapped CI for *ab* does not includes zero. As zero does not occurs between the LL and the UL, it can be concluded that only the total indirect effect is significant.

Table 6.32: Mediation effect of TRG JS FL_CF

TRG JS FL_CF				
	Coeff	*Se*	*T*	*P*
IV to Mediators (a path)	.1138	.0446	2.5513	.0113
Direct Effects of Mediators on DV (b path)	.5598	.0650	8.6120	.0000
Total Effect of IV on DV (c path)	.0972	.0540	1.7993	.0731
Direct Effect of IV on DV (c-prime path)	.0335	.0486	.6898	.4909
BOOTSTRAP RESULTS FOR INDIRECT EFFECTS	Data	Boot	Bias	SE
Indirect Effects of IV on DV through Proposed Mediators (ab paths)	.0637	.0635	-.0002	.0274
Bias Corrected and Accelerated Confidence Intervals	Lower= .0104		Upper=.1223	

6.5.3.1.20 Mediation effect of TRG JS FL_SQ

Table 6.38 shows the direct, total and the indirect effect of mediation i.e. JS on TRG andFL_SQ

Total and Direct effect output

- a path (IV to Mediators) is significant (p=.0113)
- b path (Direct Effects of Mediators on DV) is significant (p=.0000)
—c path (Total Effect of IV on DV) is not significant (p=.0192)
- c prime path (Direct Effect of IV on DV) is not significant (p=.1758)

Bootstrapped tests of the INDIRECT effects

A bias-corrected and accelerated confidence interval (CI) for *ab at* 95 per cent, the lower limit is .0153 and the upper limit is .1417. The bootstrapped CI for *ab* does not includes zero. As zero does not occurs between the LL and the UL, it can be concluded that only the total indirect effect is significant.

Table 6.33: Mediation effect of TRG JS FL_SQ

TRG JS FL_SQ				
	Coeff	*Se*	*T*	*P*
IV to Mediators (a path)	.1138	.0446	2.5513	.0113
Direct Effects of Mediators on DV(b path)	.5921	.0734	8.0620	.0000
Total Effect of IV on DV(c path)	.1419	.0602	2.3554	.0192
Direct Effect of IV on DV (c-prime path)	.0745	.0549	1.3574	.1758
BOOTSTRAP RESULTS FOR INDIRECT				
EFFECTS	Data	Boot	Bias	SE
Indirect Effects of IV on DV through Proposed Mediators (ab paths)	.0674	.0671	-.0004	.0305
Bias Corrected and Accelerated Confidence Intervals	Lower=.0153		Upper=.1417	

6.5.3.1.21 Mediation effect of TRG JS FL_SR

Table 6.39 shows the direct, total and the indirect effect of mediation i.e. JS on TRG andFL_SR.

Total and Direct effect output

- a path (IV to Mediators) is significant (p=.0113)
- b path (Direct Effects of Mediators on DV) is significant (p=.0000)
—c path (Total Effect of IV on DV) is not significant (p=.3248)
- c prime path (Direct Effect of IV on DV) is not significant (p=.8283)

Bootstrapped tests of the INDIRECT effects

A bias-corrected and accelerated confidence interval (CI) for *ab at* 95 per cent, the lower limit is .0101 and the upper limit is .0969. The bootstrapped CI for *ab* does not includes zero. As zero does not occurs between the LL and the UL, it can be concluded that the total indirect effect is significant.

Table 6.34: Mediation effect of TRG JS FL_SR

TRG JS FL_SR				
	Coeff	*Se*	*T*	*P*
IV to Mediators (a path)	.1138	.0446	2.5513	.0113
Direct Effects of Mediators on DV(b path)	.3864	.0732	5.2817	.0000
Total Effect of IV on DV(c path)	.0559	.0566	.9864	.3248
Direct Effect of IV on DV (c-prime path)	.0119	.0547	.2171	.8283
BOOTSTRAP RESULTS FOR INDIRECT EFFECTS	Data	Boot	Bias	SE
Indirect Effects of IV on DV through Proposed Mediators (ab paths)	.0440	.0434	-.0006	.0206
Bias Corrected and Accelerated Confidence Intervals	Lower=.0101		Upper=.0969	

6.5.3.1.22 Mediation effect of TRG JS FL_JP

Table 6.40 shows the direct, total and the indirect effect of mediation i.e. JS on TRG andFL_JP

Total and Direct effect output

- a path(IV to Mediators) is significant (p=.0113)
- b path (Direct Effects of Mediators on DV) is significant (p=.0000)
—c path (Total Effect of IV on DV) is not significant (p=.0183)
- c prime path (Direct Effect of IV on DV) is not significant (p=1.8251)

Bootstrapped tests of the INDIRECT effects

A bias-corrected and accelerated confidence interval (CI) for *ab at* 95 per cent, the lower limit is .0065 and the upper limit is .0723.The bootstrapped CI for *ab* does not includes zero. As zero does not occurs between the LL and the UL, it can be concluded that the total indirect effect is significant.

Table 6.35: Mediation effect of TRG JS FL_JP

TRG JS FL_JP				
	Coeff	*Se*	*T*	*p*
IV to Mediators (a path)	.1138	.0446	2.5513	.0113
Direct Effects of Mediators on DV(b path)	.2745	.0725	3.7860	.0000
Total Effect of IV on DV(c path)	.1301	.0548	2.3731	.0183
Direct Effect of IV on DV (c-prime path)	.0989	.0542	1.8251	1.8251
BOOTSTRAP RESULTS FOR INDIRECT EFFECTS	Data	Boot	Bias	SE
Indirect Effects of IV on DV through Proposed Mediators (ab paths)	.0312	.0312	-.0001	.0158
Bias Corrected and Accelerated Confidence Intervals	Lower= .0065		Upper=.0723	

6.5.3.1.23 Mediation effect of TRG JS CO_P

Table 6.41 shows the direct, total and the indirect effect of mediation i.e. JS on TRG andCO_P

Total and Direct effect output

- a path (IV to Mediators) is significant (p=.0113)
- b path (Direct Effects of Mediators on DV) is significant (p=.0185)
—c path (Total Effect of IV on DV) is not significant (p=.1077)
- c prime path (Direct Effect of IV on DV) is not significant (p=.2132)

Bootstrapped tests of the INDIRECT effects

A bias-corrected and accelerated confidence interval (CI) for *ab at* 95 per cent, the lower limit is .0029 and the upper limit is .0630. The bootstrapped CI for *ab* does not includes zero. As zero does not occurs between the LL and the UL, it can be concluded that only the total indirect effect is significant.

Table 6.36: Mediation effect of TRG JS CO_P

TRG JS CO_P				
	Coeff	*Se*	*T*	*P*
IV to Mediators (a path)	.1138	.0446	2.5513	.0113
Direct Effects of Mediators on DV(b path)	.1960	.0827	2.3688	.0185
Total Effect of IV on DV(c path)	.0995	.0616	1.6141	.1077
Direct Effect of IV on DV (c-prime path)	.0772	.0618	1.2478	.2132
BOOTSTRAP RESULTS FOR INDIRECT EFFECTS	Data	Boot	Bias	SE
Indirect Effects of IV on DV through Proposed Mediators (ab paths)	.0223	.0218	-.0006	.0141
Bias Corrected and Accelerated Confidence Intervals	Lower= .0029		Upper=.0630	

6.5.3.1.24 Mediation effect of TRG JS ER_SB

Table 6.42 shows the direct, total and the indirect effect of mediation i.e. JS on TRG and ER_SB

Total and Direct effect output

- a path (IV to Mediators) is significant (p=.0113)
- b path (Direct Effects of Mediators on DV) is significant (p=.0500)
—c path (Total Effect of IV on DV) is not significant (p=.1392)
- c prime path (Direct Effect of IV on DV) is not significant (p=.2416)

Bootstrapped tests of the INDIRECT effects

A bias-corrected and accelerated confidence interval (CI) for *ab at* 95 per cent, the lower limit is .0019 and the upper limit is .0637. The bootstrapped CI for *ab* does not includes zero. As zero does not occurs between the LL and the UL, it can be concluded that the total indirect effect is significant and the direct effect is insignificant.

Table 6.37: Mediation effect of TRG JS ER_SB

TRG JS ER_SB				
	Coeff	*Se*	*T*	*P*
IV to Mediators (a path)	.1138	.0446	2.5513	.0113
Direct Effects of Mediators on DV(b path)	.1667	.0847	1.9686	.0500
Total Effect of IV on DV(c path)	.0932	.0629	1.4831	.1392
Direct Effect of IV on DV (c-prime path)	.0743	.0633	1.1736	.2416
BOOTSTRAP RESULTS FOR INDIRECT EFFECTS	Data	Boot	Bias	SE
Indirect Effects of IV on DV through Proposed Mediators (ab paths)	.0190	.0190	.0000	.0134
Bias Corrected and Accelerated Confidence Intervals	Lower= .0019		Upper=.0637	

6.5.3.1.25 Mediation effect of ST JS FL_CF

Table 6.43 shows the direct, total and the indirect effect of mediation i.e. JS on ST and FL_CF

Total and Direct effect output

- a path (IV to Mediators) is significant (p=.0041)
- b path (Direct Effects of Mediators on DV) is significant (p=.0000)
—c path (Total Effect of IV on DV) is not significant (p=.0002)
- c prime path (Direct Effect of IV on DV) is not significant (p=.0063)

Bootstrapped tests of the INDIRECT effects

A bias-corrected and accelerated confidence interval (CI) for *ab at* 95 per cent, the lower limit is .0275 and the upper limit is .1824. The bootstrapped CI for *ab* does not includes zero. As zero does not occurs between the LL and the UL, it can be concluded that both the total indirect effect and the direct effect in this relationship are significant.

Table 6.38: Mediation effect of ST JS FL_CF

ST JS FL_CF

	Coeff	*Se*	*T*	*P*
IV to Mediators (a path)	.1597	.0552	2.8936	.0041
Direct Effects of Mediators on DV (b path)	.5598	.0650	8.6120	.0000
Total Effect of IV on DV (c path)	.2553	.0669	3.8183	.0002
Direct Effect of IV on DV (c-prime path)	.1659	.0603	2.7508	.0063
BOOTSTRAP RESULTS FOR INDIRECT EFFECTS	Data	Boot	Bias	SE
Indirect Effects of IV on DV through Proposed Mediators (ab paths)	.0894	.0824	-.0070	.0363
Bias Corrected and Accelerated Confidence Intervals	Lower= .0275		Upper=.1824	

6.5.3.1.26 Mediation effect of ST JS FL_SQ

Table 6.44 shows the direct, total and the indirect effect of mediation i.e. JS on ST and FL_SQ

Total and Direct effect output

- a path (IV to Mediators) is significant (p=.0041)
- b path (Direct Effects of Mediators on DV) is significant (p=.0000)
—c path (Total Effect of IV on DV) is not significant (p=.0001)
- c prime path (Direct Effect of IV on DV) is not significant (p=.0038)

Bootstrapped tests of the INDIRECT effects

A bias-corrected and accelerated confidence interval (CI) for *ab at* 95 per cent, the lower limit is .0315 and the upper limit is .2067. The bootstrapped CI for *ab* does not includes zero. As zero does not occurs between the LL and the UL, it can be concluded that the total indirect effect and the direct effect are significant.

Table 6.39: Mediation effect of ST JS FL_SQ

ST JS FL_SQ				
	Coeff	*Se*	*T*	*P*
IV to Mediators (a path)	.1597	.0552	2.8936	.0041
Direct Effects of Mediators on DV(b path)	.5921	.0734	8.0620	.0000
Total Effect of IV on DV(c path)	.2936	.0745	3.9393	.0001
Direct Effect of IV on DV (c-prime path)	.1990	.0681	2.9216	.0038
BOOTSTRAP RESULTS FOR INDIRECT EFFECTS	Data	Boot	Bias	SE
Indirect Effects of IV on DV through Proposed Mediators (ab paths)	.0946	.0861	-.0084	.0409
Bias Corrected and Accelerated Confidence Intervals	Lower=.0315		Upper=.2067	

6.5.3.1.27 Mediation effect of ST JS FL_SR

Table 6.45 shows the direct, total and the indirect effect of mediation i.e. JS on ST and FL_SR

Total and Direct effect output

- a path (IV to Mediators) is significant (p=.0041)
- b path (Direct Effects of Mediators on DV) is significant (p=.0000)
—c path (Total Effect of IV on DV) is not significant (p=.0050)
- c prime path (Direct Effect of IV on DV) is not significant (p=.0454)

Bootstrapped tests of the INDIRECT effects

A bias-corrected and accelerated confidence interval (CI) for *ab at* 95 per cent, the lower limit is .0198 and the upper limit is .1511. The bootstrapped CI for *ab* does not includes zero. Here also zero does not occurs between the LL and the UL, it can be concluded that the total indirect effect and the direct effect are significant.

Table 6.40: Mediation effect of ST JS FL_SR

ST JS FL_SR				
	Coeff	*Se*	*T*	*p*
IV to Mediators (a path)	.1597	.0552	2.8936	.0041
Direct Effects of Mediators on DV(b path)	.3864	.0732	5.2817	.0000
Total Effect of IV on DV(c path)	.1981	.0701	2.8280	.0050
Direct Effect of IV on DV (c-prime path)	.1364	.0679	2.0098	.0454
BOOTSTRAP RESULTS FOR INDIRECT EFFECTS	Data	Boot	Bias	SE
Indirect Effects of IV on DV through Proposed Mediators (ab paths)	.0617	.0582	-.0035	.0294
Bias Corrected and Accelerated Confidence Intervals	Lower=.0198		Upper=.1511	

6.5.3.1.28 Mediation effect of ST JS FL_JP

Table 6.46 shows the direct, total and the indirect effect of mediation i.e. JS on ST and FL_JP

- Total and Direct effect output

  - a path (IV to Mediators) is significant (p=.0041)
  - b path (Direct Effects of Mediators on DV) is significant (p=.0002)
  —c path (Total Effect of IV on DV) is not significant (p=.0431)
  - c prime path (Direct Effect of IV on DV) is not significant (p=.1632)

  Bootstrapped tests of the INDIRECT effects

A bias-corrected and accelerated confidence interval (CI) for *ab at* 95 per cent, the lower limit is .0125 and the upper limit is .1003. The bootstrapped CI for *ab* does not includes zero. As zero does not occurs between the LL and the UL, it can be concluded that only the total indirect effect is significant.

Table 6.41: Mediation effect of ST JS FL_JP

ST JS FL_JP

	Coeff	*Se*	*T*	*P*
IV to Mediators (a path)	.1597	.0552	2.8936	.0041
Direct Effects of Mediators on DV(b path)	.2745	.0725	3.7860	.0002
Total Effect of IV on DV(c path)	.1379	.0678	2.0324	.0431
Direct Effect of IV on DV (c-prime path)	.0940	.0673	1.3983	.1632
BOOTSTRAP RESULTS FOR INDIRECT EFFECTS	Data	Boot	Bias	SE
Indirect Effects of IV on DV through Proposed Mediators (ab paths)	.0438	.0409	-.0030	.0213
Bias Corrected and Accelerated Confidence Intervals	Lower=.0125		Upper=.1003	

6.5.3.1.29 Mediation effect of ST JS CO_P

Table 6.47 shows the direct, total and the indirect effect of mediation i.e. JS on ST and CO_P

Total and Direct effect output

- a path (IV to Mediators) is significant (p=.0041)
- b path (Direct Effects of Mediators on DV) is significant (p=.0185)
—c path (Total Effect of IV on DV) is not significant (p=.0008)
- c prime path (Direct Effect of IV on DV) is not significant (p=.0032)

Bootstrapped tests of the INDIRECT effects

A bias-corrected and accelerated confidence interval (CI) for *ab at* 95 per cent, the lower limit is .0055 and the upper limit is .0911. The bootstrapped CI for *ab* does not includes zero. As zero does not occurs between the LL and the UL, it can be concluded that both the total indirect effect as well as the direct effect is significant.

Table 6.42: Mediation effect of ST JS CO_P

ST JS CO_P				
	Coeff	*Se*	*T*	*P*
IV to Mediators (a path)	.1597	.0552	2.8936	.0041
Direct Effects of Mediators on DV (b path)	.1960	.0827	2.3688	.0185
Total Effect of IV on DV (c path)	.2599	.0763	3.4083	.0008
Direct Effect of IV on DV (c-prime path)	.2286	.0768	2.9776	.0032
BOOTSTRAP RESULTS FOR INDIRECT EFFECTS	Data	Boot	Bias	SE
Indirect Effects of IV on DV through Proposed Mediators (ab paths)	.0313	.0297	-.0016	.0186
Bias Corrected and Accelerated Confidence Intervals	Lower= .0055		Upper=.0911	

6.5.3.1.30 Mediation effect of ST JS ER_SB

Table 6.48 shows the direct, total and the indirect effect of mediation i.e. JS on ST and ER_SB

Total and Direct effect output

- a path (IV to Mediators) is significant (p=.0041)
- b path (Direct Effects of Mediators on DV) is significant (p=.0500)
—c path (Total Effect of IV on DV) is not significant (p=.0949)
- c prime path (Direct Effect of IV on DV) is not significant (p=.1877)

Bootstrapped tests of the INDIRECT effects

A bias-corrected and accelerated confidence interval (CI) for *ab at* 95 per cent, the lower limit is .0030 and the upper limit is .0849. The bootstrapped CI for *ab* does not includes zero. As zero does not occurs between the LL and the UL, it can be concluded that only the total indirect effect is significant.

Table 6.43: Mediation effect of ST JS ER_SB

ST JS ER_SB				
	Coeff	*Se*	*T*	*P*
IV to Mediators (a path)	.1597	.0552	2.8936	.0041
Direct Effects of Mediators on DV(b path)	.1667	.0847	1.9686	.0500
Total Effect of IV on DV(c path)	.1304	.0778	1.6761	.0949
Direct Effect of IV on DV (c-prime path)	.1037	.0785	1.3207	.1877
BOOTSTRAP RESULTS FOR INDIRECT EFFECTS	Data	Boot	Bias	SE
Indirect Effects of IV on DV through Proposed Mediators (ab paths)	.0266	.0250	-.0016	.0183
Bias Corrected and Accelerated Confidence Intervals	Lower=.0030		Upper=.0849	

6.5.3.1.31 Mediation effect of SM JS FL_CF

Table 6.49 shows the direct, total and the indirect effect of mediation i.e. JS on SM and FL_CF

Total and Direct effect output

- a path (IV to Mediators) is significant (p=.0020)
- b path (Direct Effects of Mediators on DV) is significant (p=.0000)
—c path (Total Effect of IV on DV) is not significant (p=.5527)
- c prime path (Direct Effect of IV on DV) is not significant (p=.3500)

Bootstrapped tests of the INDIRECT effects

A bias-corrected and accelerated confidence interval (CI) for *ab at* 95 per cent, the lower limit is .0326 and the upper limit is .1606. The bootstrapped CI for *ab* does not includes zero. As zero does not occurs between the LL and the UL, it can be concluded that only the total indirect effect is significant.

Table 6.44: Mediation effect of SM JS FL_CF

SM JS FL_CF

	Coeff	*Se*	*T*	*P*
IV to Mediators (a path)	.1503	.0482	3.1173	.0020
Direct Effects of Mediators on DV (b path)	.5598	.0650	8.6120	.0000
Total Effect of IV on DV (c path)	.0347	.0584	.5945	.5527
Direct Effect of IV on DV (c-prime path)	-.0494	.0528	-.9362	.3500
BOOTSTRAP RESULTS FOR INDIRECT EFFECTS	Data	Boot	Bias	SE
Indirect Effects of IV on DV through Proposed Mediators (ab paths)	.0841	.0829	-.0013	.0319
Bias Corrected and Accelerated Confidence Intervals	Lower= .0326		Upper=.1606	

6.5.3.1.32 Mediation effect of SM JS FL_SQ

Table 6.50 shows the direct, total and the indirect effect of mediation i.e. JS on SM and FL_SQ

Total and Direct effect output

- a path (IV to Mediators) is significant (p=.0020)
- b path (Direct Effects of Mediators on DV) is significant (p=.0000)

—c path (Total Effect of IV on DV) is not significant (p=.4142)

- c prime path (Direct Effect of IV on DV) is not significant (p=.5494)

Bootstrapped tests of the INDIRECT effects

A bias-corrected and accelerated confidence interval (CI) for *ab at* 95 per cent, the lower limit is .0320 and the upper limit is .1779. The bootstrapped CI for *ab* does not includes zero. As zero does not occurs between the LL and the UL, it can be concluded that the total indirect effect is significant and the direct effect is insignificant.

Table 6.45: Mediation effect of SM JS FL_SQ

SM JS FL_SQ

	Coeff	*Se*	*T*	*P*
IV to Mediators (a path)	.1503	.0482	3.1173	.0020
Direct Effects of Mediators on DV (b path)	.5921	.0734	8.0620	.0000
Total Effect of IV on DV (c path)	.0532	.0651	.8178	.4142
Direct Effect of IV on DV (c-prime path)	-.0358	.0596	-.5994	.5494
BOOTSTRAP RESULTS FOR INDIRECT EFFECTS	Data	Boot	Bias	SE
Indirect Effects of IV on DV through Proposed Mediators (ab paths)	.0890	.0884	-.0006	.0359
Bias Corrected and Accelerated Confidence Intervals	Lower= .0320		Upper=.1779	

6.5.3.1.33 Mediation effect of SM JS FL_SR

Table 6.51 shows the direct, total and the indirect effect of mediation i.e. JS on SM and FL_SR

Total and Direct effect output

- a path(IV to Mediators) is significant (p=.0020)
- b path (Direct Effects of Mediators on DV) is significant (p=.0000)
—c path (Total Effect of IV on DV) is not significant (p=.9667)
- c prime path (Direct Effect of IV on DV) is not significant (p=.3084)

Bootstrapped tests of the INDIRECT effects

A bias-corrected and accelerated confidence interval (CI) for *ab at* 95 per cent, the lower limit is .0232 and the upper limit is .1187. The bootstrapped CI for *ab* does not includes zero. As zero does not occurs between the LL and the UL, it can be concluded that only the total indirect effect is significant.

Table 6.46: Mediation effect of SM JS FL_SR

SM JS FL_SR

	Coeff	*Se*	*T*	*P*
IV to Mediators (a path)	.1503	.0482	3.1173	.0020
Direct Effects of Mediators on DV (b path)	.3864	.0732	5.2817	.0000
Total Effect of IV on DV (c path)	-.0026	.0612	-.0418	.9667
Direct Effect of IV on DV (c-prime path)	-.0606	.0594	-1.0205	.3084
BOOTSTRAP RESULTS FOR INDIRECT EFFECTS	Data	Boot	Bias	SE
Indirect Effects of IV on DV through Proposed Mediators (ab paths)	.0581	.0569	-.0012	.0234
Bias Corrected and Accelerated Confidence Intervals	Lower=.0232		Upper=.1187	

6.5.3.1.34 Mediation effect of SM JS FL_JP

Table 6.52 shows the direct, total and the indirect effect of mediation i.e. JS on SM and FL_JP

Total and Direct effect output

- a path (IV to Mediators) is significant (p=.0020)
- b path (Direct Effects of Mediators on DV) is significant (p=.0002)
—c path (Total Effect of IV on DV) is not significant (p=.2668)
- c prime path (Direct Effect of IV on DV) is not significant (p=.6755)

Bootstrapped tests of the INDIRECT effects

A bias-corrected and accelerated confidence interval (CI) for *ab at* 95 per cent, the lower limit is .0145 and the upper limit is .0953. The bootstrapped CI for *ab* does not includes zero. As zero does not occurs between the LL and the UL, it can be concluded that only the total indirect effect is significant.

Table 6.47: Mediation effect of SM JS FL_JP

SM JS FL_JP				
	Coeff	*Se*	*T*	*P*
IV to Mediators (a path)	.1503	.0482	3.1173	.0020
Direct Effects of Mediators on DV (b path)	.2745	.0725	3.7860	.0002
Total Effect of IV on DV (c path)	.0659	.0593	1.1127	.2668
Direct Effect of IV on DV (c-prime path)	.0247	.0589	.4191	.6755
BOOTSTRAP RESULTS FOR INDIRECT EFFECTS	Data	Boot	Bias	SE
Indirect Effects of IV on DV through Proposed Mediators (ab paths)	.0413	.0403	-.0009	.0189
Bias Corrected and Accelerated Confidence Intervals	Lower= .0145		Upper=.0953	

6.5.3.1.35 Mediation effect of SM JS CO_P

Table 6.53 shows the direct, total and the indirect effect of mediation i.e. JS on SM and CO_P

Total and Direct effect output

- a path (IV to Mediators) is significant (p=.0020)
- b path (Direct Effects of Mediators on DV) is significant (p=.0185)
—c path (Total Effect of IV on DV) is not significant (p=.5083)
- c prime path (Direct Effect of IV on DV) is not significant (p=.2746)

Bootstrapped tests of the INDIRECT effects

A bias-corrected and accelerated confidence interval (CI) for *ab at* 95 per cent, the lower limit is .0033 and the upper limit is .0750. The bootstrapped CI for *ab* does not includes zero. As zero does not occurs between the LL and the UL, it can be concluded that the total indirect effect is significant and the direct effect is insignificant.

Table 6.48: Mediation effect of SM JS CO_P

SM JS CO_P				
	Coeff	*Se*	*T*	*P*
IV to Mediators (a path)	.1503	.0482	3.1173	.0020
Direct Effects of Mediators on DV (b path)	.1960	.0827	2.3688	.0185
Total Effect of IV on DV (c path)	-.0441	.0666	-.6624	.5083
Direct Effect of IV on DV (c-prime path)	-.0736	.0672	-1.0948	.2746
BOOTSTRAP RESULTS FOR INDIRECT EFFECTS	Data	Boot	Bias	SE
Indirect Effects of IV on DV through Proposed Mediators (ab paths)	.0295	.0295	.0000	.0176
Bias Corrected and Accelerated Confidence Intervals	Lower= .0033		Upper=.0750	

6.5.3.1.36 Mediation effect of SM JS ER_SB

Table 6.54 shows the direct, total and the indirect effect of mediation i.e. JS on SM and ER_SB

Total and Direct effect output

- a path (IV to Mediators) is significant (p=.0020)
- b path (Direct Effects of Mediators on DV) is significant (p=.0500)
—c path (Total Effect of IV on DV) is not significant (p=.3762)
- c prime path (Direct Effect of IV on DV) is not significant (p=.6095)

Bootstrapped tests of the INDIRECT effects

A bias-corrected and accelerated confidence interval (CI) for *ab at* 95 per cent, the lower limit is .0018 and the upper limit is .0819. The bootstrapped CI for *ab* does not includes zero. As zero does not occurs between the LL and the UL, it can be concluded that only the total indirect effect is significant.

Table 6.49: Mediation effect of SM JS ER_SB

SM JS ER_SB

	Coeff	*Se*	*T*	*P*
IV to Mediators (a path)	.1503	.0482	3.1173	.0020
Direct Effects of Mediators on DV (b path)	.1667	.0847	1.9686	.0500
Total Effect of IV on DV (c path)	.0602	.0679	.8865	.3762
Direct Effect of IV on DV (c-prime path)	.0352	.0688	.5114	.6095
BOOTSTRAP RESULTS FOR INDIRECT EFFECTS	Data	Boot	Bias	SE
Indirect Effects of IV on DV through Proposed Mediators (ab paths)	.0251	.0244	-.0007	.0176
Bias Corrected and Accelerated Confidence Intervals	Lower= .0018		Upper=.0819	

6.5.3.1.37 Mediation effect of SL JS FL_CF

Table 6.55 shows the direct, total and the indirect effect of mediation i.e. JS on SL and FL_CF

Total and Direct effect output

- a path (IV to Mediators) is significant (p=.0000)
- b path (Direct Effects of Mediators on DV) is significant (p=.0000)
—c path (Total Effect of IV on DV) is not significant (p=.0000)
- c prime path (Direct Effect of IV on DV) is not significant (p=.7453)

Bootstrapped tests of the INDIRECT effects

A bias-corrected and accelerated confidence interval (CI) for *ab at* 95 per cent, the lower limit is .1927 and the upper limit is .3687. The bootstrapped CI for *ab* does not includes zero. As zero does not occurs between the LL and the UL, it can be concluded that the total indirect effect is significant.

Table 6.50: Mediation effect of SL JS FL_CF

SL JS FL_CF				
	Coeff	*Se*	*T*	*P*
IV to Mediators (a path)	.4882	.0500	9.7607	.0000
Direct Effects of Mediators on DV (b path)	.5598	.0650	8.6120	.0000
Total Effect of IV on DV (c path)	.2936	.0606	4.8468	.0000
Direct Effect of IV on DV (c-prime path)	.0203	.0625	.3252	.7453
BOOTSTRAP RESULTS FOR INDIRECT EFFECTS	Data	Boot	Bias	SE
Indirect Effects of IV on DV through Proposed Mediators (ab paths)	.2733	.2727	-.0006	.0457
Bias Corrected and Accelerated Confidence Intervals	Lower= .1927		Upper=.3687	

6.5.3.1.38 Mediation effect of SL JS FL_SQ

Table 6.55 shows the direct, total and the indirect effect of mediation i.e. JS on SL and FL_SQ

Total and Direct effect output

- a path (IV to Mediators) is significant (p=.0000)
- b path (Direct Effects of Mediators on DV) is significant (p=.0000)
—c path (Total Effect of IV on DV) is not significant (p=.0002)
- c prime path (Direct Effect of IV on DV) is not significant (p=.5991)

Bootstrapped tests of the INDIRECT effects

A bias-corrected and accelerated confidence interval (CI) for *ab at* 95 per cent, the lower limit is .2049 and the upper limit is .3998. The bootstrapped CI for *ab* does not includes zero. As zero does not occurs between the LL and the UL, it can be concluded that only the total indirect effect is significant.

Table 6.51: Mediation effect of SL JS FL_SQ

SL JS FL_SQ				
	Coeff	*Se*	*T*	*P*
IV to Mediators (a path)	.4882	.0500	9.7607	.0000
Direct Effects of Mediators on DV (b path)	.5921	.0734	8.0620	.0000
Total Effect of IV on DV (c path)	.2519	.0675	3.7302	.0002
Direct Effect of IV on DV (c-prime path)	-.0371	.0706	-.5263	.5991
BOOTSTRAP RESULTS FOR INDIRECT EFFECTS	Data	Boot	Bias	SE
Indirect Effects of IV on DV through Proposed Mediators (ab paths)	.2890	.2857	-.0034	.0497
Bias Corrected and Accelerated Confidence Intervals	Lower= .2049		Upper=.3998	

6.5.3.1.39 Mediation effect of SL JS FL_SR

Table 6.56 shows the direct, total and the indirect effect of mediation i.e. JS on SL and FL_SR

Total and Direct effect output

- a path (IV to Mediators) is significant (p=.0000)
- b path (Direct Effects of Mediators on DV) is significant (p=.0000)
—c path (Total Effect of IV on DV) is not significant (p=.1759)
- c prime path (Direct Effect of IV on DV) is not significant (p=.1460)

Bootstrapped tests of the INDIRECT effects

A bias-corrected and accelerated confidence interval (CI) for *ab at* 95 per cent, the lower limit is .1211 and the upper limit is .2729. The bootstrapped CI for *ab* does not includes zero. As zero does not occurs between the LL and the UL, it can be concluded that the total indirect effect is significant and the direct effect is insignificant.

Table 6.52: Mediation effect of SL JS FL_SR

SL JS FL_SR

	Coeff	*Se*	*T*	*P*
IV to Mediators (a path)	.4882	.0500	9.7607	.0000
Direct Effects of Mediators on DV (b path)	.3864	.0732	5.2817	.0000
Total Effect of IV on DV (c path)	.0861	.0635	1.3569	.1759
Direct Effect of IV on DV (c-prime path)	-.1025	.0703	-1.4579	.1460
BOOTSTRAP RESULTS FOR INDIRECT EFFECTS	Data	Boot	Bias	SE
Indirect Effects of IV on DV through Proposed Mediators (ab paths)	.1886	.1864	-.0022	.0380
Bias Corrected and Accelerated Confidence Intervals	Lower= .1211		Upper=.2729	

6.5.3.1.40 Mediation effect of SL JS FL_JP

Table 6.57 shows the direct, total and the indirect effect of mediation i.e. JS on SL and FL_JP

Total and Direct effect output

- a path (IV to Mediators) is significant (p=.0000)
- b path (Direct Effects of Mediators on DV) is significant (p=.0002)
—c path (Total Effect of IV on DV) is not significant (p=.0326)
- c prime path (Direct Effect of IV on DV) is not significant (p=.9773)

Bootstrapped tests of the INDIRECT effects

A bias-corrected and accelerated confidence interval (CI) for *ab at* 95 per cent, the lower limit is .0574 and the upper limit is .2243. The bootstrapped CI for *ab* does not includes zero. As zero does not occurs between the LL and the UL, it can be concluded that only the total indirect effect is significant.

Table 6.53: Mediation effect of SL JS FL_JP

SL JS FL_JP

	Coeff	*Se*	*T*	*P*
IV to Mediators (a path)	.4882	.0500	9.7607	.0000
Direct Effects of Mediators on DV (b path)	.2745	.0725	3.7860	.0002
Total Effect of IV on DV (c path)	.1320	.0615	2.1478	.0326
Direct Effect of IV on DV (c-prime path)	-.0020	.0697	-.0284	.9773
BOOTSTRAP RESULTS FOR INDIRECT EFFECTS	Data	Boot	Bias	SE
Indirect Effects of IV on DV through Proposed Mediators (ab paths)	.1340	.1341	.0001	.0406
Bias Corrected and Accelerated Confidence Intervals	Lower= .0574		Upper=.2243	

6.5.3.1.41 Mediation effect of SL JS CO_P

Table 6.58 shows the direct, total and the indirect effect of mediation i.e. JS on SL and CO_P

Total and Direct effect output

- a path (IV to Mediators) is significant (p=.0000)
- b path (Direct Effects of Mediators on DV) is significant (p=.0185)
—c path (Total Effect of IV on DV) is not significant (p=.0003)
- c prime path (Direct Effect of IV on DV) is not significant (p=.0479))

Bootstrapped tests of the INDIRECT effects

A bias-corrected and accelerated confidence interval (CI) for *ab at* 95 per cent, the lower limit is .0241 and the upper limit is .1821. The bootstrapped CI for *ab* does not includes zero. As zero does not occurs between the LL and the UL, it can be concluded that only the total indirect effect is significant.

Table 6.54: Mediation effect of SL JS CO_P

SL JS CO_P				
	Coeff	*Se*	*T*	*P*
IV to Mediators (a path)	.4882	.0500	9.7607	.0000
Direct Effects of Mediators on DV (b path)	.1960	.0827	2.3688	.0185
Total Effect of IV on DV (c path)	.2537	.0691	3.6729	.0003
Direct Effect of IV on DV (c-prime path)	.1580	.0795	1.9871	.0479
BOOTSTRAP RESULTS FOR INDIRECT EFFECTS	Data	Boot	Bias	SE
Indirect Effects of IV on DV through Proposed Mediators (ab paths)	.0957	.0920	-.0037	.0390
Bias Corrected and Accelerated Confidence Intervals	Lower= .0241		Upper=.1821	

6.5.3.1.42 Mediation effect of SL JS ER_SB

Table 6.59 shows the direct, total and the indirect effect of mediation i.e. JS on SL and ER_SB

Total and Direct effect output

- a path (IV to Mediators) is significant (p=.0000)
- b path (Direct Effects of Mediators on DV) is significant (p=.0500)
—c path (Total Effect of IV on DV) is not significant (p=.0037)
- c prime path (Direct Effect of IV on DV) is not significant (p=.1263)

Bootstrapped tests of the INDIRECT effects

A bias-corrected and accelerated confidence interval (CI) for *ab at* 95 per cent, the lower limit is .0028 and the upper limit is .1715. The bootstrapped CI for *ab* does not includes zero. As zero does not occurs between the LL and the UL, it can be concluded that the total indirect effect is significant and the direct effect is insignificant.

Table 6.55: Mediation effect of SL JS ER_SB

SL JS ER_SB

	Coeff	*Se*	*T*	*P*
IV to Mediators (a path)	.4882	.0500	9.7607	.0000
Direct Effects of Mediators on DV (b path)	.1667	.0847	1.9686	.0500
Total Effect of IV on DV (c path)	.2061	.0705	2.9256	.0037
Direct Effect of IV on DV (c-prime path)	.1248	.0814	1.5334	.1263
BOOTSTRAP RESULTS FOR INDIRECT EFFECTS	Data	Boot	Bias	SE
Indirect Effects of IV on DV through Proposed Mediators (ab paths)	.0814	.0759	-.0055	.0416
Bias Corrected and Accelerated Confidence Intervals	Lower= .0028		Upper=.1715	

6.6 Summary of results of the tested hypotheses

The summary of hypotheses is shown in Table 6.60

Table 6.56: Summary of Hypotheses related to research frame I and II

Hypotheses	***Variables***	***Significance***
H1a	os and js	Rejected
H1b	re and js	Accepted
H1c	emp and js	Rejected
H1d	trg and js	Accepted
H1e	st and js	Accepted
H1f	sm and js	Accepted
H1g	sl and js	Accepted
H1h	js and fl_cf	Accepted
H1i	js and fl_sq	Accepted
H1j	js and fl_sr	Accepted
H1k	js and fl_jp	Accepted
H1l	js and co_p	Accepted
H1m	js and er_sb	Accepted

The hypothesis related to the mediating effects of Job Satisfaction on different variables is shown in Table 6.62.

Table 6.57: Summary of Hypotheses related to mediating effects of Job Satisfaction on different variables

Hypothesis	*Variables*	*Mediation*
H2a	os and fl_cf	No
H2b	os and fl_sq	No
H2c	os and fl_sr	No
H2d	os and fl_jp	No
H2e	os and co_p	No
H2f	os and er_sb	No
H3a	re andfl_cf	Partial
H3b	re and fl_sq	Partial
H3c	re and fl_sr	Partial
H3d	re and fl_jp	Partial
H3e	re and co_p	Partial
H3f	re and er_sb	Partial
H4a	emp and fl_cf	No
H4b	emp and fl_sq	No
H4c	emp and fl_sr	No
H4d	emp and fl_jp	No
H4e	emp and co_p	No
H4f	emp and er_sb	No
H5a	trg and fl_cf	Partial
H5b	trg and fl_sq	Partial
H5c	trg and fl_sr	Partial
H5d	trg and fl_jp	Partial
H5e	trg and co_p	Partial

(Contd...)

H5f	trg and er_sb	Partial
H6a	st and fl_cf	Complete
H6b	st and fl_sq	Complete
H6c	st and fl_sr	Complete
H6d	st and fl_jp	Partial
H6e	st and co_p	Complete
H6f	st and er_sb	Partial
H7a	sm and fl_cf	Partial
H7b	sm and fl_sq	Partial
H7c	sm and fl_sr	Partial
H7d	sm and fl_jp	Partial
H7e	sm and fl_jp	Partial
H7f	sm and co_p	Partial
H8a	sl and fl_cf	Partial
H8b	sl and fl_cf	Partial
H8c	sl and fl_sq	Partial
H8d	sl and fl_sr	Partial
H8e	sl and fl_jp	Partial
H8f	sl and co_p	Partial

6.7 Summary

The data was analysed with the help of Statistical Package for Social Science version 19 (SPSS) software to do the required analysis. The reliability of different variables was measured. Demographic profile was explained on the basis of different attributes of the population. The correlation was done between different variables. It was found out that the correlation between fl_cf and fl_sq was the highest. Regression analysis showed Accepted relationships with all the variables except for organisational support and employee empowerment. The mediation test revealed full mediation in case of service technology. Next chapter deals with the findings and the conclusions.

Chapter - 7

Findings and Conclusion

7.1 Introduction

This chapter gives an insight into the major findings of the research and the conclusions. The chapter starts with discussions on the findings of the research. Section 7.2.1 discusses the results of the hypotheses tested for the research frame I and II. The section 7.2.2 deals with the results of mediation test for research frame II. Section 7.3 gives conclusions on the basis of the tested hypothesis and section 7.4 summarises the chapter.

7.2 Discussion of findings

FLSE has moved into the centre stage of airlines in the recent years. Never before has their contribution to the success of airlines has been subjected to so much of debate and discussion. The situation has developed as a result of some fundamental change that has taken place, the most important of which is the pervasive and intensive competition that airlines are facing today. To sustain the competitive advantage airlines must have a commitment for improvement, innovation and change and the most important catalyst towards developing these qualities are its employees and their capabilities. It has become very important for the airlines to recruit, care, train them on the on-going basis to improve productivity, innovation and provide them conducive environment for personal growth.

This makes the role of FLSE ever so important in ensuring the success of business. The objectives of this study were formulated keeping in mind the importance of the role played by FLSE. The primary aim of the study was to undertake research to find out the relationship between various antecedents and the consequences of FLSE commitment to service quality in airline industry of India. Another very important objective was to test whether job satisfaction mediates this relationship or not. A model on the basis of relevant review of literature was proposed and tested by using SPSS 19 and the Mediation test (proposed by Andrew F. Hayes) which gave the results for the different paths. The findings of this research are there by discussed first on the basis of individual hypothesis before giving a summary of the entire hypotheses tested.

7.2.1 Results of Hypotheses testing (Research frame I and II)

In accordance with the reviewed literature, hypotheses were developed.These hypotheses were tested using regression. Results showed that there was a negative relationship between organisational support and Job satisfaction. Indeed, the more organisational support the employees get, the less likely he/she was to get job satisfaction. The results are not consistent with the organisational support theory which states that in return for a high level of support, employees work harder to help their organisation reach its goals (Aselage and Eisenberger, 2003) because organisational support has a significant effect on job satisfaction and organisational commitment (Rhodes and Eisenberger, 2002; Aube *et. al.,* 2007; Riggle *et. al.,* 2009).Thus the findings rejects hypothesis 1a.

As expected the results showed a positive relationship between rewards and job satisfaction.That means job satisfaction depended upon the rewards, the more the rewards,the more satisfied the employees are with their job. So hypothesis 1b was accepted.The positive relationship has also been established by researchers like Bowen, Gilliland and

Folger, 1999; Brown and Peterson, 1993; (Farrell and Rusbult, 1981). Heskett, Jones, Loveman, asser, and Schlesinger (1994). They found that the perception of appropriate levels of pay and other compensation have a significant impact on frontline employees' job satisfaction and loyalty to their organisation.

By empowering employees, management relinquish control over many aspects of the service delivery (Hartline and Ferrell, 1996) to frontline employees who, because of their boundary spanning roles, can provide quick and appropriate responses to dissatisfied customers (Boshoff and Allen, 2000).The study gave a very surprising results thereby showing a negative relationship between the employee empowerment and the job satisfaction. It proved that empowerment do not always affects the level of job satisfaction and so it did not support hypothesis 1c.

Training is considered to be a systematic development of the knowledge, skills, and expertise required by a person to effectively perform a given task or job. Poorly trained employees fail to provide a high level of service quality and deal poorly with customer complaints (Bettercourt and Gwinner, 1996; Yavas *et. al.,* 2003). Hypothesis 1d was accepted as there existed a positive relationship between the training and the job satisfaction i.e. the more the training is given, the more satisfied the employees are with their jobs which could further results in their retention in a particular organisation.

A significant relationship was found in case of service technology and job satisfaction; supportive management and Job satisfaction ($r=.666$, $p<.05$ and $r=.652$, $p<.05$). It was found that the more the employees get management support and the latest technology for the service delivery, the more they get satisfied with their job. So it establishes a positive relationship between the two and hence hypothesis 1e and hypothesis 1f were accepted.

The correlations among the Job satisfaction and the servant leadership was found to be quite high($r=.814$, $p<.05$).

The regression results also showed a positive and significant relationship between them. Laub (1999) had predicted that a servant-led organisation would have higher job satisfaction. The analysis showed that as the servant leadership increases, the employees job satisfaction also increases, which establishes a positive relationship that supported hypothesis 1g. This finding also validated the work of Girard (2000) and Thompson (2003) who found a positive correlation between servant leadership and job satisfaction among the leaders and salaried levels in their respective organisational samplings. It is expected that servant leadership may impact on frontline employees' job satisfaction and organisational commitment because of its role in creating an environment conducive to delivering high quality service and handling customer complaints effectively.

The analysis also stated a positive relationship between Job satisfaction and FLSE commitment to firm. That means that more the employees get satisfied with their job, the more they get committed towards their organisation. Thus, it supports Hypothesis 1h. Many researchers agree that frontline employees who are satisfied with and committed to their jobs, share the firm's customer-oriented values, exhibit low levels of role stress, and deliver the highest level of service quality (Hartline, Maxham and McKee 2000; Singh 2000).

There is also evidence suggesting that being effective in performing a job is positively related to job satisfaction (Rust *et. al.,* 1996).The results were in the accordance to the evidences given by these researchers. The relationship between Job satisfaction and FLSE commitment towards service quality was also found to be significant which supported Hypothesis 1i. Frontline employees that have higher levels of job satisfaction are more likely to be in a positive mood and behave sensitively and considerately towards others.The results of the analysis showed a significant relationship between Job satisfaction and FLSE service recovery performance which proved the hypothesis 1j to be true.

Fitzgerald (1972) stated that employee job satisfaction relates to job performance. Satisfied employees perform better than dissatisfy employees (Boshoff & Allen, 2000). In the study also it was analysed that there exist a significant relationship between Job satisfaction and FLSE job performance, which supported hypothesis 1k.It was also found that the employees who were more satisfied by their job were more ready to help others which supported hypothesis 1l. Even researchers like Berkowitz (1972) have explained this relationship by suggesting that people who were in a good mood are more likely to engage in prosocial behaviour. It was also found that the employees who were satisfied with their jobs were ready to serve customers that were in addition to their official role requirements which satisfies hypothesis 1m. Even the recent service literature emphasises the importance of extra-role service behaviours during service encounters (Bettencourt & Brown, 1997; Kelly and Hoffman, 1997).

This research also aims to institute an understanding of the mediating effect of job satisfaction.The mediating relationship was introduced in the model where job satisfaction was introduced as a mediator for antecedents and consequences of FLSE commitment towards service delivery. In order to test the degree to which job satisfaction acts as a mediator of the relationship between all possible antecedent consequences relationships, the direct and the indirect effect were analysed.

7.2.2 Results of mediating effect of Job Satisfaction (Research frame III)

Job satisfaction was tested as a mediator between the seven antecedents and six consequences. Mediation test as outlined by Hayes (2009) was conducted for all the direct, indirect and the total effects/paths. The results of the mediated approach are as follows-

Organisational support

No direct effect between organisational support and fl_cf, fl_sq, fl_jp, fl_sp, co_p, er_sb is found. The bootstrapped CI for *ab* includes zero that means that the indirect effect is also not significant in all the cases or we can conclude that no mediation exists between organisational support and fl_cf, fl_sq, fl_jp, fl_sp, co_p, er_sb. That indicates that the job satisfaction do not mediate the relationship between organisational support and the consequences. So Hypotheses - H2a, H2b, H2c, H2d, H2e and H2f were not supported.

Rewards

No direct effect exists between reward and the consequences i.e. fl_cf,fl_sq, fl_jp, fl_sp, co_p, er_sb. the bootstrapped CI for *ab does not* includes zero that means that only the indirect effect is significant in all the cases. It is concluded that partial mediation exists between organisational support and fl_cf fl_sq, fl_jp, fl_sp, co_p, er_sb as the total effect in all the variables (consequences) is not significant. So H3a, H3b, H3c, H3d, H3e and H3f are partially supported.

Empowerment

No direct effect exists between empowerment and the consequences i.e. fl_cf,fl_sq, fl_jp, fl_sp, co_p, er_sb.The bootstrapped CI for *ab* included zero that means that the indirect effect is insignificant. As there is no direct and indirect effect, it is concluded that no mediation exists between them. That also implies that job satisfaction do not mediates the relationship between empowerment and the consequences. So the hypothesis-H4a, H4b, H4c, H4d, H4e and H4f are not supported.

Training

Inspite of the fact that no direct effect exists between training and fl_cf,fl_sq, fl_jp, fl_sp, co_p, er_sb,even then the indirect effect is significant in all the cases. The bootstrapped CI for *ab does not* includes zero. It is concluded that job satisfaction partially mediates training and fl_cf fl_sq, fl_jp, fl_sp, co_p, er_sb. H5a, H5b, H5c, H5d, H5e and H5f are partially supported.

Service technology

Direct effect exists in case of all the consequences except for fl_jp and er_sb. Indirect effect is significant in case of all variables i.e. fl_cf fl_sq, fl_sr, fl_jp, co_p. it can be concluded that a complete mediation exists between service tech and fl_cf, fl_sq, fl_sr, and co_p. As job satisfaction fully mediates the relationship between service technology and and fl_cf, fl_sq, fl_sr, and co_p, hypothesis-H6a, H6b, H6c, and H6e are supported. H6d and H6f are partially supported.

Supportive management

No direct effect exists between sm and the consequences i.e. fl_cf,fl_sq, fl_jp, fl_sp, co_p, er_sb. As the bootstrapped CI for *ab* does not includes zero, the indirect effect is significant in all the cases and we can conclude that partial mediation exists between sm and fl_cf fl_sq, fl_jp, fl_sp, co_p, er_sb. So H7a, H7b, H7c, H7d, H7e and H7f are partially supported.

Servant leadership

Direct effect is not significant in the relationship between sl and fl_cf fl_sq, fl_jp, fl_sp, er_sb. The bootstrapped ci for *ab* does not include zero in case of all the consequences which means that the indirect effect is significant in all the cases. Because of this it is concluded that a partial mediation exists between sl and the consequences as only indirect effect exists between sl and fl_cf fl_sq, fl_jp, fl_sp, er_sb. So H8a, H8b, H8c, H8d, H8e and H8f are partially supported.

7.3 Review of the results

The results of the regression analysis revealed that the organisational support and the job satisfaction are insignificantly related. In this study, organisational support focuses on help offered to frontline workers when necessary, appropriate job design, and support for frontline employees' goals and values. The discovery that employee empowerment has a significant negative influence on FLSE CSQ was not expected, as it diverges from the tenets of HRD theory, which holds that employee empowerment generates job satisfaction. The FLSE cannot handle the passenger problems by themselves as they need to get managements approval before handling passenger's problems.

However, the results are consistent with earlier studies that found rewarding an employee was a stronger predictor of employee job satisfaction (Ellinger and Keller 2003; Hannah 2004). In general, two kinds of rewards are available: financial and non-financial rewards. Rewards also range from a simple thank-you note for an exceptional service to a large reward such as wage increase and promotion. Rewards given to employees, regardless of the type, must be meaningful to the employees and the organisation.

The study also showed a significant relationship between training and job satisfaction which means that the more the training an employee's receives, the more satisfied they get. Through training, FLSE of the different airlines master the basic skills necessary to perform the daily duties of the position and develop job competence. In addition to the basic skills, more airlines are offering training such as receiving training continuously to provide good service.The training program broadens frontline employees' responsibilities and teaches proper techniques to resolve conflicts and deal with problems immediately.

Most of the FLSE feels that they have the 'state of the art' technology to enhance service quality which has resulted in a significant relationship between Service technology and job satisfaction. They feel that sufficient money is allocated for technology to support their efforts to deliver better service. The regression results are also significant for supportive management, servant leadership and the job satisfaction. They are of the view that their bosses provide them with sufficient flexibility about how they accomplish their objectives. Management also regularly spends time 'on the floor' with them and the passengers to constantly measure service quality.

As FLSE feels their future to be closely linked to that of the company, they are more committed to their company.They also feel proud to tell others about their being a part of the company and cares about the fate of their company.That is why a significant relationship between job satisfaction and FLSE Commitment to firm was found.

FLSE felt strongly about improving the service their company provides to its customers.They gained a sense of personal accomplishment in providing quality services to customers.They were willing to put in a great deal of effort to help their company deliver high-quality service to the customers. All this led to the significant relationship between job satisfaction and their commitment to service quality. FLSE handled dissatisfied passengers quite well and did not mind dealing with the complaining passengers. Satisfying complaining passengers was a great thrill to them.They also satisfied their customers' service expectations and managed their works time effectively.They are knowledgeable about their company's services and expectation of the passengers which led to the significant relationship between job satisfaction and FLSE job performance.

FLSE helped other employees who had excessive workloads and were always ready to lend a helping hand to co-workers around them. They voluntarily assisted customers even if it meant going beyond their job requirements which helped in establishing a positive relationship between Extra-role customer service behaviours, Cooperation and job satisfaction.

The conceptual model of the study places job satisfaction as a mediator of the relationship between the seven antecedents and six consequences. In order to test the degree to which job satisfaction acts as a mediator of the relationship between all possible antecedent consequences relationships, direct paths and indirect paths were added from each antecedent to each consequence.

No mediation was found in case of organisational support (antecedent) and the consequences of FLSE commitment to service quality. Same is the case with the employee empowerment and the consequences. In these cases neither direct nor indirect effects was significant.This kind of situation is also referred to suppression. As neither direct nor indirect effect was found to be significant, it is concluded that job satisfaction do not mediate these relationships and so no mediation existed between job satisfaction and the consequences (fl_cf,fl_sq, fl_jp, fl_sp, co_p, er_sb).

Job satisfaction mediated the relationship between rewards, training, service technology, supportive management and the consequences, but only partially as only indirect effect was found to be significant (bootstrapped CI for ab does not includes zero).The direct effect and the total effect were found to be insignificant, and so it was concluded that job satisfaction partially mediates the relationship between these antecedents and the consequences. Being satisfied with the received rewards, training, service technology, supportive management, will significantly reduce employees' intention to leave their employer.

Job satisfaction mediated in case of most of the antecedents (reward, training, Service technology, supportive management and servant leadership) and the consequences (fl_cf,fl_sq, fl_jp, fl_sp, co_p, er_sb). The direct and the indirect effect in case of st and sl was found to be highly significant. That is why a complementary mediation existed between these antecedents and all the consequences.

A complete mediation was found in case of st and fl_cf, st and fl_sq, st and fl_sr and st and co_p. That means job satisfaction completely mediates the relationships between service technology and fl_cf, fl_sq, fl_sr and co_p. In these cases both the direct and the indirect effects were found to be significant. However, in case of service technology and fl_jp, er_sb, both direct and the total effects were found to be insignificant.

In case of re, trg and sm only indirect effect is significant as the bootstrapped CI for *ab* does not includes zero. As far as organisational support is concerned, neither direct nor indirect effect is significant.That indicates that job satisfaction do not mediates the relationship between os and the consequences. No direct effect exists between empowerment and the consequences. The indirect effect is significant only in the case of fl_jp and fl_sp as the bootstrapped CI for *ab* does not *includes* zero. So partial mediation exists only between empowerment and fl_jp and fl_sp.

Hence, it can be concluded that whether it was a correlation, regression or a mediation analysis, service technology emerged as one of the most important variable. Job satisfaction fully mediated the relationship only between the service technology and the consequences.

Technology is being deployed to enhance the performance of the front line employee in interacting with the customer. In still other cases, technology is allowing introduction of entirely new service innovations. It is profoundly changing the nature of services and the ways in which firms interact with their customers. According to Bitner *et. al.* (1990), the influence of technology on the ability of firms to effectively: (1) customise service offerings; (2) recover from service failure; and, (3) delight customers.

Service technology came out to be an important variable in improving the performance of FLSE. The employees of the airlines undertaken for the study are satisfied with the technology provided to them by the organisation.They are satisfied with the fact that they have 'state of the art' technology to enhance service quality.They also agree with the fact that sufficient money is allocated for technology to support their efforts to deliver better service. Not only this, the management also works hard to make the systems and processes more passengers friendly.The second most important variable of the study is servant leadership.Though job satisfaction partially mediated the relationship between servant leadership and the consequences yet the correlation among the Job satisfaction and the servant leadership was found to be quite high ($r=.814$, $p<.05$).The regression results also showed a positive and significant relationship between sl and the consequences.The other variables i.e. re, trg, sm, fl_cf, fl_sq, fl_jp, fl_sp, co_p, er_sb were also found to be important as they were also partially mediated by job satisfaction.

7.4 Summary

This chapter described the major findings of the research and the conclusion. It also explained the results of the hypotheses testing for the research frame I, II. The results of mediation test for research frame III were also discussed. Overall service technology came out to be the most important antecedent. The next Chapter-8 is the last chapter of this thesis which discusses the summary, interventions, limitations, recommendations and suggestions.

Chapter - 8

Summary and Suggestions

8.1 Introduction

Domestic airlines of India contribute significantly towards the development of the country. Various changes are altering the landscape and it is essential that airlines embrace these changes for enhancing their competitiveness and sustained growth. The HRD practices are enabling airlines to develop their human resource to meet the challenges of the global world and work effectively. Airlines need to be competitive and this implies that they should be more responsive towards their employees needs and demonstrate flexibility and agility in meeting their needs. As FLSE are the face of the airlines, the organisation has high stakes on how the service employee behaves in service encounters as they are faced with multiple challenges on a daily basis. It is the manner in which these challenges are dealt with and the degree to which one can cope with the strain of boundary spanning roles, which distinguishes excellent service providers.Their attitudes and behaviours significantly influence the quality of service operations.

It is in this context that understanding of the factors which are responsible for employees certain behavior and their commitment needs to be studied. This study has examined various antecedents and the consequences of FLSE commitment towards service quality which includes organisational support, reward, empowerment, training, service technology, supportive management, servant leadership, frontline employee commitment to firm, frontline commitment to service quality, frontline employee service recovery performance,frontline commitment to job performance, cooperation, extra role customer service behaviour. In this chapter, Section 8.2 explains the summary of the study; Section 8.3 deals with the implications of the findings for the academicians, frontline employees, managers and the organisations; Section 8.4 explains recommendations and intervention strategies; 8.5 and 8.6 deals with the limitations of the study and the suggestions for future research. The last section of the last Chapter 8.7 summarises the chapter.

8.2 Summary of the study

This study provides empirical evidence regarding the effect of antecedents and consequences of FLSE commitment to service quality. Of particular importance is the emergence of certain variables that have thwart or encourage initiatives at establishing employee commitment in the organisation.The main objectives of the study were to analyse the effect of antecedents and consequences of FLSE commitment to service quality and whether job satisfaction acts as a mediator between different antecedents and the consequences.

Literature clearly indicates the factors that affect the FLSE commitment to firm which include rewards training, organisational support, empowerment and many more. These factors affect the level of job satisfaction which in turn affects the affective and the behavioural outcomes. The framework was derived from Bagozzi's (1992) reformulation of attitude theory and proposes a self-regulating process, where individuals appraise various past, present and future outcomes. These outcomes produce particular emotions that lead to various coping responses (behaviours). The framework of the Antecedents (Development and reward based activities) and the consequences (Affective and the behavioural outcomes) was developed keeping in mind the various important variables. By using frontline service employees in an airline industry as its setting, this study examines the underlying process through which a set of FLSE variables generate affective responses of job satisfaction (frontline employee feelings towards the job and organisation) as well as the behavioural outcomes (frontline employee feelings towards other employees).

The data for the study was collected from the six domestic airlines operating at the Indira Gandhi International Airport (Terminal 3) and the Domestic Airport (Terminal 1) New Delhi out of which one was a public sector airline and the other five were private sector airlines. Total of 282 data was collected from the FLSE of these airlines by a standard questionnaire on their commitment towards the service quality. This information of the 282 questionnaire was fed in the computer and analysed with the help of Statistical Package for Social Science version 20(SPSS) software.

Hypothesis were developed to see the relationship between antecedents (Development and reward based activities) and the consequences (Affective and the behavioural outcomes). The direct and the indirect effect was also estimated to see the mediation effect of job satisfaction between the antecedents and the consequences.

On the very outset, demographic analysis was done which indicated that 18.4 per cent of the respondents belonged to Kingfisher airlines, 16.3 per cent to IndiGo, 14.9 per cent to Jet airways, 18.1 per cent to Air India, 15.6 per cent to Go airlines and 16.7 per cent belonged to Spice jet. Male constituted 67.5 per cent of the total respondents. 69.1 per cent of the respondents were having a qualification of 12th with some Diploma related to the airline services. The reliability analysis was done using the Cronbach alpha which indicated the instruments' items and subscales to be reliable.The Item-Total Statistics for reliability between the variables was also done which also indicated the reliability ranging from .645 to .909.

Descriptive analysis indicated the variableflse_jp to be the most important variable with a mean of 5.89 and SD of 589. The item with the lowest mean, rated as least important by FLSE was the supportive management with the means of 5.26 and SD of .751.

The correlation and regression analysis was done and the results indicated that the fl_cf and fl_sq had the highest correlation ($r=.782$, $p<.05$) which means a high increase in fl_cf would lead to high fl_sq .This also indicates that when FLSE are committed to the goals and objectives of the airlines, they are likely to provide quality service to customers. This finding is consistent with (Boshoff and Allen, 2000, Paulin *et. al.,* 2005 and Zheng, 2009) who assert that the long-term customer relationships are built with long-term committed employees. Little and Dean (2005) and Mukherjee and Malhotra (2006) note that employee commitment contributes to employees feeling valued and consequently deliver high quality service to customers.That means, the more committed the employees are, the more the level of service quality delivery through continuous improvement. When FLSE are aligned with the goals of airlines, they perform beyond the call of duty to meet airline customer needs. FLSE task performance behaviour directed at serving customers improves as their service attitudes towards the customers will be improved.

The correlation between job satisfaction and servant leadership was also found to be quite high ($r=.770$, $p<.05$).The results are in consistent with earlier studies of researchers like Laub (1999) who predicted that a servant-led organisation would have higher job satisfaction. The finding also supported the work of Girard (2000) and Thompson (2003) who found a positive correlation between servant leadership and job satisfaction among the employees in their respective organisational samplings. The correlation between variables, Extra role customer service behaviour and organisational support was found to be the lowest. Previous studies have shown that organisational support relates to several positive work behaviours, including extra-role behaviours.The lowest correlation was among the variables empowerment and er_sb (r=.001, p>.05).

It was not surprising to see a strong relationship between rewards, training, service technology, servant leadership, supportive management and the job satisfaction. The regression results clearly indicated the significant relationships between these variables. Among them, rewards and servant leadership displayed the largest effect on FLSE's job satisfaction. In general, two kinds of rewards are available: financial and non-financial rewards. Rewards also range from a simple thank-you note for an exceptional service to a large reward such as wage increase and promotion.

Rewards given to employees' must be meaningful to them and the organisation. In other words, rewards should be based on employees' job performance and reflect the organisation's goal and service standard. Most rewards in the Asian culture, including India, are in monetary form (Stern and Associates, 2006). However, because of the growing influence of the Western style of management, rewards in the form of recognition, such as being selected as employees of the month with a certificate, are getting popular in India. This kind of recognition can increase employees' morale and make workers feel that they are appreciated and valued as a member of the organisation, leading to job satisfaction and organisational loyalty.

The study also indicated servant leadership to be an important predictor of job satisfaction. In the service literature, servant leadership behaviour is identified as a critical and integral ingredient necessary for creating and maintaining an effective climate for delivering excellent customer service (Heskett *et. al.,* 1997; Lytle *et. al.,* 1998; Schneider *et. al.,* 2005). Servant leadership has an impact on FLSEs' job satisfaction and organisational commitment because of its role in creating an environment conducive to delivering high quality service and handling customer complaints effectively.

The results demonstrated a significant relationship between training and job satisfaction which means that the more the training an employee's receives, the more satisfy the employee gets. Human resource academics and professionals together have identified training as a critical factor to improve employees' skills, firm performance, organisational survival, and considered essential for a firm to remain competitive (MacDuffie 1995; Salas & Cannon-Bowers, 2001). It is very difficult for an employee to perform well at the job place without any training; trained employees perform well as compared to untrained employees (Boudreau *et. al.,* 2001). It is very necessary for any organisation to give its employee training to get overall goals of the organisation in a better way (Heras, 2006).

Training frontline staff and getting feedback from them is absolutely essential. The presence of customer service training programs sends a strong signal to frontline employees regarding top management's commitment to service quality (Babakus *et. al.,* 2003). Customer service training has a direct impact on frontline employees' job satisfaction because of its role in developing skills to handle service failures effectively (Tax and Brown, 1998; Babakus *et. al.,* 2003). Other studies have also demonstrated that frontline employees are more committed to organisations that invest more in customer service training programs (Sweetman, 2001; Tsui *et. al.,* 1997). Berry and Parasuraman (1991) stated that although employees receive training, it is often not adequate, or not the kind of training that is required. This could results in a non-commitment of FLSE towards their job and the firm.

Supportive management has been shown to be related to a variety of work-related attitudes and outcomes. In particular, perceptions that the organisation cares about employees are positively related to work attendance (Eisenerger *et. al.,* 1986), job satisfaction (Eisenberger *et. al.,* 1997), trust in management (Whitener, 2001), and individual performance (Rhoades and Eisenberger 2002). It is viewed as important to organisations in terms of success and commitment of employees.

Most of the FLSE feels that they have the latest technology to enhance service quality which has resulted in a significant relationship between Service technology and job satisfaction. In the present scenario, service technology is considered to be the most important aspect of service organisations as Technology provides a way for customer information and data to be saved and easily accessed by employees to enhance the value of their interactions with customers. Gummesson (1994) contends that the designing of services involves a rigorous analysis of activities, processes and an interaction, which includes viewing the important role technology, will play. He considers technology to be one of the 'dynamic drawings' of the service delivery process. This therefore implies that endorsing a customer-focus is not enough; an organisation must be equipped with skilled staff and provide appropriate resources.

Service encounters can be improved through the effective use of technology; technology can make employees more effective and efficient. Quantities of information that could not possibly be remembered, filed, or sorted in the past are now available to employees with a click of a computer key (Bitner, *et. al.,* 2000).

An interesting finding is the non-significant relationship between organisational support and the job satisfaction which implies that organisational support is not a good predictor of employees'job satisfaction. In this study, organisational support focuses on help offered to frontline workers when necessary, appropriate job design, and support for frontline employees' goals and values.The discovery that employee empowerment has a significant *negative* influence on FLSE CSQ was not expected, as it diverges from the tenets of HRD theory, which holds that employee empowerment generates job satisfaction. It is possible that the FLSE might not have noticed the recognition or respect that the organisation provide to them. Perhaps the daily job routine is not interesting for them, and the airline does not define its values and goals. Most employees remain with one airline for several years as in the case of public sector airline i.e. Air India, so they lose their interest in service.

The finding simply that FLSE cannot handle the passenger problems by themselves as they need to get managements approval before handling passenger's problems. The explanations for this may be drawn from two aspects: organisational aspect and individual aspect. Some organisations are driven to implement empowerment practices because other organisations are doing it. These followers may not thoroughly understand the notion of empowerment and fail to explain it clearly to the employees. Organisations should also monitor the success and make changes when necessary once the empowerment program has been carried out (Kazlauskaite *et. al.,* 2006). If the organisation does not provide consistent support from the top, the employees will presume that the empowerment practices are just show cases and will not take it seriously. Also, some organisations would "empower" employees by assigning them additional responsibilities but not including them in the decision making process.

From the individual aspect, empowerment is not a right tool for everyone. Additional responsibilities may cause burnout and stress (Hartline and Ferrell, 1996). Employees with low internal needs for power and control may not be suitable for empowerment development. In addition, not every employee needs to be empowered. If there is a low level of uncertainty in the workplace, employees are more likely to follow the standard procedures to complete the tasks.

The relationship between the job satisfaction and the consequences of FLSE commitment to service quality was also studied. A highly significant relationship between job satisfaction and FLSE Commitment to firm was found. FLSE feels their future to be closely linked to that of the company. That is the reason why they are more committed to their company. They also feel proud to tell others about their being a part of the company and cares about the fate of their company.

A significant relationship between job satisfaction and the consequences i.e. affective and behavioural outcome was found. When the frontline of the organisation are heavily committed to the goals of the organisation, they would want the organisation to do well. The one way in which these FLSE are able to contribute to the success of the organisation is through their own individual performance. Public and private airline managers should also explicitly design and establish organisational policies pertaining to employee empowerment, education/training, and reward systems and so on in order to develop a system that will facilitate a higher level of commitment to the airline and a service-orientated performance.

The mediation analysis was conducted using bootstrapping method with bias correcting confidence variances. In the present study, the 95 per cent confidence interval of indirect effects was obtained by 1000 bootstrap resamples. The direct and the indirect effect in case of organisational support were found to be insignificant.That means job satisfaction do not mediate the relationships between organisational support and the consequences. The results of the correlation analysis also showed very low values as far as the relationship between organisational support and consequences are concerned. Full mediation resulted only in case of service technology and the consequences. That means job satisfaction fully mediates these relationships. In case of rewards, training, supportive management and servant leadership, partial mediation was observed. So overall service technology came out to be the most important variable as far as the study is concerned. Service technology support encompasses sophisticated and integrated tools provided by management to employees to free them from routine tasks so that they can devote more time to customers (Lytle *et. al.,* 1998). According to Dabholkar, (2000) service technology may also elicit positive affective responses by FLSEs because information technology has the potential to streamline processes, make procedures more accurate and efficient and reduce the risk of human error.

The other most important variable of the study was found to be a servant leadership. Servant leadership is a practical philosophy, which supports people who choose to serve first, and then lead as a way of expanding service to individuals and institutions (Greenleaf, 1970/1991). Servant-leaders set service standards by their own behavior and management styles (James, 2005; Lytle *et. al.,* 1998) and actively engage in helping, assisting and meeting the needs of employees within the work setting (Lytle and Timmerman, 2006; Schneider, 1990).

In the services literature, servant leadership behaviour is identified as a critical and integral ingredient necessary for creating and maintaining an effective climate for delivering excellent customer service (Heskett *et. al.,* 1997; Lytle *et. al.,* 1998; Schneider *et. al.,* 2005). Servant leadership has an impact on FLSEs' job satisfaction and organisational commitment because of its role in creating an environment conducive to delivering high quality service and handling customer complaints effectively.

Servant leadership is related to several positive employee outcomes, including increased job performance and satisfaction, prosocial work behaviors, leader-member exchange, and affective organisational commitment (Barbuto and Wheeler, 2006; Ehrhart, 2004; Liden, Wayne, Zhao and Henderson, 2008). Leader-member exchange and organisational commitment are important for building social cohesiveness within an organisation. Saboe (2010) also empirically proved the significant relationship between servant leadership and organisational outcomes which included Job (task) Performance, Prosocial Behaviors, Physical Well-Being, Job Satisfaction, Leader-Member Exchange, Commitment, Justice Perceptions, trust in Supervisor/Organisation.

The strong positive influence of the FLSE commitment to service quality on employees' job satisfaction and the consequences confirms the findings of previous research. The organisation manager must improve FLSE commitment to service quality because it affects employees' job satisfaction and affective and the behavioural outcome.

Providing good training programs, increasing rewards, developing the empowerment and improving the organisational support, empowering employees, increasing the management support to the employees will increase employees' job satisfaction and employees' affective and the behavioural outcomes which includes FLSE commitment to firm and service quality, FLSE service recovery performance, cooperation among the employees and the extra role customer service behaviour.

8.3 Implications of the findings

The implications of different findings in the current study are as follows.

8.3.1 For Academicians

In terms of theoretical contributions this study is one of the few studies which have been done to determine the relationship between the antecedents and the consequences of frontline employee's commitment to service quality in the public and private sector of Indian domestic airlines. The study tries to find out the impact of various Developmental and reward based activities and the consequences (Affective and the behavioural outcomes) on the employees of different airlines.

Academicians need to study the various factors responsible for the employee's commitment towards the service quality that they deliver, in detail. In general they have to study how the organisations can adopt various practices that are followed internationally without losing the positive values and culture of Indian setup. Research should also be carried out in order to integrate the factors affecting FLSE commitment with overall strategies and objectives of the concerned organisation. Finally, this study focused on only fourteen variables. Other seemingly important management service initiatives, such as information technology, diversity of workplace, mentoring, and communication, could be added in future research.

For the academic implication, schools of the hospitality and tourism in India might provide an orientation program for FLSE to develop their knowledge about the practices of service delivery. Offering courses in the field of service delivery will help the FLSE and the organisation to operate the airline effectively.

8.3.2 For Frontline Employees

Airlines which actually want to improve the effectiveness of their employees can apply the findings of this research. The employees should analyse their existing performance and try to upgrade it by enhancing their level of delivering services, sharpen skills and by setting right kind of work environment. There is a pressing need to develop practices which encourage efficiency in airline sector and for this incentive structure need to be conceived supported by appropriate training and motivation, which aligns the employee's goals and orientations with the core competencies and strategic advantages of the airline.

There is a need to adopt global best practices and adapt them to domestic environment. This largely depends on the functioning and policies of various international airlines. Managers should look inward and recognise the talent within the airline by framing a policy to spot the staff from a specific age-group, subject to suitability and eligibility, promote and develop them for the future. This will result in motivation, building commitment and loyalty among employees.

8.3.3 For Organisations and Managers

Organisations that require their employees to develop organisation commitment should provide a supportive work environment which creates a mutually beneficial environment. They should demonstrate their commitment for the employees by providing comprehensive training, rewards, support, empowerment for the development and growth of employees within the organisation and offer more than market related incentives. Organisations should provide an open and accurate communication which helps in creating an impression that the organisation cares and values the employees as a partner. Given the increasing strategic importance of FLSEs' interactions with customers, it is critical for service organisations to develop a better understanding of how to help and encourage FLSEs to provide the kinds of service experiences that differentiate their firms from competitors.

The major strength of the present study is that the researcher has extended the previous organisational research on the employee perspective to that of the customer. As this research applies FLSE commitment in the service delivery situation, service organisations should devote far more managerial effort to improving employees service delivery and commitment.

Managers interested in fostering communication among their employees can gain by seeking guidance from the growing literature on high commitment towards service quality.The airline managers must be attentive to employees' needs in order to provide commitment and satisfaction. Committed and satisfied employees contribute to the success of the airline industry company. The managers must, at least, keep the consistency or increase employees' job satisfaction. They should select and adopt the practices that would contribute to the perception of the organisational commitment to the employees.

They should explicitly design and establish organisational policies pertaining to employee empowerment, education/ training, and reward systems and so on in order to develop a system that will facilitate a higher level of commitment to the airlines. Moreover, the management team must demonstrate the extra role service behaviours that will be recognised by the organisation (Bettencourt and Brown, 1997). Thus, employees would be encouraged to practice these behaviours in order to earn recognition.

Managers should emphasis employees commitment to service delivery by communicating clear organisational policies. By not taking into consideration the important variables, managerial action to improve individual and organisational performance may fail (Babakus *et. al.,* 2003; Lytle and Timmermann, 2006).

8.4 Recommendations and intervention strategies

The findings represent a step forward in the discovery of interventions that may help frontline employees and managers to better understand and take appropriate steps to improve service employees' job-related attitudes and behaviours. Based on the research findings and learning's thereof, the following intervention strategies are recommended in the Indian context.

Firstly, insignificant effect of organisational support on airline employees' job satisfaction was found. In this study, organisational support focuses on help offered to frontline workers when necessary, appropriate job design, and support for frontline employees' goals and values. This insignificant result may be partly associated with the high power distance between supervisors and subordinates. In the airline industry, managers are more likely to be valued and respected than frontline personnel, and airline managers with authoritative leaderships are least likely to place a high priority on the well-being of frontline employees and assisting in their job. Although the organisational culture is changing slowly, and some of the airlines are adopting Western management styles, it takes a long time for employee perceptions to change. Indian frontline personnel are more likely to recognise strong organisational support (i.e., they feel they receive enough help at work, their job is designed to be rewarding, and their goals and values are as important as managers' goals and values) in the future.

Although the result of the study does not support a relationship between organisational support and employees' job satisfaction, past research presented a positive relationship. Therefore, the management should improve other kinds of organisational support such as educational resources, materials, equipment, and corporate philosophy (Kim, Leong and Lee, 2004). The organisation should reinforce the idea that "people are the key to our success" (Schneider *et. al.*, 1994). These kind of new working environments may develop employees' interest and increase their value to the organisation. When employees trust the organisation, they will be satisfied in their jobs and consequently provide the prosocial service behaviors (Randall, Cropanzano, Bormann and Birjulin,1999). This result may also build cooperation among employees.

To motivate employees it is important that the employees are provided with both intrinsic as well as extrinsic rewards. Examples of intrinsic rewards are feelings of achievement and personal growth, while extrinsic rewards include outcomes such as salary, status, job security and fringe benefits. A properly designed reward structure is management's most powerful tool for mobilising organisational commitment to successful strategy execution. It is equally important to regularly assess the rewards that motivate employees and are of vital importance to all business firms. In addition, if employees expect their efforts to be rewarded fairly, they are more likely to provide extra services to customers.

Empowering employees has become important for the service business. On the other hand, not many employees know how to use their empowerment. In India, employees like to follow the leader, so employees are uncomfortable using their authority without obtaining permission from a supervisor. Empowerment training would show employees how to exercise their empowerment. Moreover, the airline management should encourage frontline employees to use their empowerment to prevent service failures. But at the same time, the manager should monitor the employees' empowerment because sometimes employees exploit their empowerment by soliciting rewards from customers in exchange for privileges. Bowen and Lawler (1995) and Argyris (1998) state that empowerment cannot be effective if it is not aligned with appropriate rewards and training. In other words, training and rewards systems are necessary for empowered frontline hospital staff to be effective in their jobs. Similarly, Hart *et. al.* (1990) and Forrester (2000) argue that training is unlikely to produce the intended results unless reward mechanisms are also in place.

Training programs will improve employees' job satisfaction and service performance. It clarifies several service issues that employees may not know, teaches the practices that will improve customer satisfaction, and increase employee satisfaction in return. Additional training programs about service quality or the airline service culture should be offered to the employees. Moreover, the airlines should provide regular training programs. Otherwise, employees can become distracted, and the training program would not be effective. Training programs should take place twice to three times a year and must be relevant to job description programs and service quality programs. Managers should consider monitoring training, because it will remind employees of their service commitment to customers.Training in communication skills will increase employees' job satisfaction, because they can communicate with customers efficiently, provide the right services, and satisfy the customers. It is important that the training function is made an effective organisational intervention by establishing a clear policy of training and development within the framework of total human resource development. The training establishments need to be actively involved in the total training process starting from the identification of training needs, evaluation of training effectiveness and the benefits of training to the end-users viz. the internal and external customers.

The utilisation of technology is critical to creating a service system for the delivery of service quality excellence. It elicits positive attitudinal and behavioural responses by frontline employees because information technology has the potential to streamline processes, make procedures more accurate and efficient, and reduce the risk of human error. As it is considered an important asset in assessment of quality and skill provided in airline facilities, there is a need for introduction of new technology, skill building and strong base of FLSE.

Servant leadership impacts frontline employees' job satisfaction and organisational commitment because of its role in creating an environment conducive to deliver high quality service and handle customer complaints effectively. As the employees who perceive servant leadership behaviours in the organisation get more satisfied with their jobs, it is important to promote factors that provide a satisfying work environment to FLSEs, namely leadership behaviours associated with servant leadership, could help retain employees who may otherwise choose to retire early or leave the profession altogether.

The primary apprehension of the airline should be to foster cohesive team work and create commitment to improve the efficiency of its human capital. More than operational skills today there is a need of 'soft skills' to attend the needs and requirement of the customers at the counter.

The core function of HRD in the airline industry is to facilitate performance improvement, measured not only in terms of certain indicators of operational efficiency but also in terms of quality of services provided. The technical skill, attitude and knowledge of the personnel play an important role in determining the competitiveness of an airline. Airlines have to understand that the capital and technology which is considered to be the most important pillars of airlines are replicable but not human capital, which needs to be viewed as a valuable resource of competitive advantage. The primary concern of the airline should be to bring in proper integration of human resource management strategies with the business strategies.

Morale boosting of the employees have been over looked by the organisations. Human beings even if satisfied of material wellbeing need to be appraised and encouraged constantly. Airlines should realise this need and should take steps to keep their work force motivated through proper encouragement like man of the month awards, repeat get-togethers, conferences, sports events, dinners, company sponsored travel, reunions, etc. This is the way through which sense of belongingness could be created among the employees.

Such actions as improving the working environment, management helping and meeting the needs of employees within the work setting, engaging in information technology and concern for staff welfare could further strengthen airline staff organisational commitment.

Encouraging supervisors and frontline managers to coach employees by setting expectations, giving constructive feedback, asking questions rather than providing solutions, and communicating the importance of expectations relative to the broader goals of the firm appear to be effective practices for improving FLSE job-related attitudes and behaviours.To overcome the public sector's hierarchical structure which gives preference to seniority over performance is not the best environment to attract the best talent from among the young.The main focus should be on the coping of service related issues and problems which directly or indirectly affects the performance of FLSE.

Overall, the findings of the study have interesting implications for practice and suggest significant areas for future research.

8.5 Limitations of the study

A critical examination of the conceptual framework and interpretation reveals certain limitations of the study. Limitations are inherent in all research investigations and it is important that these should be brought to light. Some of the limitations of the present study may be enumerated as follows:

- The study was confined to Delhi and only six domestic airlines were taken for the study.
- Random error in measurement of factors of antecedents and consequences may have influenced the correlation and regression results of the present study.

- The study focused on 14 variables. There may be some other factors, which have not been included and show equal degree of relationship, such as diversity of workplace, mentoring, and communication etc. could be added in future research. It is an undeniable fact that if other practices were included in the study, the result might have revealed a higher contribution towards the study. The results of this research would not be accepted as being completely applicable to all services because it focused on domestic airline services only.
- The generalisation occurring from this study is more indicative than conclusive and limited to a particular group of FLSE who have been included. In other words, the limitation comes from the non-probability sampling technique that has been used for the study.The sampling techniques used should have been representative of the sample population by adopting the simple random sampling technique but as a result of time and the cost involved, a non-probability sample was adopted so as to get the information quicker from the airlines.
- The research was limited to front line staffs of the airline due to time limit and difficulty in reaching the management. The front line staffs does not represent the perception of the companies as a whole, thus the overview of this research is limited.
- Inter sectorial differences was studied with only Indian public and private airlines.
- The employees of only domestic airlines have been considered. The results could have been different if the perception of foreign airlines had been included.
- Because of the recession in the airline industry, some airlines have been laying off employees in India. The employees' perceptions about their organisation and job satisfaction may therefore be prejudiced. The collected data may be biased and could affect the accuracy of these results. Future research may need to

take the longitudinal approach or use other samples to limit the amount of bias in the results.

- It was impossible to verify the accuracy and honesty of the employees' self-reported data. However, the anonymity of the responses and the confidentiality assurance the researchers gave to the participants may have reduced any bias that could have occurred because of the method they adopted in the study.
- The results in this study might only be applied to the airline industry in India. The influences of different cultures or industries must be investigated. For future research, using the different samples may produce different results.

Despite these limitations, this study contributes to the literature by investigating the contributions of various antecedents and their consequences on FLSE commitment to service quality in the airline industry of India.

8.6 Suggestions for Future Research

The conducted study has significant relevance for understanding the various antecedents and consequences of FLSE commitment to service in Indian public and private sector airlines and its implication on employees and organisational effectiveness. The refinements and extension of the present problems may be undertaken. Further work on the general framework is required. Specifically, it would be of value to examine further variables within the objective, event, and dispositional classes of antecedents; broaden the domain of consequences to include more objective data; to examine possible recursive effects between job satisfaction, antecedents and consequences, and to replicate our effects in other settings. It would also be interesting to investigate how the observed relationships differ across job types.

The study may give a broader picture if data is collected from different regions of the country, for it may bring into light various factors which have not been studied till date.

The various factors which have been undertaken for this study could be studied by including international airlines operating in the country and it could then be compared with the Indian public and private sector airlines.

It would also be useful to examine whether job satisfaction mediates the relationship between more objective indicators of the antecedents and consequences. Studies can be done on the impact of change process on employee commitment like how it changes with the changes in the national political systems and new economic policies, downsizing, mergers, acquisitions, layoffs, leadership transitions, technology transfer, privatisation, change in market etc. are some of the variables whose impact on the employees commitment could be investigated.

A longitudinal study of various antecedents and the consequences with larger sample size and different types of airlines with distinctive characteristics would certainly yield better results. A comparative study of employees from the private and the public sector, in order to examine whether this mediation effect (or some other mediation or moderation effect) is viable, is strongly recommended. Lastly, the role of government, support associations and public private initiative in implementing the various practices in this regard can be studied.

This descriptive research presents us with some interesting results that warrant further investigation into whether these antecedents may cause the consequences. The extant literature does not provide us with a logical conceptual model from which to proceed in this area. This researcher has reviewed and consolidated prior research and current theoretical models from several fields of study. This consolidation prompted a framework that can guide future research aimed at explaining and predicting service employee's behaviour that can also be managerially useful. This research is a small step in that direction, and one that hopefully, will encourage additional exploration in this area.

8.7 Summary

This is the last chapter that explains the summary of the study which summarises the results of the correlation, regression test. Of all the variables, service technology has emerged as the most important variable. Implications of the findings have also been discussed. Recommendations and intervention strategies are also outlined so as to enhance the employee commitment. Finally the suggestions were given for the future research work.

References

Aaker, D.A., Kumar, V. and Day, G.S. (2000). *Marketing Research*, (7th ed.). New York: John Wiley and Sons.

Abrahams, M., (1983) 'A service quality model of air travel demand: An empirical study', *Transportation Research,* Vol.17A (5), pp. 385-393.

Ahmed, Irfan, and Parasuraman, A. (1994), "Environmental and Positional Antecedents of Management Commitment to Service Quality: A Conceptual Framework," in Advances in *Services Marketing and Management*, Vol. 3, Teresa A. Swartz, David E. Bowen, and Stephen W. Brown, eds., Greenwich, CT: JAI Press, 69–93.

Aldrich, H. and Herker, D. (1977) 'Boundary Spanning Roles and Organisation Structure', *Academy of Management Review*, 2 (2), 217-30.

Alexandrov, A. Babakus E. and Yavas U. (2007) 'The Effects of Perceived Management Concern for Frontline Employees and Customers on Turnover Intentions Moderating Role of Employment Status', *Journal of Service Research* Vol. 9, No. 4: 356-371.

Aliosha, A. Babakus, E. and Yavas, U. (2007) 'The Effects of Perceived Management Concern for Frontline Employees and Customers on Turnover Intentions-Moderating Role of Employment Status', *Journal of Service Research* May 2007 Vol. 9, No. 4: 356-371.

Allen, N. J. and Meyer, J. P. (1990) 'The Measurement and Antecedents of Affective, Continuance and Normative Commitment to the Organisation', *Journal of Occupational Psychology*, Vol. 63, pp. 1-18.

Allison JJ, Wall TC, Spettell CM, Calhoun J, Fargason CA, Kobylinski RW, Farmer R, Kiefe C.(2000) The art and science of chart review. *Journal of Quality Improvement.*; 26(3):115-136.

Allison, JJ. Wall TC. Spettell CM. Calhoun J. Fargason CA. Kobylinski RW. Farmer R., Kiefe C. The art and science of chart review. *Journal of Quality Improvement.* 2000; 26 (3):115-136.

Alotaibi, K.F. (1992) 'An empirical investigation of passenger diversity, airline service quality, and passenger satisfaction', *Unpublished Ph.D. thesis.* Arizona State University, AZ.

Argyris, C. (1998), "Empowerment: the emperor's new clothes", *Harvard Business Review,* Vol. 76, No. 3, pp. 98-105.

Ariffin, A. A. M. Salleh, A. H. M. Norzalita, A. A. and Asbudin, A. A. (2010) 'Service Quality and Satisfaction for Low Cost Carriers', *International Review of Business Research Papers,* Vol. 6, No.1 February, pp. 47-56.

Armstrong, M. (2006) 'Handbook of Human Resource Management Practice (10th Edition)'. *London, GBR: Kogan Page, Limited,* p. 4.

Arnett, D.B., Laverie, D.A., and Mclane, C. (*2002*) 'Using job satisfaction and pride as internal-marketing tools', *Cornell Hotel and Restaurant Administration Quarterly,* 43(2), pp. 87-96.

Aselage, J. and Eisenberger, R. (2003) 'Perceived organisational support and psychological contracts: A theoretical integration', *Journal of Organisational Behavior,* Vol. 24, No. 5, pp. 491-509.

Ashill J, Janet Carruthers And Jayne Krisjanous (2006) 'The effect of management commitment to service quality on frontline employees' affective and performance outcomes: an empirical investigation of the New Zealand public healthcare sector',*Int. J. Nonprofit* Volume. pp. 271–287 Published online in Wiley Inter Science.

Ashilla J, Michel Rod And Janet Carruthersb (2008) 'The Effect of Management Commitment to Service Quality on Frontline Employees' Job Attitudes, Turnover Intentions and Service Recovery Performance in a New Public Management Context', *Journal of Strategic Marketing* Vol. 16, No. 5, December 2008, 437–462.

Aube, C. Rousseau, V. and Morin, M.E. (2007) 'Perceived organisational support and organisational commitment: The moderating effect of locus of control and work autonomy', *Journal of Managerial Psychology,* Vol. 22, No. 5, pp. 479-495.

Aziz, A. (2008) 'The Effects of Emotional Dissonance and Employee's Empowerment on Service Quality and Customer Satisfaction Perception: Customer Level Analysis', *Int. Journal of Economics and Management* 2(2): pp. 237-258.

Babakus, E. Yavas, U. Karatepe, O. M., and Avci, T. (2003) 'The effect of management commitment to service quality on employees' affective and performance outcomes', *Journal of the Academy of Marketing Science*, 31, 272-286.

Babakus, E., Yavas, U., Karatepe, O., and Avci, T. (2003). "The effect of management commitment to service quality on employees' affective and performance outcomes". *Journal of the Academy of Marketing Science,* 20(10), 1-15.

Babakus, E., Yavas, U., Karatepe, O.M. and Avci, T. (2003), "The effect of management commitment to service quality on employees' affective and performance outcomes", *Journal of the Academy of Marketing Science*, Vol. 31, No. 3, pp. 272-86.

Babin, Barry J., and James S. Boles (1996) 'The Effects of Perceived Co-Worker Involvement and Supervisor Support on Service Provider Role Stress, Performance and Job Satisfaction', *Journal of Retailing,* 72 (Spring), 57-75.

Bagozzi, R.P. (1992). Theoretical Advances in Social Psychology, *Social Psychology Quarterly* Vol. 55, No. 2., pp. 178-204.

Bagozzi, R. P. (1992). The Self-Regulation of Attitudes, Intentions, and Behavior Social Psychology Quarterly, Vol. 55, No. 2, Special Issue: *Theoretical Advances in Social Psychology.* (Jun., 1992), pp. 178-204.

Bansal, H. S. Morris, B. Mendelson, Sharma, B. (2001) 'The impact of internal marketing activities on external marketing outcomes', *Journal of Quality Management* Volume: 6, Issue: 1, Publisher: Elsevier, pp. 61-76.

Barbee, C. and Bott, V. (1991) 'Customer Treatment as a Mirror of Employee Treatment', *Advanced Management Journal*, 5, 27-31.

Barber, L, Hayday, S and Bevan S M, 'From People to Profits', *IES Report* 375, 1999.

Barbuto, J. E., Jr., and Wheeler, D. W. (2006). Scale development and construct clarification of servant leadership. *Group and Organisation Management*, 31(3), 300-326.

Baron, Reuben, M. and Kenny, D. A. (1986) 'Moderator-Mediator Variables Distinction in Social Psychological Research: Conceptual, Strategic, and Statistical Considerations', *Journal of Personality and Social Psychology*, 51 (6), 1173-82.

Bateman, T.S. and Organ, D.W. (1983) 'Job satisfaction and the good soldier: The relationship between affect and employee citizenship', *Academy of Management Journal*, 26, 587-595.

Beck, C. Beck, E. (1986) 'The Manager's open door and the communication climate', *Business Horizons* 29(1): 15-20.

Becker, T.E. and Billings, R.S. (1993) 'Profiles in commitment: An empirical test', *Journal of Organisation Behavior,* 14, 177-190.

Bejou, D. Edvardsson, B.O. and James P. R. (1996) 'A Critical Incident Approach to Examining the Effects of Service Failures on Customer Relationships The Case of Swedish and U.S. Airlines', *Journal of Travel Research,* Vol. 35, No. 1: 35-40.

Benoy, J.W. (1996) 'Internal marketing builds service quality', *Journal of Health Care Marketing,* Vol. 16 No. 1, pp. 54-59.

Berkowitz, L. (1972) 'Social norms, feelings, and other factors affecting helping and altruism', In L. Berkowitz (ed.), *Advances in Experimental Social Psychology.* Academic Press, New York, 6, 63-108.

Berry, L L Parasuraman A, Zeithaml V. (1994) 'Improving service quality in America: lessons learned; executive commentary', *The Academy of Management Executive* 8(2): 32-53.

Berry, L. L. and Parasuraman, A., (1991). Marketing Services, Competing Through Quality, New York, The Free Press.

Bettencourt LA, Gwinner KP. (1996) 'Customisation of the service experience: the role of the frontline employee', *International Journal of Service Industry Management* 7(2): 3-20.

Bettencourt, L. A., and Brown, S. W. (1997) 'Contact employees' relationships among workplace fairness, job satisfaction and prosocial behaviors', *Journal of Retailing,* 73, 39-62.

Bettencourt, L.A. and Brown, S.W. (2003) 'Role Stressors and Customer-Oriented Boundary-Spanning Behaviors in Service Organisations', *Journal of the Academy of Marketing Science,* 31 (4), 394-408.

Bettencourt, L.A., Brown, S.W. and Mackenzie, S.B. (2005) 'Customer-oriented boundary spanning behaviors: Test of a social exchange model of antecedents', *Journal of Retailing,* 81 (2), 141-57.

Bettencourt, L.A., Gwinner, K.P. and Meuter, M.L. (2001) 'A Comparison of Attitude, Personality, and Knowledge Predictors of Service-Oriented Organisational Citizenship Behaviors', *Journal of Applied Psychology,* 86 (1), 29-41.

Bitner, M. Booms, B. Tetreault, M. (1990) 'The service encounter: diagnosing favourable and unfavourable incidents', *Journal of Marketing* 54: 71-84.

Bitner, M., Brown, S. and Meuter, M. (2000). 'Technology Infusion in Service Encounters' *Journal of the Academy of Marketing Science.* 28(1), 138-149.

Blau, P. (1964) 'Exchange and power in social life' Wiley, New York.

Borucki, C. C. And Burke, M.J. (1999) 'An examination of service-related antecedents to retail store performance', *Journal of Organisational Behavior J. Organiz.* Behav. 20, 943-962 .

Boshoff, C., and Allen, J. (2000) 'The Influence of Selected Antecedents on Frontline Staff's Perception of Service Recovery Performance', *International Journal of Service Industry, 11*(1), pp. 63-82.

Boudreau, Boswell, W.R., Judge, T.A. 2001. 'Effects of personality on executive career success in the United States and Europe'. *Journal of Vocational Behavior*, 58, 53-81.

Boulding, William, Kalra, A. Staelin, R. and Valarie A. Zeithaml (1993) 'A Dynamic Process Model of Service Quality: From Expectations to Behavioral Intentions' *Journal of Marketing Research,* 30 (1), 7-27.

Bowen, D, Lawler E. (1995) 'Empowering service employees', *Sloan Management Review* 36: 73-84.

Bowen, D. E., Gilliland, S. W., and Folger, R. (1999) 'HRM and service fairness: How being fair with employees spills over to customers', *Organisational Dynamics,* 27, 7-23.

Bowen, D., and Schneider, B. (1988). 'Services marketing and management: Implications for organisational behavior'. *Research in organisational behavior,* 10, 43-80.

Bowen, Gilliland, and Folger 1999 Schwepker Jr. and Michael D. Hartline (2005) 'Managing the Ethical Climate of Customer-Contact Service Employees', *Journal of Service Research,* May 2005, Vol. 7, No. 4, 377-397.

Boyd, H.W., Jr., Westfall, R and Stasch, S.F. (2003). *Marketing Research-Text and Cases* (7th ed.). Illinois: Richard D Irwin Inc.

Brady K, Clay M. Voorhees and Michael J. Brusco (2011) 'Service Sweethearting: Its Antecedents and Customer Consequences', *Journal of Marketing.*

Brady, Michael K., and Joseph J. Cronin, Jr. (2001) 'Customer Orientation: Effects on Customer Service Perceptions and Outcome Behaviours', *Journal of Services Research,* 3 (February), 241-251.

Bradya, K. Christopher J. Robertson,(2001) 'Searching for a consensus on the antecedent role of service quality and satisfaction: an exploratory cross-national study', *Journal of Business Research* 51 (2001) 53-60.

Brief, A. P., and Motowidlo, S. J. (1986) 'Prosocial organisational behaviors', *Academy of Management Review*, 11, 710-725.

Brown S, Peterson A. (1993) 'Antecedents and consequences of sales person job satisfaction: meta-analysis and assessment of causal effects', *Journal of Marketing Research* 30: 63–77.

Brown, S. P., and Peterson, R. A. (1993) 'Antecedents and consequences of sales person job satisfaction: Meta analysis and assessment of causal effects', Journal of Marketing Research, 30, 63-77.

Bryman, A and Bell, E. (2007) *Business research methods,* 2nd edition. Oxford university press.

Burke, Gc. (1989) 'Understanding the dynamic role of the hospital executive: the view is better from the top', *Hospital and Health Services Administration* 34(1): 99-112.

Burmann, C., and Konig, V. (2011) 'Does internal brand management really drive brand commitment in shared-service call centers?', *Journal of Brand Management*, 18(6), 374-393.

Carrière, J., Bourque,C. (2009) "The effects of organisational communication on job satisfaction and organizational commitment in a land ambulance service and the mediating role of communication satisfaction", *Career Development International*, Vol. 14 Iss: 1, pp. 29-49.

Caruana, A., and Calleya, P. (1998) 'The effect of internal marketing on organisational commitment among retail bank managers', *The International Journal of Bank Marketing,* Vol. 16, No. 3, pp. 108-16.

Chanda, R. and Gupta, P. (2011) 'Service Sector Liberalisation in India: Key Lessons and Challenges South African Institute of International Affairs' *SAIIA Occupational paper* series No. 88, 5-29.

Chang, Y.H., and Yeh, C.H. (2002) 'A survey analysis of service quality for domestic airlines', *European Journal of Operational Research*, 139(1), 166-177.

Chebat, J. C., Babin, B., and Kollias, P. (2002). 'What makes contact employees perform? Reactions to employee perceptions of managerial practices'. *Journal of Bank Marketing,* 20(7), 325-332.

Chen, K.J. (1997) 'Consumer tolerance zone: Implications on Philippine Airlines domestic service delivery', *Journal of Global Marketing,* 11(2), 93-105.

Chen, K.R. and Liu, Y.C. (2002) 'The study of domestic airline service quality promotion', *Journal of quality*, 44-54.

Cherati H, Mahdavi I, Rezaeian J (2013), "The Mediating Role of Job Satisfaction between Spiritual Intelligence and Organisational Commitment", *International Journal of Research in Organisational Behaviour and Human Resource Management,* Vol. 1, No. 1, 2013, pp. 1-11.

Cheung F.Y. and To W.M., (2010) 'Management commitment to service quality and organisational outcome', *Managing Service Quality*, Vol. 20 Iss: 3, pp. 259-272.

Chiang, C. F. and Soo Cheong (Shawn) Jang (2008) 'The Antecedents and Consequences of Psychological Empowerment: The Case of Taiwan's Hotel Companies', *Journal of Hospitality & Tourism Research,* February 2008, Vol. 32, No. 1, 40-61.

Chih, H. Tsung-Ju Yang, Ling-Chu Huang and Che-Hao Hsu (2009) Customer orientation behaviours of frontline employees: Moderating Roles of Emotional Intelligence, Proceeding IACSIT-SC '09 *Proceedings of the 2009 International Association of Computer Science and Information Technology* - Spring Conference, pp. 249-253.

Cho, K. and Larry, J. Menor. (2010) 'Toward a Provider-Based View on the Design and Delivery of Quality E-Service Encounters', *Journal of Service Research* Vol. 13, No. 1, 83-95.

Clark, R.A., Hartline, M.D., and Jones, K.C. (2008) 'The effects of leadership style on hotel employees,, commitment to service quality', *Cornell Hospitality Quarterly*, pp.1-23.

Coelho, F. and Augusto, M. (2010) 'Job Characteristics and the Creativity of Frontline Service Employees', *Journal of Service Research* Vol. 13, No. 4, 426-438.

Cohen, A. (1991) 'Career stage as a moderator of the relationship between organisational commitment and its outcomes: A meta analysis', *Journal of Occupational Psychology*, Vol. 64, pp. 253-268.

Cohen, A. (1993) 'Age and tenure in relation to organisational commitment: A meta-analysis', *Basic and Applied Social Psychology,* Vol. 14, pp. 143-159.

Conger, J. A. and Kanungo, R. B. (1988) 'The Empowerment Process: Integrating Theory and Practice', *Academy of Management Review*, 13, 471-82.

Curry, J.D. Wakefield, J. Price and Mueller, C. (1986). 'On the Causal Ordering of Job Satisfaction and Organisational Commitment', *Academy Management Journal.* 29: 445-470.

Dabholkar, P. (2000) 'Technology in service delivery: implications for self-service and service support', *In Handbook of Services Marketing and Management,* Swartz TA, Iacobucci D (eds). Sage Publications: Thousand Oaks; 103-110.

Dean, A.L. (2007) 'The Impact of the Customer Orientation of Call Center Employees on Customers' Affective Commitment and Loyalty', *Journal of Service Research* Vol. 10, No. 2, 161-173.

Dolatabadi R and M. Safa (2010) 'The Effect of Directive and Participative Leadership Style on Employees' Commitment to Service Quality', *International Bulletin of Business Administration,* pp. 31-42.

Dubinsky, Alan J., Roy D. Howell, Thomas N. Ingham, And Danny Bellenger (1986), 'Sales Force Socialisation', *Journal of Marketing,* 50 (October), 192–207.

Economic Survey (2012-13) 'Service sector has insulated India from global slowdown', *Economic times.*

Ehrhart, M. G. (2004). Leadership and procedural justice climate as antecedents of unit level organisational citizenship behavior. *Personnel Psychology, 57,* 61-94.

Eichengreen, B. and Gupta, P.(2011) 'The service sector as India's road to economic growth', *national bureau of economic research,* (NBER) working paper series.

Eisenberger, R. Huntington, R. Hutchison, S. & Sowa, D. (1986) 'Perceived organisational support', *Journal of Applied Psychology, 71,* 500-507.

Eisenberger, R. P., Cummings, J., Armeli, S., and Lynch, P. (1997). Perceived organisational support, discretionary treatment and job satisfaction. *Journal of Applied Psychology,* 82(5), 812-820.

Ellinger D, Alexander E. Ellinger and Scott B. Keller (2003) 'Supervisory coaching behavior, employee satisfaction, and warehouse employee performance: A dyadic perspective in the distribution industry', *Human Resource Development Quarterly,* Vol. 14, Issue 4, pp. 435-458.

Ellinger, D. Robert, G. Hamlin, Rona, S. Beattie, Yu-Lin, Wang, and Mcvicar,O.() 'Managerial Coaching as a Workplace Learning Strategy Professional and Practice-based Learning', 1, Volume 5, Supporting Workplace Learning, Part 2, pp. 71-8.

Ellinger, Alexander E., Musg-rove, Carolyn (Casey) Findley, Ellinger, Andrea D., Bachrach, Daniel G., Wang, Yu-Lin and Ayþe Banu Elmadað Baþ (2012), "Influences of organisational investments in social capital on service employee commitment and performance", *Journal of Business Research*, http://dx.doi.org/10.1016/j.jbusres.2012.03.008.

Elmadað Baþ" Wang. (2012) 'Influences of organisational investments in social capital on service employee commitment and performance', *Journal of Business Research.*

Elliott, K. and Roach, D. W. (1993) 'Service quality in the airline industry: are carriers getting an unbiased evaluation from consumers? *Journal of Professional Service Marketing'*, 9(2), 71-82.

Elmadag, A.B., Ellinger, A.E., and Franke, G.R. (2008) 'Antecedents and consequences of frontline service employee commitment to service quality', *Journal of Marketing Theory and Practice*, Vol.16, No. 2, pp. 95-110.

Etherington, L D. and Var, T.(1984) 'Establishing a measure of airline preference for business and non-business travellers', *Journal of travel Research*, Vol. 22(4) pp. 22-27.

Fang, E. Palmatier, R. W. and Grewal, R. (2011) 'Effects of customer and innovation asset configuration strategies on firm performance', *Journal of Marketing Research*, 48(3), 587-602.

Farh, J. Podsakoff, P.M. and Organ, D.W. (1990) 'Accounting for organisational citizenship behavior: Leader fairness and task scope versus satisfaction', *Journal of Management*, 14, 705-721

Farrell, D. and Rusbult, C. E. (1981) 'Exchange variables as predictors of job satisfaction, job commitment, and turnover: The impact of rewards, costs, alternatives, and investments' *Organisational Behavior and Human Performance*, 27, 78-95.

Farzad, A. Nahavandi, N. Caruana, A. (2008) 'The Effect of Internal Marketing on Organisational Commitment in Iranian Banks', *American Journal of Applied Sciences* 5 (11): 1480-1486.

Fitzgerald, S.M. (1972) 'A career development study of elementary school teachers', (Doctoral Dissertation, University of Minnesota). *Dissertation Abstracts International, 33, 3452A.*

Forrester, R. (2000) 'Empowerment: rejuvenating a potent idea', *Academy of Management Executive* 14(3): 67-80.

Frankfort-Nachmias, C. and Nachmias, D. (1996), *Research Methods in the Social Sciences*, 5th edition New York: St. Martin's Press.

Frick, R. A. (1997) 'The application of total quality management on service quality in banking', *The Journal of Bank Cost and Management Accounting* 10(3): 3-29.

Friedman, R. A. and Podolny, J. (1992) 'Differentiation of boundary spanning oles: labor negotiations and implications for role conflict', *Administrative Science Quarterly,* Vol. 37, pp. 28-47.

Fu, F. Q. W. Bolander and Jones, E. (2009) 'Managing The Drivers of Organisational Commitment and Salesperson Effort: An Application of Meyer and Allen's Three-Component Model', *Journal of Marketing Theory and Practice.* 17 (4): 335-350.

Gaspari, A. and Taga, H. (2011) 'Internal Marketing and Service Quality: The Case Study Of Albanian Sea – Side Hotels', *Journal of Marketing and Management,* 2 (1), 1-10.

Gera, R. (2011) 'Modelling the service antecedents of favourable and unfavourable behaviour intentions in life insurance services in India An SEM study', *International Journal of Quality and Service Sciences* Vol. 3, No. 2, pp. 225-242.

Geralis, M. Terziovski, M. (2003) 'A quantitative analysis of the relationship between empowerment practices and service quality outcomes', *Total Quality Management* 14(1): 45-62.

Getty, M. and Getty, L. (2000) Proceedings *of the Human Factors and Ergonomics Society Annual Meeting,* Vol. 44 No. 12, 2523-2526.

Ghorbani, M. (2013) 'Study of the Relationship Between Management Commitment to Service Quality (MCSQ) and Services Receiving Performance in Public and Private Hospitals', *World Applied Sciences Journal,* 21 (8): 1167-1175.

Gilbert, D. Child, D. and Bennett, M. (2001) 'A qualitative study of the current practices of 'no-frills' airlines operating in the UK', *Journal of Vacation Marketing* Vol. 7, No. 4, 302-315.

Girard, S. H. (2000) 'Servant leadership qualities exhibited by Illinois public school district superintendents' *Dissertation*, UMI No. 9973347, University, City, ST.

Goleman, Daniel. (2000) 'Leadership That Gets Results', *Harvard Business Review*, 78 (2), 78-90.

Gounaris, S. Stathakopoulos, V. Athanassopoulos, A. (2003) Antecedents to perceived service quality: an exploratory study in the banking industry', *International Journal of Bank Marketing* 21 (4), 168-190.

Gountas, Walker, R. (2009) 'Employee perspectives of service quality in the supermarket sector', *Journal of Services Marketing*, Vol. 23 Iss: 6, pp. 407-421.

Gourdin, K. (1988) 'Bringing quality back to commercial travel', *Transportation journal* Vol. 27(3), pp. 23-29.

Greenfield, D. (2012) 'Competition and Service Quality: New Evidence from the Airline Industry', *Northeastern University* January 2012.

Greenleaf, R. (1970/1991). The servant as leader. Indian apolis, In: The Greenleaf Centre.

Gronroos, C (1990) 'Service Management: A Management Focus for Service Competition', *International Journal of Service Industry Management,* Vol. 1, Iss: 1, pp. 6-14.

Gronroos, C., (1988) "*Service quality: the six criteria of good perceived service quality*", Review of Business, Vol. 9, No. 3, *1988*, pp. 10-13.

Gronross, C. (1983) 'Strategic management and marketing in the service sector', *Marketing Science Institutes working paper series.* Cambridge, MA: Marketing Science Institute.

Gudergan, Siegfried, Lings, Ian (2010) '*International Journal of Services Technology and Management,* Volume 14, Numbers 2-3, pp. 208-216(9).

Güleryüz, G. Güney, S. Aydin, E.M. Aºan, O. (2008), "The mediating effect of job satisfaction between emotional intelligence and organisational commitment of nurses: a questionnaire survey", *Int J Nurs Stud.*; 45(11):1625-35.

Gummesson, E., (1994). Service Management: An Evaluation and the Future. *International Journal of Service Industry Management*, 5(1), 77-96.

Gupta, M. and Kumar, A. "Customer Satisfaction with Low Cost Airlines in India: An Empirical Study", *South Asian Journal of Tourism and Heritage* (2009), Vol. 2, No. 1.

Guzzo, Richard, A. Richard, D. Jette, and Raymond, A. Katzell. (1985) 'The Effects of Psychologically Based Intervention Programs on Worker Productivity: A Meta-Analysis', *Personnel Psychology,* 38 (2), 275-291.

Hair, J. F. Jr. Rolph E. Anderson, Ronald, L. Tatham and William, C. Black. (1998) *Multivariate Data Analysis,* 5th edition, Prentice Hall, Inc.

Hair, J.F., Anderson, R.E., Tatham, R.L. and Black, W.C. (2006), Multivariate Data Analysis, 6th ed., Prentice-Hall, Upper Saddle River, NJ.

Hansen, H. Sandvik, K. and Selnes, F. (2003) 'Direct and Indirect Effects of Commitment to a Service Employee on the Intention to Stay', *Journal of Service Research,* Vol. 5, No. 4, 356-368.

Harris, C. and Ogbonna, E. (2002) 'Exploring Service Sabotage-The Antecedents, Types and Consequences of Frontline, Deviant, Antiservice Behaviors', *Journal of Service Research,* February Vol. 4 and No. 3, 163-183.

Harris, L. C., and Ogbonna, E. (2000) 'The response of front-line employees to market-oriented culture change', *European Journal of Marketing*, 34, 318-340.

Harris, C. and Emmanuel, Ogbonna. 'Exploring Service Sabotage-The Antecedents, Types and Consequences of Frontline, Deviant, Antiservice Behaviours', *Journal of Service Research,* February 2002, Vol. 4, No. 3, 163-183.

Hart, C.W., Heskett, J.L. and Sasser, W.E. (1990). The Profitable Art of Service Recovery, *Harvard Business Review*, July/August, 148-156.

Hartline, M, Maxham, Jg, Mckee, Do. (2000) 'Corridors of influence in the dissemination of customer- orientated strategy to customer contact service employees', *Journal of Marketing* 64: 35-50.

Hartline, M. D. and Ferrell, O. C. (1996) 'The management of customer-contact service employees: An empirical investigation', *Journal of Marketing,* 60, 52-70.

Hashim, R. A. and Mahmood, R. (2011) 'Transformational Leadership Style and Academic Staffs' Commitment to Service Quality at Malaysian Universities', *Journal of Marketing Theory and Practice*, Vol.16, No. 2, pp. 95-110.

Hayes, A. F. Beyond Baron and Kenny: Statistical Mediation Analysis in the New Millennium. Communication Monographs, Vol. 76(4), Dec 2009, 408-420.

Hayes, B. E. (1994) 'How to measure empowerment', *Quality Progress, 27,* 41-46.

Haynes, R. and Percy, J. (1994) 'Perception paradox: Airline service quality issues', *Proceedings of Decision Sciences Institute, Annual Meeting*, 3, 1950-1952.

Heras, I. 2006. How quality management models influence company results conclusions of an empirical study based on the Delphi method. *Total Quality Management & Business Excellence*, 17(6), 775-794.

Heskett, J. L., Jones, T. O., Loveman, G. W., Sasser, W. E., and Schlesinger, L. A. (1994) 'Putting the service-profit chain to work', *Harvard Business Review,* 72, 164-174.

Heskett, J., Sasser, T., and Schlesinger, L. (1997). The service profit chain: How leading companies link profit and growth to loyalty, satisfaction, and value. New York: Free Press.

Hmeidan, T. A. 'The effect of perceived work environment on frontline employees' service recovery performance: the case of four and five star hotels in Jordan', *European Scientific Journal,* April 2013 edition, Vol. 9, No. 11, pp. 130-142.

Hoang, T. Rao,S. Hill, and Nhat, V. L, 'The Influence of Service Culture on Customer Service Quality: Local vs. Foreign Service Firms in .merging Markets' *Proceedings of the Australian and New Zealand Marketing Academy Conference (ANZMAC 2010), 'Doing more things less', held the the University of Canterbury, 29 Nov-1 Dec 2010 / P. Ballantine and J. Finsterwalder* (eds.): pp. 1-11.

Hoffman, K. D. and Bateson, J. E. G. (1997). Essentials of Services Marketing Fort Worth, TX. The Dryden Press.

Huang, (2009) 'The Effect of Airline Service Quality on Passengers' Behavioural Intentions Using servqual scores: 'a Taiwan case Study', *Journal of the Eastern Asia Society for Transportation Studies*, Vol. 8.

Hur, W. M. Tae, W. M. Kyoon, J. (2013) 'The role of perceived organisational support on emotional labor in the airline industry', *International Journal of Contemporary Hospitality Management,* Vol. 25 Iss: 1, pp. 105-123.

Huselid, Mark A. (1995) 'The Impact of Human Resource Management Practices on Turnover, Productivity and Corporate Performance', *Academy of Management Journal,* 38 (3), 635-672.

James, L.R. and Brett, J. M. (1984) 'Mediators, moderators, and tests of mediation', *Journal of Applied Psychology,* 69(2), 307-321.

James, N. and Finklea, II (2005) 'High flyers A study on competition price and service quality in the European Aviation Industry', *Thesis Jönköp I N G international b u s i n e s s school jönköping university.*

James, W. (2005). The impact of corporatisation and national competition policy. *Leadership and Organisation*, 26(4), 289-309.

Jaworski, Bernard, J. and Kohli, A. K. (1993) 'Market Orientation: Antecedents and Consequences', *Journal of Marketing*, 57 (July), 53-70.

Jean-Charles Chebat, Barry Babin, Paul Kollias, (2002) "What makes contact employees perform? Reactions to employee perceptions of managerial practices", *International Journal of Bank Marketing*, Vol. 20 Iss: 7, pp. 325-332.

Jin-Woo, P. Robertson, R. and Wu, C.L.(2005) 'Investigating the Effects of Airline Service Quality on Airline Image and Passengers' Future Behavioural Intentions: Findings from Australian international air passengers',*The Journal of Tourism Studies* Vol. 16, No. 1, pp. 2-11.

Johnson, T. Ventura, R. (2004) 'Applied informatics for quality assessment and improvement', *Journal of Nursing Care Quality* 19(2): 100-105.

Johnston, M. W. Parasuraman, A. Futrell, C.M. and Black W.C. (1990) 'A Longitudinal Assessment of the Impact of Selected Organisational Influences on Salespeople's Organisational Commitment During Early Employment', *Journal of Marketing Research*. 27 (3): 333-344.

Jong, D. *et. al.,* (2006) 'Linking Employee Confidence to Performance: A Study of Self-Managing Service Teams', *Journal of the Academy of Marketing Science,* Vol. 34 No. 4, 576-587.

Julie, M. Haysa, Arthur, V. Hill, B. (2001) 'A preliminary investigation of the relationships between employee motivation/vision, service learning and perceived service quality', *Journal of Operations Management,* 335–349, Elsevier.

Kandampully, J. (2002) 'Service management the new paradigm in hospitality', *Australia: Pearson Education.*

Karatepe, Osman, M. 'Core self-evaluations, exhaustion, and job outcomes: A study of frontline hotel employees in Iran', *Tourism and Hospitality Research,* October 2011, Vol. 11 No. 4, 248-257.

Karatepe, O.M. (2013) 'Perceptions of organisational politics and hotel employee outcomes: The mediating role of work engagement', *International Journal of Contemporary Hospitality Management*, Vol. 25, Iss: 1, pp. 82-104.

Kasper, H. *et. al.* (2006) ' Services Marketing Management – A Strategic Perspective', 2nd edition, John Wiley & Sons Ltd.

Kaynak, E. Kucukemiroglu, O, and Kara. A. (1994) 'Consumers' perceptions of airlines: A correspondence analysis approach in a global airline industry', *Management International Review*, 34, 235-254.

Kazlauskaitc, R., Buciuniene, I. and Turauskas, L. (2006), "Building Employee Commitment", *Baltic Journal of Management*, Vol. 1, No. 3, pp. 300-314.

Kelley, S.W. and Hoffman, K.D. (1997) An investigation of positive affect, prosocial behaviors and service quality. *Journal of Retailing*, *73*(3), 407-427.

Kelley, Scott, W. (1992) 'Developing Customer Orientation Among Service Employees', *Journal of the Academy of Marketing Science*, 20 (Winter), 27-36.

Kelly, J. and Kelly, C. (1990) 'Them and Us: Social Psychology and the New Industrial Relations', *British Journal of Industrial Relations*, 29 (1), 345-360.

Kim J, Tavitiyaman, P. and Kim, B.G. (2009) 'The effect of management commitment to service on employee service behaviours: the mediating role of job satisfaction, *Journal of Hospitality & Tourism Research*, Vol. 33, No. 3, August, 369-390.

Kim, W. G., Leong, J. K., and Lee, Y. K. (2005) 'Effect of service orientation on job satisfaction, organisational commitment, and intention of leaving in a casual dining chain restaurant', *International Journal of Hospitality Management, 24,* 171-193.

Kimura, T.(2012), "Transformational leadership and job satisfaction: The mediating effects of perceptions of politics and market orientation in the Japanese context", *Int. Journal of Business Science and Applied Management*, Volume 7, Issue 1, 2012.

Kivel, J. and Chu, H. (2001) 'Delivering Quality Service: Diagnosing Favorable and Unfavorable Service Encounters in Restaurants', *Journal of Hospitality & Tourism Research* Vol. 25, No. 3, 251-271.

Kuokkanen, L Leino-Kilpi, H. Katajisto, J. (2003) 'Nurse empowerment, job-related satisfaction, and organisational commitment', *Journal of Nursing care Quality* 18(3): 184-192.

Kwong, S.T, Luk, G.A., Fullgrabe, L. (2013) 'Trust in customer-salesperson relationship in China's retail sector', *International Journal of Retail & Distribution Management*, Vol. 41, Iss: 3, pp. 226-248.

Lambert, S.D. (2002) My HR Network Re-energizing Your Organisation after Layoffs, http://www.nehra.com/attachments/articles/Reener gizing% 20after%20layoffs.ppt.

Landy, F. W. (1985). 'The psychology of work behavior, (3rd ed.). Homewood, IL: Dorsey Press.

Laschinger, H, Shamian, J. Thomson, D. (2001) 'Impact of magnet hospital characteristics on nurses' perceptions of trust, burnout, quality of care, and work satisfaction', *Nursing Economics* 19(5): 209-220.

Lashley, C. (1997) 'Empowering Service Excellence: Beyond the Quick Fix', *London: Cassell.*

Lashley, C. (2001b) 'Feeling Empowered: Emotional Labour or Just a Nice Job?', *International Journal of Customer Relationship Management* (September/October), 121-33.

Laub, J. A. (1999) Assessing the servant organisation: Development of the organisational leadership assessment (OLA) instrument', *Unpublished Dissertation*, Florida Atlantic University, Boca Raton.

Law, R. and Leung,R. (2001) 'A Study of Airlines' Online Reservation Services on the Internet', *Journal of Travel Research,* Vol. 39, No. 2 202-211).

Lee, (1999) 'The influence of switching costs on customer retention: a study of the cell phone market in France', *European Advances in Consumer Research,* Vol. 4, pp. 277-283.

Leong, C. C. (2008) 'An Importance-Performance Analysis to Evaluate Airline Service Quality: The Case Study of a Budget Airline in Asia', *Journal of Quality Assurance in Hospitality & Tourism*, Vol. 8, No. 3.

Lewis, B, Gabrielsen, G. (1998) 'Intra-organisational aspects of service quality management: the employees' perspective', *The Service Industries Journal* 18(2): 64-89.

Liao, H. (2007) 'Do it Right This Time: The Role of Employee Service Recovery Performance in Customer-perceived Justice and Customer Loyalty After Service Failures', *Journal of Applied Psychology,* 92(2), 475-789.

Liden, R. C., Wayne, S. J., Zhao, H., and Henderson, D. (2008). Servant leadership: Development of a multidimensional measure and multi-level assessment. *The Leadership Quarterly,* 19, 161-177.

Lin, C and Lin, C.Y. (2011) 'What makes service employees and customers smile: Antecedents and consequences of the employees' affective delivery in the service encounter', *Journal of Service Management*, Vol. 22, Iss: 2, pp.183-201.

Lindberg, M. Löfgren, E. [2009) Service Quality and Customer Preferences-A study of interactional service quality in the airline industry', *Dissertation Umeå School of Business.*

Little, M. M. and Dean, A.M. (2006). "Links between service climate, employee commitment and employee service quality capability", *Managing Service Quality,* 16(5): 460-476.

Liu, Ben Shaw-Ching, Sudharshan, D. and Hamer, L.O. (2000) 'After-Service Response in Service Quality Assessment: A Real-Time Updating Model Approach', *Journal of Services Marketing,* 14 (2), 160-177.

Liu, C. (2006), 'The Effect of Organisational Vision on Service Quality Delivery', *The Service Industries Journal,* Vol. 26, No. 8, pp. 849-859.

Locke, E. A. (1976) 'The nature and causes of job satisfaction', In M. D. Dunnette (Ed.), *Handbook of industrial and organisational psychology* (pp. 1297-1350). Chicago: Ran McNally.

Loveman, Gary W. (1998) 'Employee Satisfaction, Customer Loyalty, and Financial Performance: An Empirical Examination of the Service Profit Chain in Retail Banking', *Journal of Service Research,* 1 (August), 18-31.

Lu, H., A. E. While and K. L. Barribal. (2007) 'A Model of Job Satisfaction of Nurses: a Reflection of Nurses' 'Working Lives in Mainland China', *JAN: Original Research.* 468-479.

Lucas, G. H., Babakus, E., and Ingram, T. N. (1990) 'An empirical test of the job satisfaction turnover relationship: Assessing the role of job performance for retail managers', *Journal of the Academy of Marketing Science*, 18, 199-208.

Luk, G. A. Sherriff, T.K. Lorna, F. (2013) "Trust in customer-sales person relationship in China's retail sector", *International Journal of Retail & Distribution Management*, Vol. 41, Iss: 3, pp. 226-248.

Luria, G., Iddo, G. and Yagil, D. (2009) 'Employees' Willingness to Report Service Complaints', *Journal of Service Research,* November Vol. 12, No. 2, 156-174.

Lytle, R, Hom, P. Mowka, M. (1998) 'SERV*OR: managerial measures of organisational service orientation', *Journal of Retailing* 74(4): 1–15.

Lytle, R.S. and Timmermann, J.E. (2006), "Service orientation and performance: an organisational perspective", *Journal of Services Marketing*, Vol. 20, No. 2, pp. 136-47.

MacDuffie, J.P. (1995). Human resource bundles and manufacturing performance: organisational logic and flexible production systems in the world auto industry, *Industrial and Labor Relations Review*, 48, 197-221.

Mahmoud, E. Rice, G. (1998) 'Information systems technology and healthcare quality improvement', *Review of Business* 19(3): 8-12.

Malhotra, N. & Mukherjee, A. (2004) 'The relative influence of organisational commitment and job satisfaction on service quality of customer-contact employees in banking call centers', *Journal of Services Marketing,* 18, 162-174.

Malhotra, N.K. (2007). Marketing Research–An applied orientation, 5th Edition. Prentice Hall of India.

Malhotra, N.(2012) 'Service quality of frontline employees: A profile deviation analysis', *Journal of Business Research,* pp. 1-7.

Malik, O.F. Waheed, A. Malik, K. R. (2010) "The Mediating Effects of Job Satisfaction on Role Stressors and Affective Commitment", *International Journal of Business and Management,* Vol. 5, No. 11, pp. 223-235.

Manojlovich, M. Spence, Laschinger, H. K. (2002) 'The relationship of empowerment and selected personality characteristics to nursing job satisfaction', *Journal of Nursing Administration* 32(11): 586-595.

Manus, T. M. and Graham, M.D. (2003) 'Creating a Total Rewards Strategy', American Management Association, New York. Marketing success', *Journal of Services Marketing,* 1, 39-46.

Martin, C. and N. Bennett. (1996) 'The Role of Justice Judgments in Explaining the Relationship Between Job Satisfaction and Organisational Commitment', *Group Organisational Management.* 21 (1): 84-104.

Martin, C. and N. Bennett. (1996) 'The Role of Justice Judgments in Explaining the Relationship Between Job Satisfaction and Organisational Commitment', *Group Organisational Management.* 21 (1): 84-104.

Masdek, M. Aziz, Y.A. and Khairil, Wahidin. (2011) 'Potential Antecedents and Outcomes of Frontline Employees' Service Recovery

Performance', *Int. Journal of Economics and Management* 5(1): 114-139.

Mathies, C. and Marion, Burford. (2011) *Gender Differences in the Customer Service Understanding of Frontline Employees.* University of New South Wales.

Mathieu, J. E., and Zajac, D. M., (1990). A review and meta-analysis of the antecedents, correlates and consequences of organisational commitment. *Psychological Bulletin*, 108(2), 171-194

Mathieu,V. (2003) 'Employees commitment to service offering strategy implementation University Aix-Marseille III.

Maxham, J.G. and Netemeyer, R.G. (2002) 'A Longitudinal Study of Complaining Customers' Evaluation of Multiple Service Failures and Recovery Efforts', *Journal of Marketing*, 66, 57-71.

Mazzeo, M.J. (2003) 'Competition and Service Quality in the U.S. Airline Industry' *Review of Industrial Organisation* 22: 275–296.

Mcneely, B.L. Meglino, B.M. (1994) 'The role of dispositional and situational antecedents in prosocial organizational behavior: An examination of the intended beneficiaries of prosocial behavior', *Journal of Applied Psychology*, 79, 836-844.

Megha Gupta and Amit Kumar, "Customer Satisfaction with Low Cost Airlines in India: An Empirical Study", *South Asian Journal of Tourism and Heritage* (2009), Vol. 2, No. 1.

Mende, M. and Bolton, R. N. (2011) Why Attachment Security Matters-How Customers' Attachment Styles Influence Their Relationships With Service Firms and Service Employees, Journal of Service Research, August, Vol. 14, No. 3, 285-301.

Meyer, J. Paunonen, S. Gellatly I, Goffin, R. Jackson, D. (1989) 'Organisational commitment and job performance: it's the nature of the commitment that counts', *Journal of Applied Psychology* 74(1): 152-156.

Mishra, S. (2010) 'Internal Marketing–A Tool to Harness Employees' Power in Service Organisations in India'. *International journal of Business and Management,* Vol. 5, No. 1, pp. 185-193.

Mitra, D. (2010) 'A Comparative Study Between Indian Public And Private (Low Cost) Airlines With Respect To Their Passenger Service', *International Review of Business Research Paper,* Vol. 6, No. 6, pp. 48-65.

Motowidlo, S.J. (1984) 'Does job satisfaction lead to consideration and personal sensitivity?', *Academy of Management Journal*, 27, 910-915.

Mowday, R. Steers, R. Porter, L. (1979) 'The measurement of organisational commitment', *Journal of Vocational Behavior,* 14: 224-247.

Mukherjee, A. and Malhotra, N. (2006). Does role clarity explain employee-perceived service quality? A study of antecedents and consequences in call centres, *International Journal of Service Industry Management*, 17(5): 444-473.

N. Bhat, (1995) A Multivariate Analysis of Airline Service Quality, pp. 1-7.

Natalisa, and Subrato, B. (2003) 'Effects of management commitment on service quality to increase customer satisfaction of domestic satisfaction of domestic airlines in Indonesia', *Singapore management review,* pp. 85-104.

Nicholas J. Ashill*, Janet Carruthers and Jayne Krisjanous (2006) 'The effect of management commitment to service quality on frontline employees' affective and performance outcomes: an empirical investigation of the New Zealand public healthcare sector Int', *J. Non-profit Volunt. Sect. Mark.* 11: 271-287. No. 2, pp.1, 3346.

Noelker, S. Farida, K. Ejaz, Heather, L. Menne, and Joshua, G. Bagaka's, (2009) 'Factors Affecting Frontline Workers' Satisfaction With Supervision', *Aging Health* Vol. 21, No. 1, 85-101.

Olle Strömgren (2007). Analysing Service Quality. A Study among peruvian Resort Hotels. *Master's Thesis,* pp. 21-23.

Ömer, O. (2012), "Relationship between organisational commitment and ethical climate: the mediating role of job satisfaction dimensions (A Study in A Group of Companies in Turkey)", *Journal of WEI Business and Economics, December*, Vol. 1, No. 1.

Organ, D. W. (1990) 'The motivational basic of organisational citizenship behavior', In B. M. Straw and L. L. Cummings (Eds.), *Research in organisational behaviour* (Vol. 12, pp. 43-72), Greenwich, CT: JAI Press.

Organ, D.W., and Ryan, K. (1995) 'A meta-analytic review of attitudinal and dispositional predictors of organisational citizenship behavior', *Personnel Psychology*, 48, 775-802.

Ostrowski, P.L., O'Brien, T.V. and Gordon, G.L. (1993) 'Service quality and customer loyalty in the commercial airline industry', *Journal of Travel Research, Fall,* 16-24.

Ottenbacher, M. and Gnoth, J. (2005) 'How to Develop Successful Hospitality Innovation', *Cornell Hospitality Quarterly,* May, Vol. 46, No. 2, 205-222.

Parasuraman, A. (2002) 'Service quality and productivity: A synergistic perspective', *Managing Service Quality*, Vol. 12, Iss: 1, pp. 6-9.

Parasuraman, A. (1987) "Customer-Oriented Corporate Cultures are Crucial to Services Marketing Success", *Journal of Services Marketing*, Vol. 1, Iss: 1, pp. 39-46.

Parish, J.T. Leonard L. Berry and Shun Yin Lam (2008) 'The Effect of the Service scape on Service Workers', *Journal of Service Research,* February, Vol. 10, No. 3, 220-238.

Patrick, J. (2000). 'Training'. In N. Chmiel (Ed.), *Introduction to work and organisational psychology*, 100-125. Oxford, UK: Blackwell.

Patrick, J. Montana, and Bruce, H. Charnov, (2000) 'Training And Development', *Management. Barron's Educational Series,* pp. 225.

Patton, M. Q. (2002) 'Qualitative Research & Evaluation Methods', Sage Publications, Thousand Oaks.

Paul, J. Vella, John Gountas, Rhett Walker, (2009) "Employee perspectives of service quality in the supermarket sector", *Journal of Services Marketing*, Vol. 23, Iss: 6, pp. 407-421.

Paulin, M. Ferguson, R. J. and Bergeron, J. (2006) 'Service climate and organisational commitment: The importance of customer linkage'. *Journal of Business Research*, 59, 906-915.

Peccei, Riccardo and Patrice, Rosenthal. (2001) 'Delivering Customer-Oriented Behavior Through Empowerment: An Empirical Test of HRM Assumptions', *Journal of Management Studies,* 38 (September), 831–857.

Pfeffer J. (1994) 'Competitive Advantage Through People: Unleashing the Power of the Work Force', *Harvard Business School Press*: Boston, MA.

Pi-Chuan, Hsu, Wan-Ju and Wang, Kuang-Cheng (2012) 'Enhancing the commitment to service quality through developmental and rewarding systems: CSQ consistency as a moderator', *International Journal of Human Resource Management*; Apr 2012, Vol. 23, Issue 7, pp. 1462-1480, 19p.

Pimpakorn, and Paul, G. P. (2010) 'Customer-oriented behaviour of front-line service employees: The need to be both willing and able', *Australasian Marketing Journal, Vol.* 18, Issue: 2, pp. 57-65.

Ping He. (2008) 'Dissertation An Investigation of the Antecedents and Consequences of Affective Commitment in a U.S. Hospitality Organisation. *Faculty of the Virginia Polytechnic Institute and State University.*

Polly, L. (2002) 'Social exchange and customer service: The relationship between perceived organisational support, leader–member exchange, and customer service behavior', *Unpublished doctoral dissertation, Louisiana State University and Agricultural & Mechanical College.*

Porter, L. Steers, R. Mowday, M. and Boulian, P. (1974) 'Organisational Commitment, Job Satisfaction, and Turnover among Psychiatric Technicians', *Journal of Applied Psychology.* 59: 603-609.

Potluri and Zeleke (2009) 'Evaluation of customer handling competencies of Ethiopian employees', *African Journal of Business Management,* April, Vol. 3 (4), pp. 131-135.

Poznanski, P. J. and Bline, D.M. (1997) 'Using Structural Equation Modeling to Investigate the Causal Ordering of Job Satisfaction and Organisational Commitment among Staff Accountants', *Behavioral Research in Accounting.* 9: 154-171, 1997.

Preacher, K.J. and Hayes, A.F. (2004) 'SPSS and SAS procedures for estimating indirect effects in simple mediation models', *Behavior Research Methods, Instruments, & Computers,* 36 (4), 717-731.

Prentice, C. and Brian, King. (2011) 'The Influence of Emotional Intelligence on the Service Performance of Casino Frontline Employees', *Tourism and Hospitality Research,* January, Vol. 11, No. 1, 49-66.

Prince, J.T. and. Simon, D.H. (2009) 'Multimarket Contact and Service Quality: Evidence From On-Time Performance In The U.S. Airline Industry', *Academy of Management Journal,* Vol. 52, No. 2, 336-354.

Psomas, E.L. Angelos, Pantouvakis, Dimitrios P. Kafetzopoulos, (2013) "The impact of ISO 9001 effectiveness on the performance of service companies", *Managing Service Quality,* Vol. 23, Iss: 2, pp. 149-164.

Puffer, S.M. (1987) 'Prosocial behavior, non-compliant behavior, and work performance among commission sales people', *Journal of Applied Psychology,* 72, 615-621.

Punjaisri, K. and Wilson, (2007) 'The role of internal branding in the delivery of employee brand promise', *Journal of Brand Management* 15, 57-70.

Rahim, M. *et. al.,* (2011) 'Motivational Orientation as an Internal Marketing Tool in Service Training: A Study of Service Delivery in a Hospital', *International journal of business management* Vol. 6, No. 2, 93-100.

Ramseook and Lukea (2010) 'Service quality in the public service'. *International journal of management and marketing research,* Vol. 3, No. 1, pp. 37-50.

Randall, M. L. Cropanzano, R. Bormann, C. A. & Birjulin, A. (1999) 'Organisational politics and organisational support as predictors of work attitudes, job performance, and organisational citizenship behavior' *Journal of Organisational Behavior,* 20, 159-174.

Rashid, M.Z.A. Sambasivan, M. and Johari, J. (2003) 'The influence of corporate culture and organisational commitment and performance', *Journal of Management Development*, Vol. 22, No. 8, pp. 708-728.

Rhoades, L. and Eisenberger, R. (2002) 'Perceived organisational support: A review of the literature', *Journal of Applied Psychology*, Vol. 87, No. 4, pp. 698-714.

Riggle, R.J. Edmondson, D.R. and Hansen, J.D. (2009) 'A meta-analysis of the relationship between perceived organisational support and job outcomes: 20 years of research', *Journal of Business Research,* Vol. 62, No. 10, pp. 1027-1030.

Rogers, J.D. Clow, K.E. Kash, T.J. (1994) 'Increasing Job Satisfaction of Service Personnel', *Journal of Services Marketing* 8(1): 14-26.

Rogg, K. L Schmidt, C.S. Schmidt, N. (2001) 'Human resource practices, organisational climate and customer satisfaction', *Journal of Management,* 27: 431-449.

Rust, R.T. Stewart, G.R. Miller, H. Pielack, D. (1996) 'The satisfaction and retention of frontline employees: a customer satisfaction measurement approach', *International Journal of Service Industry Management,* 7(5): 62-80.

Rust, Roland, (2004) 'Editorial: A Call for a Wider Range of Service Research', *Journal of Service Research'*, 6 (3), 211.

Saboe, K.N. (2010) Prioritizing those who follow: Servant leadership, needs satisfaction, and positive employee outcomes, University of South Florida Scholar Commons, Graduate School Theses and Dissertations Graduate School.

Salas, E., and Cannon-Bowers, J. A. (2001). The science of training: A decade of progress. *Annual Review of Psychology*, 52, 471-499.

Samad, S. (*2011*) 'Predictors of Employee Willingness to Engage with Customer Oriented Behavior', *European Journal of Social Sciences,* Vol. 22, No. 4, 611-619.

Schneider (Ed.), Organisational climate and culture (pp. 383-412). San Francisco, CA: Jossey Bass.

Schneider, B. (1980). The service organisation: Climate is crucial. *Organisational Dynamics,* 9 (Autumn), pp. 52-65.

Schneider, B. (1990) 'The climate for service: an application of the climate construct. In Organisational Climate and Culture', *Schneider B (ed.). Jossey Bass: San Francisco*; 383-412.

Schneider, B. and Bowen, D.E. (1995) 'Winning the Service Game is Crucial', *Harvard Business School Press, Boston*, MA.

Schneider, B. Bowen, D. (1985) 'Employee and customer perceptions of service in banks: replication and extension', *Journal of Applied Psychology,* 70 (3): 423-433.

Schneider, B. White, S. Paul, M.C. (1998) 'Linking Service Climate and Customer Perceptions of Service Quality: Test of a Causal Model'. *Journal of Applied Psychology,* Vol. 83 (2): 150-163.

Schneider, B., Ehrhart, M., Mayer, D., Saltz, J., and Niles-Jolly, K. (2005). Understanding organisation–customer links in service settings. *Academy of Management Journal*, 48(6), 1017-1032.

Schneider, Benjamin and David E. Bowen, (1985) "Employee and Customer Perceptions of Service in Banks: Replication and Extension," *Journal of Applied Psychology,* 70: 423-433.

Schneider, Benjamin, and David, E. Bowen, (1993) 'The Service Organisation: Human Resources Management Is Crucial', *Organisational Dynamics*, 21 (Spring), 39-53.

Schneider, Jill, K. Wheeler, and Jonathan, E. Cox (1992) 'A Passion for Service: Using Content Analysis to Explicate Service Climate Themes', *Journal of Applied Psychology,* 77 (3), 705-716.

Scholl, R.W. Cooper, E.A. and Mckenna, J.F. (1987) 'Referent selection in determining equity perceptions: Differential effects on behavioral and attitudinal outcomes', *Personnel Psychology,* 40, 113-124.

Schultz, Don. E. (2002) 'Study Internal Marketing for Better Impact', *Marketing News*, 36 (21), 8-10.

Schwepker, Jr. and Michael, D. Hartline (2005) 'Managing the Ethical Climate of Customer-Contact Service Employees', *Journal of Service Research,* May, Vol. 7, No. 4, 377-397.

Scott, S. G. and Bruce, R. A. (1994) 'Determinants of innovative behavior: A path model of individual innovation in the workplace', *Academy of Management Journal,* 37, 580-607.

Sekaran, U. (2003) 'Research Methods for Business: A Skill Building Approach', 4 edn. New York, John Wiley and Sons Inc service support. In T.A. Swartz and D. Iacobucci (Eds.), *Handbook of services marketing.*

Shamdasania, P., Mukherjeeb, A., Malhotrac, N. (2008), "Antecedents and consequences of service quality in consumer evaluation of self-service internet technologies", *The Service Industries Journal*, 28(1), pp. 117-138.

Shipchandler, E. Sita, C, Rao, A. and Stanbury, J. (2001) 'Improving Service Delivery in a Globally Competitive Environment'. *The Journal of Business Perspective,* Vol. 5, No. 2, 1-6.

Shrout, P. E., and Bolger, N. (2002). Mediation in experimental and non-experimental studies: New procedures and recommendations. *Psychological Methods*, 7, 422-445.

Sim, K. L. Song, C. J. Larry, N. Killough, (2010) 'Service quality, service recovery, and financial performance: An analysis of the US airline industry', in Marc J. Epstein, John Y. Lee (ed.) *18 (Advances in Management Accounting),* Volume 18, Emerald Group Publishing Limited, pp. 27-53.

Singh, J. (2000) 'Performance Productivity and Quality of Frontline Employees in Service Organisations', *Journal of Marketings* Vol. 64, No. 2, pp. 15-34.

Singh, Parth, (April 15, 2012) 'Service tax trends in India'Available at SSRN: *http://ssrn.com/*2040206.

Singh, P. (2003) 'Strategic Reward Systems at Southwest Airlines Compensation' *Benefits Review,* Vol. 34, No. 2, 28-33.

Slåtten, Svensson,G. Sværi, S. (2011) 'Service quality and turnover intentions as perceived by employees: Antecedents and consequences', *Personnel Review,* Vol. 40, Issue: 2, pp. 205-221.

Smith, C.A. Organ, D.W. and Near, J.P. (1983) 'Organisational citizenship behavior: Its nature and antecedents', *Journal of Applied Psychology*, 68, 653-663.

Sohail, M. S. and Shaikh, N.M. (2004) 'Quest for excellence in business education: A study of student impresssions of service quality', *The International Journal of Educational Management,* Vol. 18, No. 1, pp. 58-65.

Spector, P. (1997) 'Application, assessment, causes and consequences'. CA: Sage Publishers.

Subagyo,T.H. (2002) Cranfield University, College of Aeronautics PhD Thesis.

Sultan, F. and Simpson, M. C. (2000) 'International service variants: airline passenger expectations and perceptions of service quality', *Journal of service marketing*, Vol. 14, No. 3, 188-216.

Sun, P. C. Hsu, W.J. and Wang, K.C. (2012) 'Enhancing the commitment to service quality through developmental and rewarding systems: CSQ consistency as a moderator', *The International Journal of Human Resource Management,* Vol. 23, Issue 7.

Susskind, A. M. Borchgrevink, C. P. Kacmar, K. M. and Brymer, R. A. (2000) 'Customer service employees' behavioral intentions and attitudes: An examination of construct validity and a path model', *International Journal of Hospitality Management*, 19, 53-77.

Sweetman, K. (2001). Employee loyalty around the globe. *Sloan Management Review*, 42(2), 1-16.

Tavitiyaman, P. Kim, J. and Kim, W.G. (2009) 'The Effect of Management Commitment To Service On Employee Service Behaviors: the Mediating Role of Job Satisfaction', *Journal of Hospitality & Tourism Research*, Vol. 33, No. 3, August, 369-390.

Tax, S.S., Brown, S.W. and Chandrashekaran, M. (1998). Customer Evaluations of Service Complaint Experiences: Implications for Relationship Marketing. *Journal of Services Marketing*, 62, 60-76.

Tett, Robert, P. and John, P. Meyer, (1993) 'Job Satisfaction, Organisational Commitment, Turnover Intention, and Turnover: Path Analyses Based on Meta-Analytic Findings', *Personnel Psychology*, 46 (2), 259-293.

Thompson, R. S. (2003) 'The perception of servant leadership characteristics and job satisfaction in a church-related college', *Unpublished dissertation, Indiana State University, Terre Haute, IN.*

Tsai, C. (2008) 'Leadership style and employee's job satisfaction in international tourist hotels', *Advances in Culture, Tourism and Hospitality Research*, Vol. 2, No. 2, pp. 293-332.

Tsai, Y and Wu, S.W. (2011) 'Using internal marketing to improve organisational commitment and service quality', *Journal of Advanced Nursing,* pp. 1365-2648.

Tsui, A., Pearce, J., Porter, L., and Tripoli, A. (1997). Alternative approaches to the employee–organisation relationship: Does investment in employee-pay off? *Academy of Management Journal*, 40(5), 1089-1121.

Udo, J. G., Guimaraes,T. and Igbaria. M. (1997) 'An Investigation of the Antecedents of Turnover for manufacturing plant managers', *International Journal of Operation Production Management.* 17 (9): 912-930.

Upenieks, V. (2003) 'What constitutes effective leadership? Perceptions of magnet and non-magnet nurse leaders', *Journal of Nursing Administration* 33 (9): 456-467.

Vandaele, D and Paul, G. (2006) 'Working Paper Performance Implications of In-role and Extra-role Behavior of Frontline Service Employees', *Department of Management Information, Operations Management and Technology Policy, Faculty of Economics and Business Administration, Ghent University.*

Vandam, K. (2005) 'Employee Attitudes toward Job Changes: An Application and Extension of Rusbult and Farrell's Investment Model', *Journal of Occupational and Organisational Psychology.* 78 (2): 253-273.

Vandenberg, R.J., and Lance, C.E. (1992). Examining the causal order of job satisfaction and organisational commitment. *Journal of Management,* 18(1), 153-167.

Venkatesh, B. and Nargundkar, R. (2006) 'Service Quality Perceptions of Domestic Airline Consumers in India: An Empirical Study', *Vilakshan, XIMB Journal of Management,* pp. 114-124.

Vicky, E. (2004) 'An investigation of service delivery: The difference between frontline employees and customers perception of the service delivery within the New Zealand real estate industry', *Dissertation Auckland University of Techn*ology.

Walker Information Inc (2000), Employee commitment and the bottom line: *Ethical Issues in the Employer-Employee Relationship,* Work, USA.

Wangenheim, V, Evanschitzky, H. and Wunderlich, M. (2007) 'Does the employee–customer satisfaction link hold for all employee groups?' *Journal of Business Research,* 690-697.

Wanous, J.P., and Lawler, E.E. (1972) 'Measurement and meaning of job satisfaction', *Journal of Applied Psychology, 56,* pp. 95-105.

Webster, C. (1990) 'Toward the measurement of the marketing culture of a service firm", *Journal of Business Research,* Vol. 21, pp. 345-62.

Weun, S., Beatty, S.E. and Jones, M.A. (2004). The impact of service failure severity on service recovery evaluations and post-recovery relationships. *The Journal of Services Marketing,* 18(2), 133-146.

Whitener, E. (2001). Do human resource practices affect employee commitment? A cross-level analysis using hierarchical linear modeling. *Journal of Management*, 27, 515-535.

Whiting A, Naveen Donthu and Andrew M. Baker (2011) 'Investigating the immediate and long-term effects of job stressors on frontline service employees', *International Journal of Research in Marketing*, Vol. 28, Issue 4, December 2011, pp. 319-331.

Yang, F.-H., and Chang, C.-C. (2008). Emotional labour, job satisfaction and organisational commitment amongst clinical nurses: A questionnaire survey. *International Journal of Nursing Studies*, 45(6), 879-887.

Yavas, U, Karatepe, O.M. and Babakus, E. (2011) 'Do customer orientation and job resourcefulness moderate the impact of interrole conflicts on frontline employees' performance?', *Tourism and Hospitality Research*, April, Vol. 11, No. 2, 148-159.

Yavas, U. Karatepe, O.M. Avci, T. and Tekinkus, M. (2003) 'Antecedents and outcomes of service recovery performance: an empirical study of frontline employees in Turkish banks', *The International Journal of Bank Marketing*, Vol. 21, Nos. 4/5, pp. 255-65.

Ye and Liang (2010) 'The Employees Roles on Service Delivery: Case Study on Haibin Hotel & Westin Hotel Dissertation', University of Gavle, Sweden.

Yi and Gong,T. (2006) 'The Antecedents and Consequences of Service Customer Citizenship and Badness Behavior', *Seoul Journal of Business*, Vol. 12, No. 2, 145-176.

Yiing, L.H. and Ahmad, K.Z.B. (2008) 'The moderating effects of organisational culture on the relationships between leadership behaviour and organisational commitment and between organisational commitment and job satisfaction and performance', *Leadership and Organisational Development Journal*, Vol. 30, No.1, pp. 53-86.

Yoon, M. Beathy, S. Suh, J. (2001) 'The effect of work climate on critical employee and customer outcomes: an employee-level analysis'. *International Journal of Service Industry Management*, 12(5): 500–522.

Young, C. Lawrence, C. and Lee, M. (1994) 'Assessing service quality as an effective management tool: The case of the airline industry', *Journal of Marketing Theory and Practice*, Vol. 2(2), pp. 76-96.

Zeithaml, V. A., Bitner, M. J. and Gremler, D. D. (2009), Services Marketing: Integrating Customer Focus Across the Firm, 5th edition, New York: McGraw-Hill.

Zeithaml, V. Berry, L. Parasuraman, A. (1996) 'The behavioral consequences of service quality', *The Journal of Marketing,* 60(2), 31-46.

Zeithaml, V.A. and Bitner, M.J. (2003), 'Services Marketing: Integrating Customer Focus Across The Firm', McGraw Hill, New York.

Zeithaml, Valarie, A. Bitner, M. J. and Gremler. (2006) 'Integrating Customer Focus Across the Firm'. *Services Marketing,* New York.

Zeithaml, Valarie, Leonard L. Berry, and Parasuraman, A. (1996), 'The Behavioral Consequences of Service Quality', *Journal of Marketing,* 60 (April), 31-46.

Zerbe, W.J. Dobni, D., and Rel, G.H. (1998) ' Promoting employee service behaviour: The role of perceptions of human resource management practices and service culture', *Canadian Journal of Administrative Science*s, 15(2), pp.165-179.

Zheng, C. (2009), 'Keeping talents for advancing service firms in Asia', *Journal of Service Management*, 20(5): 482-502.

http://en.wikipedia.org/wiki/Air_india accessed on 5/6/11

http://en.wikipedia.org/wiki/GoAir accessed on 5/6/11

http://en.wikipedia.org/wiki/IndiGoaccessed on 5/6/11

http://en.wikipedia.org/wiki/Jet_Airways accessed on 5/6/11

http://en.wikipedia.org/wiki/Kingfisher_Airlinesaccessed on 5/6/11

http://en.wikipedia.org/wiki/spicejetaccessed on 5/6/11

Index